A FRENCH COMPANION

A Handbook for English Speakers
Travelling and Living in France

Helen Caradon

Acknowledgements

Among the many people who have contributed to the rich texture of my experience of France on which this book is based, I'd like to mention Patricia and Jacques Alaniesse, Anne and Lindon Amison, the Battut family, Susan Baxter, Eliane Berthaud, Michel Boisnoir, Maïthé Champagnat, Miss Isabelle Clarke, Gary Cook, Val and Les Dawson, Edith and Thierry Gavard-Lefevre, Francine Grégory, Sabine Grailles, Sylvie Hertzel, Hans Hoek, Colette and Harvey Jacobsen, Meg and the late Clive Jones, Anne Metcalfe, Trish and Len Rawlins, Margaret and Michael Payne, Mary Penney, Marie and Daniel Perret, Gilles Quentin, Barbara and Tim Ray, Dominique and Raymond Veulliez, Robert Walt, and Wendy and Martin Warner.

Thanks also for their interest and encouragement to Angela and Eric Dunn, Hilary and Phil Nesbit, and Jacqueline Rutherford and John Chadwick, of the Quercy branch of the Association France-Grande Bretagne. Additional thanks for reading the text, to Susan Baxter, Eliane Berthaud, Eric Boyer, Sabine Grailles and my sister Rosemary Hamilton, and to Jane Tatam of Amolibros for her invaluable technical support.

The book will be updated regularly and readers' comments are welcome, specially if they are constructive! The author may be contacted at afrenchcompanion@aol.com.

Although every effort has been made to provide accurate up-to-date information and useful practical advice in this book, neither the author, the publisher nor the distributors can accept any liability for any problem, mishap or misunderstanding arising therefrom.

Distributed by Gazelle Book Services Ltd
Hightown, White Cross Mills, South Road, Lancaster, England LA1 4XS
tel: +44 (0) 152 468765   fax: +44 (0) 152 463232   www.gazellebooks.co.uk

British Library Cataloguing in Publication Data
A catalogue record for this book is available from the British Library

ISBN. 0-9547802-0-5

Typeset by the author
This book production has been managed by Amolibros, Milverton, Somerset
Printed and bound by Advance Book Publishers, Oxford, England

Cover illustration adapted by kind permission from an original watercolour of a street in Beynac in the Dordogne, by Olga Taranova (06 64 92 82 47).

Contents

✣ Introduction

This slim volume is one result of the many eventful and mostly happy years I have spent in France, for the most part in the southwest, in the Dordogne and the Lot. During this time I have met many compatriots, some of whom have settled here already, and some who come to France regularly and would like to live here on a permanent basis. A few of those I have met speak the language effortlessly, have made friends among the locals, and have grasped how the weird and wonderful administrative system functions – to say nothing of how the occasionally weird and often wonderful citizens of this remarkable country operate and how they regard life, the universe, the neighbours, and everything else. Not all however are in this happy position, and it is for the sake of these hopeful souls that I have put this book together.

Let me make clear however what this book is *not*: it is not a technical guide to the complexities of the administration or to the procedures of buying a property or starting a business. It does talk about many of the issues that need to be grappled with in the house hunting and buying process for instance, but it does not claim to be exhaustive on the legal front. Everyone planning to settle in France permanently is strongly advised to do their own research on technical topics such as the small print of house purchase, the inheritance and tax system, etc, which are explained in detail elsewhere (see suggested titles on p. 159), and to take expert professional and legal advice before making any major commitments. Moreover the French administrative and legal system is in an ongoing process of change and adjustment, in the face of issues such as immigration, unemployment and public safety, so inevitably as rules and regulations are modified there is a need to obtain the most up to date information.

What this book does provide is a wealth of advice, tips and insights that will be endlessly useful whether you're planning your first or your tenth visit to France, as well as lots of inside information that may well spare you numerous headaches, *faux pas* and even mishaps, if and when you decide to stay here. Tips for example on addressing people correctly in various circumstances (something the French are very sensitive about), making the most of the phone and post systems, staying out of trouble on the road, shopping choices, getting proper health care, changing a gas bottle, writing official letters, gardening in the heat, obtaining the right kind of firewood and avoiding being ripped off by your builder. As several friends have said on reading the drafts of the book, "If only I'd known all this when I first arrived . . . !"

Some topics I have deliberately not dealt with: one is the food, wine and restaurant scene which is very well covered already in dozens of other publications, and another is the area of schools and education. My only experience in this field is indirectly through families whom I know, and since my basic principle has been to work from firsthand experience, I have left this one out – the more readily because it is relevant for only a minority of people who consider settling in France. Similarly I have said nothing about the sports scene, although the French are in fact very sporty and there are plenty of good sports facilities in most of the country, particularly for the martial arts and for *les sports extrêmes* such as hang gliding, canyoning, etc.

And then there's the challenge of doing all this enjoying, exploring and/or setting up home in another language. How many times have I heard a plaintive, "Well, I did do some French at school, but that's not what they actually *say*, is it . . ." Exactly. But fear not, help is at hand.

Probably the most useful parts of this book are the model conversations tailor made for various situations you may encounter while you are over here, whether as a visitor or a resident: booking a room in a hotel or *chambre d'hôte*, renting a *gîte*, getting your car fixed, ordering your Sunday croissants at the baker's, inviting French friends to a party, talking about your family, reporting a fault on the phone line, describing a malaise to the doctor, writing a note to a French friend or asking at the *brico* for some urgently needed widget.

Some of these conversations are fairly simple, others more complex, but all are very specially based on the things people *do* actually say in the situations indicated, and in other similar contexts. They are amplified by lists of vocabulary relevant to each topic covered and a selection of appropriate phrases (see those on cars, pp. 37-9, on shopping, pp. 52-3, on houses, pp. 93 & 101ff.). So look on these as recipes for successful communication, where you can mix the ingredients provided to suit the event or situation you need to deal with. And if you are really stuck in a situation where you can't make yourself understood, you can just show the person on the page of this book what you are trying to say.

The sharp eyed reader will notice from the parallel translations of the conversations that the two versions do not always match. Sometimes this is inevitable because there are not always exact equivalents in the two languages. In other places this is because French, with its largely Latin and Greek vocabulary base, is full of words and phrases which sound to an English ear rather formal, if not actually pompous, but which are in fact perfectly standard usage because in French there is no alternative. So although I have kept the two versions parallel as far as possible, some of these expressions are matched with an English phrase equivalent in tone even if not in actual words.

One point you'll notice in the conversations which may be unfamiliar to those fed on textbook French: the use of the pronoun *on*, which is nowadays very prevalent and becoming more so, however much the purists may deplore it. It's used in two ways: somewhat like 'one' in formal English, to denote 'they' = people in general: *En France on mange à midi* = 'In France people eat at noon'; and to denote 'we'. Strangely enough for people who generally like to dramatise, the French often refer to themselves as *on*, both when they talk about their habits: *On y va souvent* = 'We go there often', and when they talk about what they've been doing: *Hier on a dîné chez Marcel* = 'We had dinner at Marcel's yesterday.' Often you can tell from the context if the *on* means 'people in general' or if it means 'us':

On s'amuse bien sur la plage. *People have a good time/enjoy themselves on the beach.*
On s'est bien amusé sur la plage. *We had a good time/enjoyed ourselves on the beach.*

On is sometimes used too when talking about days of the week:

Quel jour on est aujourd'hui? On est jeudi. *What day is it today? It's Thursday.*

NB: *On* is always followed by a verb and adjectives in the singular, even when it obviously means 'we'.

In some of the vocabulary lists you will note occasional words in square brackets. These are warnings of mistakes or confusions to avoid: for instance you might ask at the *boulangerie* for "*une pièce de gâteau*", but unfortunately *une pièce*, by itself, means 'a room', 'a document' or 'a coin', so what you should ask for is "*une part de gâteau*" – but then the confusion is understandable since something sold by the piece is *à la pièce*, though *une pièce détachée* is 'a spare part' . . . when you know how, it's a piece of cake!

The companion volume to this one, *French for Enjoying France* (in preparation), focuses on the language itself, giving clear explanations of the basic grammar rules by which it functions, for the benefit of those who have forgotten or never really grasped them. These rules give you a framework for expressing your own needs and ideas, and understanding them will enable you to make the best use of the conversations in the handbook. The grammar book also explains many of the points of difference which English speakers are often baffled or confused by. It is designed principally for re-beginners, but even if your French is fairly competent, you'll probably find in it a lot of useful reminders, and a good selection of current language and expressions. Either or both will provide you with many months of useful and, I hope, enjoyable and rewarding study.

The effort put into learning will be repaid a thousand times over, since the sooner you become comfortable with the language, the sooner you'll be able to move on from being an observer and a consumer, to being a participant and becoming involved in local life. Most French people appreciate foreigners who speak their language well, and if you can do so you will find a warmer welcome, will be taken more seriously, and will be that much closer to making the most of your choice to settle in a different country and a different culture.

1 Meeting and Greeting

As everyone who wants to get on well with French people needs to know from the beginning, they are very sensitive, after generations of conditioning, to the style in which they are addressed. As in any sophisticated social group, there are many unwritten and unwriteable rules about the style of speech and vocabulary which are appropriate in different circumstances, ranging from the ridiculously flowery phrases used to close a formal letter to the most elliptical of café slang, and it would take a foreigner years to fathom them all. But there are two more obvious rules to remember, which should help you start on the right foot and avoid the *faux pas* that might give unintended offence.

The French and their names

First of all, the French use surnames more than a Brit would expect: in general usage everyone is Monsieur Somebody or Madame Somebody, unless or until they become close friends. (Women are *madame* over the age of 25 or so, whether married or not.) In formal situations this seems normal, but it is true on social occasions as well. So don't assume you can call a French person by their first name, however friendly they may be, until they invite you to do so. And when you introduce yourself, give your family name clearly as well as your first name so that they can use it and not feel obliged reciprocally to let you use their first name.

This may seem odd to those of us used to being on first-name terms very readily with people we consider in the same group as ourselves – for instance guests met at a friend's house - but that is not at all in the French tradition. It's not unusual for the friendliest of neighbours to be calling each other Madame Whatever even after thirty years of living side by side. It's seen as a mark of respect, so don't be surprised or offended if your neighbours, especially in the country, ignore your requests to call you by your first name and insist on using your surname.

There is a halfway stage, often used respectfully for older people: if the locals address your neighbour as Monsieur Henri or Madame Delphine, you can probably do the same. When you meet someone you have already been introduced to, it's more polite to greet them with their surname – *"Bonjour, Madame Dubois"* – than with just *"Bonjour"*. Likewise *"Bonjour, madame/ monsieur"* is appropriate when you want to be polite to someone whose name you do not know.

One peculiarity to listen for when a French person introduces themselves is that they may tell you their family name first and their first name second: Didier Desmoulins, for example, may introduce himself as Desmoulins Didier. Maybe it's from all those generations of filling in forms, or else from the days when people identified themselves mainly by their clan or family and only secondarily by their individual name, as the Romans did. You will often see this presentation too on shop signs and on artisans' vans.

In any case, it's advisable to do the same when you are giving your name to anyone official, since that's what they will be expecting to hear. If your name is Paul Martin or Martin Paul, good luck to you! (NB: first name = *prénom*, surname = *nom de famille*, *surnom* = nickname – you have been warned.) Another oddity is that on official forms a married woman is often identified by her maiden name (*le nom de jeune fille*), so be prepared for this if you sign a legal document, apply to be in the health system, etc. And speaking of legal documents, a solicitor (*le notaire*) is addressed not as *Monsieur* or *Madame* but as *Maître*. One other detail to notice: a couple, eg Monsieur and Madame Chavanne, are 'les Chavanne', without an added s.

Tu or vous

Rule number 2: as you probably know already, there are two styles of saying 'you', the more formal using *vous* and the informal using *tu*. Each has its own verb forms and pronouns, and it's really important to get the details of each one right. Generally, *tu* is for close friends, family and children, and everyone else is *vous*. The golden rule when talking to a French person, in any situation, is to use the more formal *vous* style unless and until they specifically invite you to *tutoyer*, ie use *tu*.

This will only happen if you are already on first-name terms, and it seems that this switch to the more familiar comes about after the first few meetings or not at all. Being invited to *tutoyer* is a significant mark of friendship, and though someone who has not yet suggested it may bristle if you say *tu* to them, someone who *has* done so may be equally offended if you forget and call them *vous* the next time you meet. They might also conclude that they have offended you in some way. So if you want things to go smoothly, remember who is which!

Greetings and goodbyes

As anyone who has been in the country more than ten minutes has noticed, the French also kiss each other when they say hello and goodbye. Though kiss is not really the word, it's usually a peck in midair while they are cheek to cheek, more or less, often without any other body contact - first to one side then to the other, usually right cheeks then left. The number of pecks varies with the region, so as always, if you want to be accepted, do as the locals do! Those who don't peck usually shake hands, so this is a safe move if you want to be polite or friendly but not too familiar. And don't try to hug anyone, even a close friend – the French don't, except on the football field! Though men, especially politicians wanting to look affable, will be seen on occasion giving each other a sort of semi-ritual embrace, gripping the upper arms and leaning to touch chests, again first to one side then to the other.

Something else you will no doubt notice fairly soon is that when entering a shop, café or even the post office, the well brought up French person will give a general greeting to the assembled company, so if you want to help keep up a delightful custom, you can do the same. It's usually a simple *"Messieurs – dames"* (ie *messieurs, mesdames*), sometimes said on leaving too. However this generally happens only in smaller places, not in very busy or impersonal ones. The limit seems to be about 10 people present – if there are more than that, there is a different atmosphere and people don't bother. Similarly, in a restaurant it's polite to say *"Bonjour/Bonsoir"* and *"Au revoir"* to the people at nearby tables when you arrive and when you leave. Someone who is about to start eating, even on a picnic, will be wished *"Bon appetit"*.

At the end of a social gathering everyone is expected to go round and say goodbye to everyone else present, even if they haven't actually talked to them all. This can be maddening because it can take ages for everybody to go through the ritual, including the kisses, handshakes, thanks, final snippets of gossip, arrangements for next time, etc, etc. But if you want to avoid offending your hosts, and to be considered worth inviting again, don't skip it - there is a not very polite expression, *filer à l'anglaise,* which means to do the opposite of this, ie to disappear without telling anyone, and by implication, without facing your obligations. (The suspicion is obviously mutual, hence the expression 'to take French leave'!)

To say goodbye at the end of a phone call with a close friend you can say *"Je t'embrasse"* ('I send you a kiss') or *"Gros bisous"* ('big kisses'). These can go on a note or postcard too, or else: *Cordialement* = cordially, *Amicalement* = 'friendlily', *Pensées amicales/chaleureuses* = friendly/warm thoughts. You might plan to say *"Meilleurs voeux*" for 'best wishes', but in fact it means 'season's greetings', and people only say this for the New Year. (More on wishes, p. 15, and more letter phrases on pp. 132-5).

Useful vocabulary

saluer	*to greet*	une bise, un bisou	*a kiss of greeting*
serrer la main	*to shake hands*	un baiser	*a kiss*
faire la bise	*to kiss in greeting*	[NB: baiser (verb)	*to have sex* (slang)]
embrasser	*to kiss*		

Weather chat

If you want to say more than hello or goodbye when you meet somebody, the weather is always a safe topic – the French talk about it at least as much as the Brits do.

Il fait beau aujourd'hui, n'est-pas?	*It's a lovely day, isn't it?*
Il fait un peu frisquet aujourd'hui, n'est-pas?	*It's a bit chilly today, isn't it?*
Quelle chaleur!	*How hot it is!*
Quel plaisir, une journée comme ça!	*What a pleasure to have a day like this!*
Le soleil/La pluie est le/la beinvenu(e), n'est-ce pas?	
	The sunshine/rain is very welcome, isn't it?

Saying hello

Formally

A: Bonjour, Madame/Monsieur Martin!
   Good morning, Madame/Monsieur Martin!

B: Bonjour, Madame/Monsieur Dubois!
   Good morning, Madame/Monsieur Dubois!

A: Comment allez-vous?
   How are you?

B: Très bien, merci. Et vous-même?
   Very well thank you. And you?

A: Ah oui, pas mal, pas mal du tout.
   Oh, not bad, not bad at all.

B: C'est bien. Il fait vraiment doux aujourd'hui, n'est-ce pas?
   That's good. It's really mild today, isn't it?

A: C'est vrai, c'est le beau temps qui revient!
   It's true, it's the fine weather coming back!

B: Pourvu que ça dure! Alors, passez une bonne journée!
   Let's hope it lasts! Well, have a good day!

A: Merci, vous de même, au revoir!
   Thank you, the same to you, goodbye!

B: Merci, au revoir!
   Thank you, goodbye!

Informally

A: Salut Alain, ça va?
Hello Alain, everything OK?

B: Salut Janine! Oui, ça va bien. Et toi?
Hello Janine! Yes, everything's fine. And you?

A: Oui, pas de problème.
Yes, no problem.

B: Tant mieux.
So much the better.

A: Avec ce beau temps!
Specially with this fine weather!

B: Tu as raison, on a une belle journée aujourd'hui.
You're right, it's a beautiful day today.

A: Ça fait du bien, n'est-ce pas?
It does you good, doesn't it?

B: Tout à fait, il faut en profiter!
Absolutely, let's make the most of it!

A: À bientôt, alors!
See you soon, then!

B: À plus, bye!
See you soon, bye!

Other things to say when you say hello

Questions

formal

Comment allez-vous?	*how are you?*
Vous allez bien?	*are you well?*
Vous vous portez bien?	*are you feeling well?*

middling

Tout va bien?	*is everything all right?*
Ça se passe bien chez vous?	*is everything going well at home?*
Et la petite famille?	*how are the children/the family?*

informal

(Comment) ça va?	*how's things?/how's it going?*
Ça va bien?	*everything OK?*
Tu vas bien?	*are you OK?*
Comment tu vas?	*how's you?*

Answers

positive

Très bien, merci	*very well, thank you*
Impeccable/Formidable, merci!	*fine/terrific, thanks!*
Sans problème!	*no problem!*
Ça roule!	*just great!*

middling

Comme ci, comme ça!	*so-so!*
Pas mal	*not bad*
On ne peut pas se plaindre	*I can't complain*
Ça pourrait être pire	*it could be worse*

negative

Pas trop	*not so good*
Pas vraiment	*not really*
Pas très bien	*not very well*
Pas du tout	*not at all*
Ce n'est pas terrible	*it's not great*
C'est affreux!	*it's awful!*
C'est la galère!	*it's a real slog!*
C'est la cata!	*it's a catastrophe!*

Other comments

Vous avez/tu as bonne mine!	*you're looking well!*
Vous avez/tu as l'air très en forme!	*you're looking really fit!*

Un petit bonjour de ma part à Suzanne/Alain	*say hello to Suzanne/Alain from me*
Mes amitiés à Madame/Janine/Henri	*greetings to Madame/Janine/Henri*
Meilleurs souvenirs à votre femme/mari	*remember me to your wife/husband*
Reply: Merci, je ne manquerai pas (de le lui dire)	*thank you, I won't fail (to tell her/him)*

When saying goodbye

Bonne journée/fin de journée/soirée = *have a good day/rest of the day/evening*

Bon après-midi = *have a good afternoon*

Bon voyage/retour = *have a good journey/journey home*

Bonne route = *have a good drive*

Bonne continuation = *good continuing* (to someone in the middle of doing something)

Bon courage = *be of good courage!* (to someone dealing with something challenging)

Portez-vous/Porte-toi bien = *take care, stay well*

À tout de suite, à tout à l'heure = *see you shortly* (within a few hours)

À bientôt = *see you soon* (within a few hours or days)

À plus (tard) = *see you later* (pronounced *plus* when on its own)

À la prochaine = *until we meet again* (said to those you know personally)

À ce soir/samedi (or time/day agreed for the next meeting) =

see you this evening/Saturday, etc

Au plaisir de vous revoir = *until we have the pleasure of meeting again*

Other polite phrases

In spite of the invasions and erosions of modern slang and anti-culture, the French on the whole still maintain a traditional courtesy and correctness in their dealings with each other, and your dealings with them will go that much more smoothly if you can produce an appropriately polite turn of phrase. (See also the section on Asking for Help in the Appendix, pp. 147-8.)

Please

Pardon, madame/monsieur . . .	*excuse me, madame/monsieur . . .*
S'il vous plaît, madame/monsieur . . .	*please, madame/monsieur . . .*
Est-ce qu'on peut . . .	*could I/we . . .*
Est-ce que vous pourriez . . .	*could you . . .*
Est-ce que c'est possible/faisable de . . .	*is it possible/feasible to . . .*
Je pourrais vous demander de . . . ?	*could I ask you to . . .*
Je voudrais/prendrais bien un café, s'il vous plaît.	*I'd like to have a coffee please.*
Si cela ne vous gêne pas/dérange pas	*if you don't mind, if it doesn't bother you*
Si vous me permettez	*if you'll allow me*
Si vous êtes d'accord	*if you agree*
Allez-y, je vous en prie	*go ahead, after you, help yourself*

Thank you

Merci bien/beaucoup	*thank you very much*
Un grand merci pour . . .	*a big thank you for . . .*
Je vous remercie pour . . .	*thank you very much for . . .*
Vous êtes très gentil(le)	*you're very kind*
C'est très aimable à vous/de votre part	*it's very kind of you*
C'etait un vrai régal	*it (the meal) was a real treat/feast*
C'était fameux	*the meal was delicious/yummy* (informal)

Mes/Nos remerciements pour votre gentillesse/accueil/hospitalité.
My/Our thanks for your kindness/welcome/hospitality.

Nous vous sommes très reconnaissants de cet accueil chaleureux.
We really appreciate your warm welcome.

C'est avec un réel plaisir que nous avons passé cette soirée sympathique avec vous/parmi vous.
It's been a real pleasure for us to spend this enjoyable evening with you/with you all.

Grâce à votre venue, nous avons tous passé une soirée merveilleuse.
Thanks to your coming, we've all had a wonderful evening.

Apologies

Désolé(e), excusez-moi	*sorry, excuse me*
Veuillez m'excuser	*please excuse me*
Désolé(e), c'était de ma faute	*sorry, it was my fault*
Désolé(e), ce n'était pas exprès	*sorry, it wasn't on purpose*
Désolé(e), je n'ai pas compris le message	*sorry, I didn't understand the message*

Désolé(e), je n'ai pas capté votre nom, vous pouvez le répéter?
Sorry, I didn't catch your name, could you repeat it?

Nos excuses pour ce retard, on avait un empèchement.
Our apologies for being late, something happened that held us up.

Toutes mes/nos excuses pour cette erreur/ce malentendu/cet incident.
My/our deepest apologies for this mistake/misunderstanding/mishap.

Replies and reassurances

De rien	*you're welcome, it's nothing*
Je vous en prie	*you're welcome, don't mention it*
Il n'y a pas de quoi	*don't mention it* (= there's nothing to thank me for)
C'est normal!	*that's normal!* (= what you're thanking me for wasn't exceptional)
Ce n'est rien	*it's nothing*
Ce n'est pas grave	*it's not serious, it doesn't matter*
Pas de problème!	*no problem!*
Ne vous inquiétez pas	*don't worry*
Ne vous en faites pas	*don't fret about it*
Ça va s'arranger	*it will sort itself out*
On va s'en occuper	*we/I'll take care of it/deal with it*
On va se débrouiller	*we'll cope with the situation, we'll find a solution*

Agreeing

Bien sûr	*of course*
Sûrement	*surely*
Certainement	*certainly*
Tout à fait!	*absolutely!*
Vous avez (bien) raison	*you're (quite) right*
D'accord! Entendu!	*fine, agreed!*
Ça marche!	*fine, okay, let's go for it!*
On fait comme ça.	*that's what we'll do* (confirming an arrangement)

Accepting

Pourquoi pas?	*why not, fine!*
Je ne dirais pas non	*I wouldn't say no, I don't mind if I do*
Oui, j'aimerais/je voudrais bien	*yes, I'd like to very much*
Volontiers	*gladly, willingly*
Avec plaisir	*with pleasure*
Avec le plus grand plaisir	*with the greatest of pleasure*

Refusing

Merci/Merci non/Non merci	*no thank you*
Merci non, rien de plus	*no thank you, nothing more*
Merci, j'en ai eu largement assez	*thanks, I've really had plenty*
[Je suis plein<u>e</u>	*I'm pregnant* – doesn't mean 'I'm full'!]
Désolé(e), je ne peux pas	*sorry, I can't*
Désolé(e), mais je n'ai pas le temps	*sorry, but I don't have time*
Désolé(e), je suis pressé(e)/occupé(e)	*sorry, I'm in a hurry/busy*
Ce n'est pas possible en ce moment	*it's not possible at the moment*

Je ne préfère pas	*I'd rather not*
Je ne me vois pas faire ce genre de chose	*I can't see myself doing that sort of thing*
Jamais de la vie!	*not on your life!*

Introductions

A: Je vous/te présente mon ami(e) . . .   *I present my friend . . .*
B: Enchanté(é).   *Very pleased.*

A: J'ai le plaisir de vous présenter mes amis/voisins/. . . Mme et M. Xxxx.
   It's my pleasure to introduce (to you) my friends /neighbours / . . . Mrs and Mr Xxxx.
B: Ravi(e) de vous connaître.   *Delighted to meet you.*
B: Ravi(e) de faire votre connaissance.   *Delighted to make your acquaintance.*

A: Permettez-moi de me présenter. Je suis Peter Watson. Et vous êtes Madame . . . ?
   Allow me to introduce myself. I'm Peter Watson. And you are Madame . . . ?

B: Ferrier, Sylviane Ferrier – je suis une cousine de la mariée.
   Ferrier, Sylviane Ferrier - I'm a cousin of the bride.

A: Enchanté de vous rencontrer, Madame Ferrier.
   Very pleased to meet you, Madame Ferrier.

B: Pour moi aussi, c'est un plaisir.
   It's a pleasure for me too.

Wishes

Congratulations	*Félicitations*
Get well soon	*Bon rétablissment*
Good luck	*Bonne chance*
Happy Birthday	*Joyeux Anniversaire*
Happy Christmas	*Joyeux Noël*
Happy New Year	*Bonne Année*
Season's Greetings	*Meilleurs Voeux*
Welcome!	*Soyez le bienvenu/la bienvenue/les bienvenus.*

We wish you a pleasant stay.	*Nous vous souhaitons un agréable séjour.*
I hope you will soon be better.	*Je vous souhaite un prompt rétablissement.*
Sincere condolences.	*Sincères condoléances.*

With all my sympathy at this painful time.
Avec toute ma sympathie en ce moment douloureux.

Our thoughts are with you at this difficult time.
Nos pensées amicales vous suivent en ce moment difficile.

My husband/wife joins me in offering you our best congratulations.
Mon mari/Ma femme se joint à moi pour vous exprimer nos meilleures félicitations.

Congratulations on your lovely new home, and our best wishes for many years of happiness and prosperity within it.
Félicitations pour la réussite de votre belle maison, et tous nos voeux de bonheur et de prosperité pour les années qui vous y attendent.

❧❧

2 People

Whether you are in the country for a few days or a few years, there are bound to be occasions when you want to explain something about yourself and what you are doing, where are you from, etc. The French are generally curious and enthusiastic about meeting other people, so be prepared for a little interrogation! But the niceties are still observed; if someone asks you a more personal question they will usually add *"si ce n'est pas indiscret"* ("if you don't mind my asking").

Of course we could never provide a full range of possible scenarios but here are a few samples. Maybe, like many before you, you will start in the first holidaymaker scenario, will become a regular visitor returning to the scene, will succumb to the charm and discover the house of your dreams, and one fine day will find yourselves in the role of meeting your new neighbours.

En vacances - On holiday

A: Bonjour, madame/monsieur, comment allez vous aujourd'hui?
Hello, madame/monsieur, how are you today?

B: Très bien merci.
Very well thank you.

A: Et ça vous plaît, notre belle région?
And do you like this wonderful region of ours?

B: Ah oui, ça nous plaît beaucoup. Le paysage est superbe.
Oh yes, we like it a lot. The landscape is wonderful.

A: C'est vrai, c'est très beau par ici. Vous êtes en vacances, je suppose?
You're right, it's really beautiful here. You're on holiday, I suppose?

B: Oui, pour une semaine, puis on va à Paris.
Yes, for a week, then we're going to Paris.

A: Bien sûr, la belle Paris! Et c'est votre première visite?
Of course, beautiful Paris! And is it your first visit?

B: C'est notre première fois ici en Bourgogne, mais on vient chaque année en France, pour découvrir une autre région.
It's our first time here in Burgundy, but we come to France every year, to explore another part of it.

A: Et est-ce que vous avez des préférences?
And do you have any favourites?

B: C'est difficile à dire, il y a tant de beaux endroits dans ce pays. Et tant de bons restaurants, et de bons vins!
It's hard to say, there are so many wonderful places in this country. And so many good restaurants, and good wines!

A: Là vous êtes bien placés pour les découvrir!
Well, you're in the right place to find out about them!

B: Tout à fait!
Absolutely!

A: Et les enfants, ils s'amusent bien aussi?
And are the children enjoying themselves too?

B: Bien sûr, on a fait du VTT, puis on a passé une journée merveilleuse sur la rivière. Mais ils n'aiment pas encore les escargots!
Very much so, we've been mountain biking, and we spent a marvellous day on the river. But they're not very keen yet on snails!

A: Quel dommage, c'est une de nos spécialités! Ça va venir!
What a pity, it's one of our specialities! It'll happen one day!

B: Cela m'étonnerait – mais on ne sait jamais!
I'd be surprised – but you never know!

A: Donc, bonne continuation pour vos vacances.
Well, enjoy the rest of your holidays.

B: C'est très gentil, monsieur, merci. Et bonne continuation à vous!
That's very kind of you, monsieur, thank you. And all the best to you!

A: Au revoir, et bonne route!
Goodbye, have a good journey!

B: Au revoir!
Goodbye!

Chez nous - The local scene

A: Ah bonjour, c'est Madame Bennett, n'est-ce pas? On vous reconnaît maintenant dans le coin!
Oh hello, it's Mrs Bennett, isn't it? We know your faces now around here!

B: Bonjour, Madame Fauvel, oui, on est revenu, comme vous le voyez!
Hello, Madame Fauvel, yes, we've come back, as you can see!

A: Et vous êtes là pour un petit moment?
And are you here for a while?

B: Oui, on va rester un mois entier cette fois.
Yes, we're staying a whole month this time.

A: Vous vous plaisez ici, alors?
So you like it here, then?

B: Bien sûr, et nous sommes ravis d'être de retour.
Of course, and we're delighted to be back.

A: Vous avez pris le même gîte chez Madame Sylvie?
Have you taken the same gîte at Madame Sylvie's?

B: Oui, ça nous convient tellement bien, surtout avez la belle piscine.
Yes, it suits us very well, specially with the lovely pool.

A: Et les enfants, comme ils ont grandis!
And the children, how they've grown!

B: C'est vrai, ça pousse!
It's true, you can't stop them getting bigger!

A: Ils ont quel âge maintenant?
And how old are they now?

B: Jamie a onze ans et Caroline bientôt neuf. Un petit bonjour à Madame, les enfants?
Jamie's 11 and Caroline will soon be 9. Are you going to say hello to Madame, children?

J: Bonjour madame!

C: Bonjour!

A: N'oubliez pas que c'est la fête du village ce weekend.
Don't forget it's the village fête this weekend.

B: Ah, ça tombe bien! On s'est tellement bien amusé l'année dernière.
That's well timed! We had such fun last year.

A: C'ést vrai, c'était une fête formidable, malgré le temps un peu morose.
It's true, it was a great party, in spite of the slightly gloomy weather.

B: Espérons du mieux pour cette année. Et votre mari s'occupe du méchoui, comme d'habitude?
Let's hope for better things this year. And your husband's looking after the spit roast, as usual?

A: Bien sûr, il organise déjà son équipe. Puis il y aura le fanfare, les feux d'artifice, et tout le reste. Vous serez parmi nous, j'espère?
Of course, he's already getting his team together. Then there'll be the brass band, the fireworks and all the rest of it. You'll be there with us, I hope?

B: Vous pouvez compter sur nous, on ne le manquerait pour rien au monde.
You can count on us, we wouldn't miss it for anything in the world.

A: C'est bien. Bonne journée, alors, et à vendredi soir!
That's good. Well, have a good day, and see you on Friday evening!

B: Merci, vous de même, Madame Fauvel, et à vendredi!
Thanks, the same to you, Madame Fauvel, and till Friday!

Une histoire vraie – A true story

A: Depuis combien de temps vous êtes en France?
How long have you been in France?

B: Nous sommes venus plusieurs fois en vacances au cours des années, puis l'année dernière on a décidé de venir nous installer définitivement.
We've come several times on holiday over the years, then last year we decided to come and move here for good.

A: Et est-ce que vous avez mis beaucoup de temps à trouver une maison?
And did it take you a long time to find a house?

B: Non, pas du tout, nous avons trouvé notre maison idéale après seulement trois jours de recherche.
No, not at all, we found our ideal house after only three days of looking.

A: Ce n'est pas vrai!
It's not true!

B: Mais si! Vous imaginez bien, on ne s'y attendait pas.
Yes it is! You can imagine, it's not what we expected.

A: Et vous avez vraiment décidé tout de suite de l'acheter?
And did you really decide right away to buy it?

B: Ah oui, c'était le coup de foudre!
Oh yes, it was love at first sight!

A: Et ensuite?
And then what happened?

B: Tout s'est mis en place assez rapidement, donc on y est installé maintenant depuis sept mois.
Everything was arranged fairly quickly, so we've been in it now for 7 months.

A: Et est-ce qu'il y avait des travaux à faire?
And was there any work to do in the house?

B: Pas vraiment, juste quelques petits aménagements pour la rendre plus convenable.
Not really, just a few small changes to make it more convenient.

A: Quelle belle histoire!
What a great story!

B: Oui, on a eu beaucoup de chance.
Yes, we were very lucky.

A: Alors, profitez-en bien!
Well, make the most of it!

B: Merci – on a bien l'intention de le faire!
Thank you, we certainly intend to!

A la rencontre des voisins – Meeting the neighbours

A: Monsieur Lachaise, j'ai le plaisir de vous présenter Madame et Monsieur Bernard, dont je vous ai parlé. Enfin c'est définitif, et c'est eux qui achètent la maison.
Mr Lachaise, it's my pleasure to introduce Madame and Monsieur Bernard, who I've told you about. At last it's all settled, and it's they who are buying the house.

B: Enchanté de faire votre connaissance, Madame et Monsieur, et toutes mes félicitations! J'espère de tout mon cœur que vous serez très contents ici.
Delighted to make your acquaintance, Madame and Monsieur, and all my congratulations! I hope with all my heart that you'll be very happy here.

C (Mr Bernard): Enchanté, Monsieur Lachaise, et merci, vous êtes très gentil!
Delighted, Monsieur Lachaise, and thank you, you're very kind!

D (Mrs Bernard): C'est un plaisir pour nous aussi de vous rencontrer, Monsieur Lachaise. Madame Mornay nous a tant parlé de vous. Vous êtes voisins depuis longtemps, n'est-ce pas?
It's a pleasure for us too to meet you, Monsieur Lachaise. Madame Mornay has told us so much about you. You've been neighbours for a long time, haven't you?

B: Ah oui, ça fait pas mal d'années maintenant qu'on partage ce joli coin et profite de son calme et de sa verdure.
Oh yes, for quite a few years now we've shared this delightful spot and enjoyed its quiet and its greenness.

C: C'est ça qui nous attire aussi, après tant d'années de vie citadine.
That's what appeals to us too, after so many years of city life.

B: Vous êtes de quelle région en Angleterre?
Which part of England do you come from?

C: D'une ville près de Birmingham, en plein centre du pays.
From a town near Birmingham, right in the middle of the country.

B: Et vous avez des enfants qui viennent vous joindre ici?
And do you have any children who'll come and join you here?

D: Nous avons trois enfants, deux fils et une fille, tous adultes maintenant. Mais ils viendront de temps en temps bien sûr. Et notre aîné devient bientôt papa, donc il y aura des petits aussi un de ces jours!
We have three children, two sons and a daughter, all grown up now. But they'll come now and again, of course. And our eldest is soon going to be a dad, so there'll be some little ones around one of these days!

A: C'est bien, ça fait de la vie, les petits!
That's good, little ones liven the place up!

C: Oui, on a pensé à eux aussi en choississant une maison avec un grand jardin, et pas de souci pour la circulation.
Yes, we had them in mind too when we chose a house with a big garden, and no worries about the traffic.

B: Là vous avez bien choisi, la circulation ici est vraiment minime, n'est-ce pas, Nadine?
There you've made a good choice, the traffic around here is minimal, isn't it, Nadine?

A: C'est le cas de le dire, la route est très peu fréquentée. Idéale pour apprendre à faire du vélo, par exemple.
You can certainly say so, the road is hardly used. Ideal for learning to ride a bike, for instance.

D: On a déjà remarqué votre beau jardin, Monsieur Lachaise. Vous êtes vraiment expert, on dirait.
We've already noticed your lovely garden, Monsieur Lachaise. It looks as if you're a real expert.

B: Expert non, mais cela me plaît, et ça m'occupe aussi. Depuis que ma femme est disparue, vous savez . . .
Not really expert but I enjoy it and it keeps me busy. Since I lost my wife, you know -

A: Et votre potager, Henri, c'est toujours plein à craquer!
And your vegetable garden, Henri, it's always full to bursting!

B: Il faut le dire, la famille en profite aussi, ils viennent assez souvent me rendre visite, et faire des emplettes!
I must say, the family take advantage of it too, they come fairly often to visit me, and to fill up their shopping basket!

D: Ils habitent près d'ici?
Do they live near here?

B: C'est ma fille cadette et sa famille qui sont à 20 kilomètres, près de Montferrand.
It's my youngest daughter and her family who live 20km away, near Montferrand.

C: Vous pourriez nous conseiller peut-être, car nous avons envie de faire un potager, mais de ce côté-là, on n'est que des débutants.
Perhaps you could give us some advice, because we want to start a vegetable garden, but with that kind of thing we're only beginnners.

B: Avec beaucoup de plaisir. Donc vous serez là toute l'année?
With great pleasure. So you're going to be here all year?

C: Pas tout de suite, nous avons encore des engagements en Angleterre, et puis il y aura quelques travaux à faire dans la maison. Mais dès le printemps prochain on envisage d'être là pour la plupart de l'année.
Not right away, we still have some commitments in England, and then there'll be some work to do on the house. But from next spring we plan to be here for most of the year.

A: C'est une très bonne nouvelle, on a besoin de nouveaux habitants pour faire vivre notre commune.
That's very good news, we need some new residents to keep our commune alive.

D: On fera ce qu'on peut!
We'll do what we can!

B: Donc vous n'êtes pas encore à la rétraite?
So you haven't retired yet?

C: Si, mais depuis trois mois seulement. L'entreprise est gérée maintenant par quelqu'un d'assez compétent, mais il a encore besoin d'un petit conseil de temps en temps.
Yes, but only 3 months ago. The company is run now by someone who's fairly competent, but he still needs a little advice now and again.

B: Un bon chef, ça ne s'improvise pas!
A good boss isn't made overnight!

C: Vous avez bien raison.
You're quite right.

> A: Alors Monsieur et Madame Bernard, Henri, allons arroser cette heureuse occasion!
> *Well Monsieur and Madame Bernard, Henri, let's drink to this happy occasion!*
>
> D: Avec plaisir, Madame Mornay.
> *With pleasure, Madame Mornay.*
>
> B: Volontiers, Nadine.
> *Gladly, Nadine.*
>
> A: Voilà, mes amis, à la santé de tous!
> *Here we are, my friends, here's good health to you all!*
>
> B, C, D: À la vôtre!
> *And to yours!*

Meeting the neighbours

While on the subject of neighbours, it is worth knowing that when you arrive to settle in a French community, especially in a village, it is up to you as the newcomer to make a move towards meeting your new neighbours. It is no use waiting anxiously behind your lace curtains to see if any of them are coming to knock on your door, because they are sitting behind theirs, waiting for you to come and do the knocking.

So, once you've had a day or two to collect your wits, prepare a couple of sentences to give them an idea of who you are and where you have come from, and sally forth. (For some relevant phrases see the conversations above, and Talking about the Family, pp. 28-9.) No doubt you'll have had some contact with some of the locals already from your previous visits, which will give you a starting point. And they will no doubt have heard something about you from the previous owners of your house, if it's not a new one, and will be all agog to find out more. One other point to remember: don't call during the time people are likely to be at table. A good moment is usually between 1.30 and 2pm, or between 5.30 and 6.30pm.

And once you're really settled in and have been in residence for a while, you might like to invite them to something.

Invitations

1 At home

> A: Bonjour, Madame Bouvier, comment allez-vous?
> *Hello, Madame Bouvier, how are you?*
>
> B: Très bien, merci, Madame Gilbert, et vous-même?
> *Very well, thank you, Madame Gilbert, and you?*
>
> A: Impeccable, tout se passe bien chez nous – en effet nous préparons une petite fête pour l'anniversaire de Jim, et ça nous ferait grand plaisir de vous voir parmi nous.
> *Fine, all's well with us – in fact we're planning a little party for Jim's birthday, and we'd be delighted if you would come and join us.*

B: C'est gentil, ce serait un plaisir pour nous aussi. C'est pour quand?
That's kind of you, it would be a pleasure for us too. When is it?

A: Pour le dimanche 15, à midi – on va préparer un barbecue, donc on espère du beau temps pour la journée!
On Sunday the 15th, for lunch – we're going to do a barbecue, so let's hope the weather's good that day.

B: Ah oui, ça!
As for that . . . !

A: Donc vous pouvez venir, tous les deux?
So will you both be able to come?

B: Je vais voir avec Jacques, qu'il n'a rien d'autre prévu - s'il y a un problème je vous rappelle, mais je ne crois pas, donc vous pouvez compter sur nous!
I'll check with Jacques that he doesn't have any other plans – if there's a problem I'll ring you, but I don't think so, so you can count on us!

A: C'est très bien! Je suis ravie que vous pouvez venir. Et ce sera l'occasion de vous présenter nos voisins de l'autre côté qui viennent de s'installer.
That's great! I'm delighted you can come. And it will be a chance to introduce to you our neighbours on the other side, who have just moved in.

B: Ah oui, vous m'en avez parlé, n'est-ce pas? Je serais contente de les connaître.
Oh yes, you told me about them, didn't you? I'd be pleased to meet them.

A: Oui, ils ont l'air très sympa. Et d'ici là on se reverra, sans doute.
Yes, they seem very likeable. And between now and then we'll see each other again, no doubt.

B: Ah oui, bien sûr, au moins sur le marché!
I'm sure, at least at the market!

A: Comme d'habitude, n'est-ce pas? Alors, Madame Bouvier, au plaisir de vous revoir!
As we usually do, don't we? So, Madame Bouvier, until we have the pleasure of meeting again!

B: De même, Madame Gilbert, au plaisir, et bonne soirée!
And the same to you too, Madame Gilbert, good evening!

2 To a restaurant

A: Bonsoir Jean-Luc, c'est Paul à l'appareil – comment ça va?
Good evening Jean-Luc, it's Paul here – how are you?

B: Salut, Paul! Oui, ça va, ça va . . . et Jacqueline? Et vous-même?
Hello, Paul! Things are all right . . . and how's Jacqueline? And yourself?

A: Ah oui, ça va. Vous savez que le frère de Jacqueline et sa belle-soeur sont là chez nous en ce moment.
Oh, we're fine. You know that Jacqueline's brother and sister-in-law are staying with us at the moment?

B: C'est sympa! C'est leur première visite ici?
That's nice! Is it their first visit here?

A: Oui, depuis qu'on s'est installé – et ils sont ravis par tout ce qu'ils découvrent dans la région, surtout les bons restaurants!
Yes, since we moved in – and they're thrilled with everything they're discovering in the area, specially the good restaurants!

B: C'est vrai, côté restos, ici on est vraiment gâté, n'est-ce pas?
It's true, as for restaurants, we're really spoiled here, aren't we?

A: Justement . . . Dîtes, on a voulu essayer ce nouveau bistro à St Rémy – est-ce que vous en avez entendu parler?
Exactly . . . Tell me, we wanted to try that new bistro in St Rémy – have you heard anything about it?

B: Ah oui, effectivement, nos voisins y sont allés il y a quinze jours. Apparemment c'est un très bon chef, et le cadre aussi est agréable – et même les prix sont plus ou moins abordables!
Oh yes, in fact our neighbours went there a couple of weeks ago. Apparently the chef is really good, and the setting is pleasant too – and even the prices are more or less affordable!

A: C'est ce que j'ai entendu dire aussi. Donc est-ce que ça vous dirait de vous joindre à nous pour un petit dîner là-bas, la semaine prochaine?
That's what I've heard too. So would you fancy joining us for dinner there next week?

B: Bien sûr, avec beaucoup de plaisir!
Of course, with great pleasure!

A: Très bien! On a pensé faire ça mardi ou mercredi, si cela vous convient?
Good! We were thinking of doing it on Tuesday or Wednesday, if that suits you?

B: Mercredi on ne peut pas, nous avons déjà un autre engagement, mais mardi, pourquoi pas?
Wednesday we can't, we've already got something else on, but Tuesday would be fine.

A: D'accord, on y va pour mardi. Et qu'est-ce qu'on fait pour y aller – vous venez ici d'abord, puis on va à St Rémy ensemble?
Great, let's go for Tuesday. And what shall we do about getting there – do you want to come here first, and then we'll go into St Rémy together?

B: Oui, c'est une bonne idée, une voiture de moins à garer. Vers quelle heure pensez-vous?
Yes, that's a good idea, one less car to park. About what time were you thinking of?

A: Disons 19 heures 30 pour un petit apéro ici, et ensuite aller au resto vers 8 heures?
Let's say 7.30 for a little drink here first, then to go to the restaurant about 8?

B: Parfait! Nous, on n'aime pas dîner trop tard.
Perfect! We don't like eating too late.

A: Nous non plus. Donc on fait comme ça?
We don't either. So we'll do that then, shall we?

B: Ça marche! Merci d'avoir pensé à nous – et bon weekend! À mardi!
Yes, fine with us! Thanks for thinking of us – and have a good weekend! See you on Tuesday!

A: Merci, vous aussi – et à mardi, au revoir!
Thanks, you too – and till Tuesday, good-bye!

B: Au revoir!
Good-bye!

Useful vocabulary

un cocktail	*cocktail/cocktail party*
un petit verre, un apéro	*a drink (before lunch or dinner)*
le déjeuner	*lunch*
le thé	*tea*
le goûter	*tea with eats, afternoon snack*
le dîner	*dinner*
une fête de famille	*a family party*
une soirée	*an evening party* - where you can hear yourself speak
un boum	*a party* - where you probably can't!
faire la fête	*to have a party, have a good time*
fêter un événement	*to celebrate an event*
inviter quelqu'un prendre un verre	*to invite someone for a drink*
prendre l'apéro chez les voisins	*to have pre-dinner drinks with the neighbours*
dîner avec des amis	*to have dinner with some friends (in a restaurant)*
dîner chez des amis	*to have dinner with some friends at their home*
pendre la crèmaillère	*to hold a housewarming ('hang the pot-chain over the hearth')*

recevoir les voisins/enfants, etc *to entertain/'receive' the neighbours/children, etc*

descendre/rester chez quelqu'un *to stop off/ stay with someone ('get down', as from a coach)*

rendre visite à quelqu'un *to visit someone* [visiter = *go round a town, monument, etc*]

1: Marianne et Jacques nous ont invités à fêter les fiançailles de leur fils.
Marianne and Jacques have invited us to their son's engagement party.

2: On a accepté leur invitation avec plaisir.
We've accepted the invitation with pleasure.

3: On a reçu les Chavanne hier soir, c'était une soirée géniale.
The Chavannes came to dinner yesterday, we had a great evening.

4: On va recevoir les enfants pour une semaine, ils arrivent jeudi soir.
The children are coming to stay for a week, they arrive Thursday evening.

5: Sur la route ils vont rester la nuit chez Sue et Michel.
On the way they're going to stay the night at Sue and Michel's.

6: Notre fille et notre gendre viennent pour les grandes vacances, avec les deux petits.
Our daughter and son-in-law are coming for the summer holidays, with the two children.

25

More invitations

M. et Mme Chauvet ont le plaisir de vous inviter à l'occasion des fiançailles de leur
   fils Julien, le samedi 12 septembre à . . .
*M. et Mme Chauvet have the pleasure to invite you on the occasion of the engagement of their
son Julien, on Saturday 12 September at . . .*

Nous allons fêter l'inauguration de notre maison/pendre la crèmaillère le *(date, etc)*
We are going to hold the house-warming of our new home on . . .

Nous serions très heureux si votre femme et vous pourriez être des nôtres.
We would be very happy if you and your wife could join us.

Nous serions très heureux de vous voir parmi nous.
We would be very pleased if you could join us.

Merci de nous honorer de votre présence.
We hope to have the pleasure of your company.

Accepting

Nous vous remercions de votre aimable invitation et nous nous faisons une joie
   d'accepter.
We thank you for your kind invitation and we are delighted to accept.

Merci pour l'invitation, nous nous ferions une joie de venir.
Many thanks for the invitation, we'll look forward to coming.

NB: If you're asked for pre-dinner drinks, don't outstay your welcome, since your
hosts will probably be planning to eat by 8pm or thereabouts. If you are invited to
dinner at someone's home it is customary to take a bunch of cut flowers.

In fact cut flowers or an interesting pot plant make a good thank-you gesture in any
circumstances, but don't give anyone chrysanthemums! In mid October gorgeous pots
of chrysanths begin to carpet the country, and you might think they'd make a
wonderful gift: but in fact these are all destined for the cemetery, where every right
thinking family goes on November 1, Toussaint (the Feast of All Souls), to put flowers
on the graves of their nearest and dearest. Some friends who unwittingly took a
splendid pot of same to their neighbours as a thank you for their warm welcome are
still being teased about it 14 years later by said neighbours . . . who obviously forgave
them after all!

Refusing

Désolé(e), nous ne sommes pas libres/disponibles ce jour-là/ce soir-là – peut-être une
   autre fois?
I'm sorry but we aren't free that day/that evening – maybe some other time?

J'aimerais bien dire oui, mais malheureusement ce n'est pas possible.
I'd love to say yes, but unfortunately it's not possible.

C'est très gentil de votre part, mais malheureusement je ne suis pas là ce week-end.
It's very kind of you, but unfortunately I won't be here this weekend.

Cela aurait été un plaisir, mais je suis en déplacement cette semaine-là.
It would have been a pleasure, but I'm away on a (business) trip that week.

Who's Who

les étrangers/ères *foreigners, strangers* (in many places this includes Parisians!)
les gens du coin/d'ici *the locals*
les habitant(e)s *inhabitants*
les résident(e)s *residents*
les voisin(e)s *neighbours*
les vacanciers/ères *holidaymakers*

l'homme	*man*	le garçon	*boy*
le mari	*husband*	le fils	*son*
le père	*father*	le frère	*brother*
la femme	*wife, woman*	la fille	*girl, daughter*
la mariée	*bride*	la sœur	sister
la mère	*mother*		
		la tante	*aunt*
le bébé	*baby* (m or f)	l'oncle	*uncle*
le/la petit(e)	*little one*	le/la cousin/e	*cousin*
l'enfant (m or f)	*child*	le neveu	*nephew*
le gosse, môme	*kid* (m or f)	la nièce	*niece*

les parents	*parents, relations in general*
la/le grand-mère/père	*grandmother/father*
les grands-parents	*grandparents*
le papie, la mamie	*grandpa, grandma*
les arrière-grands-parents	*great-grandparents*
le petit-fils/la petite-fille	*grandson/daughter*
les petits-enfants	*grandchildren*
[les jeunes enfants	*little/young children*]
les arrière-petits-enfants	*great-grandchildren*
l'époux/se	*spouse, husband/wife*
la belle-mère	*mother-in-law* or *stepmother*
le beau-père	*father-in-law* or *stepfather*
les beau-parents	*parents-in-law* or *step-parents*
le gendre	*son-in-law*
le beau-fils	*stepson*
la belle-fille, la bru	*daughter-in-law* or *stepdaughter*
l'ainé/ée	*the eldest*
le/la cadet/te	*the youngest*
le benjamin	*the youngest*
un(e) enfant unique	*an only child*
la famille nucléaire	*the nuclear family*
la famille récomposée	*the step family*
les enfants d'un premier mariage	*children from a first marriage*
les liens de parenté/de sang	*family/blood ties*
la nouvelle géneration	*the next generation*

un type, mec	*a chap, guy, bloke*
les gars	*the lads*
une nana	*an attractive single girl, a bird, chick, etc*
un vieux garçon	*a confirmed bachelor*
une vieille fille	*a confirmed spinster*
une vieille dame/femme	*an old lady/woman*
un vieux monsieur	*an old gentleman*
un vieil homme	*an old man*
Madame Machin	*Mrs What'sername*
Monsieur un Tel	*Mr So-and-So*
célibataire	*single (does not mean 'celibate'!)*
marié(e)	*married*
séparé(e)	*separated*
divorcé(e)	*divorced*
veuf/veuve	*widower/widow*
les petits	*small children*
les jeunes (gens)	*youngsters*
les adolescents/ados	*teenagers*
les gens d'un certain âge	*the middle-aged*
les personnes âgées	*older people*
les gens du troisième âge	*the over 70s*
les aînés	*the elderly*
les vieux	*the old*
l'âge (m)	*age*
l'anniversaire (f)	*birthday*
l'anniversaire de mariage	*wedding anniversary*
les noces	*wedding*
la lune de miel	*honeymoon*
le mariage	*marriage*
la séparation	*separation*
le divorce	*divorce*
la naissance	*birth*
le décès, la mort, disparition	*death (see below)*

Talking about the family

This description gives you a framework for talking about your family. The vocabulary above will help you adapt it to your own circumstances.

1: Nous avons trois enfants, deux fils et une fille, qui sont tous mariés. L'ainé Alan est ingénieur, et lui et sa famille habitent au nord d'Angleterre.
We have three children, two sons and a daughter, who are all married. The eldest Alan is an engineer, and he and his family live in the north of England.

2: Notre gendre est chef, et lui et notre fille Marian gèrent ensemble un restaurant dans un quartier huppé de Londres.
Our son-in-law is a chef, and he and our daughter Marian run a restaurant together in a smart part of London.

3: Le cadet Jeremy est pilote de ligne, donc il est souvent absent, mais le plus c'est que sa famille ont la possibilité de partir en voyage tous ensemble sans se ruiner.
The youngest Jeremy is a pilot, so he is often away, but the bonus is that his family have the chance to go on trips together without spending a fortune.

4: Notre fille a deux enfants, un garçon qui a quatre ans et une fillette de dix-huit mois.
Our daughter has two children, a little boy who is four and a little girl of eighteen months.

5: Et ils ont des cousins: nos fils ont chacun deux enfants aussi, Alan a deux filles et Jeremy deux garçons.
And they have cousins: our sons each have two children too, Alan has two daughters and Jeremy two sons.

6: Nos petits-enfants sont pour nous une véritable joie, et nous serons ravis de les recevoir ici - avec leurs parents, bien sûr.
Our grandchildren are a real delight to us, and we will be thrilled to welcome them here – with their parents of course.

7: Mon père est décédé il y a quatorze ans, et ma mère l'a suivi trois ans plus tard. Elle n'aimait pas la vie de veuve, sans lui.
My father died fourteen years ago, and my mother followed him three years later. She didn't enjoy living as a widow without him.

8: Ils se sont mariés en 1940, donc ils ont pu fêter leur cinquantième anniversaire de mariage.
They were married in 1940, so they were able to celebrate their fiftieth wedding anniversary.

9: Par contre, les parents de mon mari/ma femme sont toujours en vie, et ils viennent nous rendre visite ici assez souvent.
On the other hand, my husband's/wife's parents are still alive, and they come and visit us here fairly often.

10: Alan et sa femme attendent un autre enfant pour la fin de l'été, donc on va rentrer pour l'accouchement, et Lilian va rester chez eux quelque temps pour les aider avec le bébé.
Alan and his wife are expecting another child at the end of the summer, so we're going back for the birth, and Lilian's going to stay a while to help them with the baby.

Talking about death

Though the French don't generally bother much with euphemisms, they do often refer to someone's death (*la mort* or *le décès*) as their *disparition* ('disappearance'), much as we talk of 'losing' someone:

Depuis la disparition de sa femme il ne sort pas beaucoup.
Since he lost his wife he doesn't go out much.

And if the death of someone famous is commemorated:

C'est le dixième anniversaire de sa disparition. *It's the tenth anniversary of his death.*

Otherwise 'to die' = *mourir*, 'to decease' = *décéder* (in past, *être décédé(e)* - see example above).

To be born = *naître* (also with *être*):

Notre voisine était née dans ce village. *The woman next door was born in this village.*

Relationships

In addition to the vocabulary indicated above, there are certain nuances in describing relationships you might one day be glad to know:

un/e ami/e = a friend, unspecified.

un/e ami/e d'école = a schoolfriend, past or present.

un petit ami = boyfriend, *une petite amie* = girlfriend, regardless of the physique of the persons concerned.

mon copain = close male friend, buddy, mate; when referred to by a girl or young woman, probably but not necessarily indicates an intimate boyfriend.

ma copine = close female ditto; when referred to by a man, chap or bloke, usually signifies an intimate girlfriend.

mes copains/copines = my best close friends, the gang.

les petits copains = the 'old boy' network.

mon pote = my chum, pal (whether m or f).

un/une compagne = a partner, usually of the live-in variety; a neutral term used also by officialdom for unmarried partners.

NB: *sa* compagne = *his* partner, *son* compagne = *her* partner.

un conjoint = a spouse m or f (in officialese)

un/une partenaire = ditto, less often a business partner.

un/e connaissance = an acquaintance.

Asking people's names

Children are normally addressed as *tu*, so to ask a child their name you can say:

"Comment tu t'appelles?"

To ask someone for the name of another person (or thing) you can say:

"Comment s'appelle-t-il/elle?"

But to ask an adult their own name it is more polite to say:

"Vous êtes Madame/Monsieur . . . ?" and wait for their reply.

A little warning about genders

Due to the peculiarities of French grammar it is not easy in some contexts to grasp if a male or female person is being referred to, a distinction which can be rather useful when relationships are the topic of discussion . . . The trickiest arise from the rule that French possessive pronouns agree with the gender of the object or person *possessed*, rather than the gender of its or their *possessor*. Thus in English we can say clearly, 'his parents', 'her father', and know exactly what we mean, but *ses parents* could be his or hers, and a father of a son or a daughter will always be *son père*, as a mother will always be *sa mère*. One way to avoid confusion is to describe 'her parents' as *ses parents à elle*, and 'his parents' as *ses parents à lui*, and so on.

Then take a sentence like *Elle est venue avec son ami*. Here the *son* (usually denoting masculine) is used because of the following vowel, so only the rest of the tale will reveal if she came with *une amie* (f) or *un ami* (m) - in which case most French people will assume he's her partner. Likewise consider the sentence *Il est venu avec son ami*, and consider its possible meanings - if it's *avec sa copine* then all is clear!

Moreover various classes of persons are lumbered with a grammatical gender that has nothing to do with their actual gender. Thus 'a person' of any kind and in any garb is always *une personne*, a victim is always *une victime*, a tourist is always *un touriste*, a cabinet minister is always *le ministre*, a mayor *le maire*, etc. Since public attitudes have moved on while the language has stood still, oddities have appeared such as Madame le Maire, Madame le Ministre, Madame le Juge.

In addition to those mentioned above, others can choose whether to be m or f: *un/une collègue* = a colleague or business partner, *un/une propriétaire* = an owner, *un/une locataire* = a tenant or lodger, for instance. Another curious fish is *le* or *la professeur*, although a masculine *-eur* (eg *vendeur*) usually becomes a feminine *-euse* (eg *vendeuse*) – but that's quite far enough to go along this thorny path.

Talking about jobs

This is not the place for an exhaustive list of jobs (*les métiers*) and professions (*les professions*), but here are a few you might want to know, for conversation or for filling in those forms. Some of these names have feminine forms, which are indicated in the list. Otherwise the name can be used for either ms or fs doing the job in question.

Note that when you tell someone your job you don't put in the article: I'm a painter = *je suis peintre* (not <u>un</u> *peintre*), he's in management = *il est cadre*.

patron	*boss*
directeur/trice d'entreprise	*company director*
cadre	*someone in management*
gérant/e	*manager/ess* (of business or shop)
responsable	*person in charge*
comptable	*accountant*
sécretaire	*secretary*

antiquaire, brocanteur	*antique dealer*	restaurateur	*restaurant owner*
avocat	*barrister*	scientifique	*scientist*
bijoutier	*jeweller*		
coiffeur/se	*hairdresser, barber*	artiste	*artist*
commerçant/e	*trader, shopkeeper*	écrivain	*writer*
dentiste	*dentist*	ferronnier	*wrought iron smith*
enseignant/e	*teacher*	musicien	*musician*
garagiste	*garage owner*	orfèvre	*goldsmith*
hôtelier	*hotel owner*	peintre	*painter* (artistic or otherwise)
informaticien/ne	*'computerer'*	potier	*potter*
ingénieur	*engineer*	restaurateur	*restorer*
instituteur/trice	*school teacher*	sculpteur	*sculptor*
journaliste	*journalist*	tisserand	*weaver*
mechanicien	*mechanic*		
médecin	*doctor*	agriculteur, fermier/ère	*farmer*
notaire	*solicitor*	berger/ère	*shepherd/ess*
photographe	*photographer*	éleveur	*farmer with animals*
pilote	*pilot*	jardinier	*gardener*
politique	*politician*	maraîcher	*market gardener*
professeur	*teacher* or *professor*	paysagiste	*landscape gardener*

3♠ Travelling

Driving

The French road system is already excellent, and is continually being upgraded. However, having ever smoother and straighter roads in front of them does induce people to drive way above the speed limit, and you should stay alert *at all times* when you are at the wheel. The good news is that thanks to recent publicity campaigns and the installation of hidden radar cameras which dish out tickets automatically, French drivers are at last slowing down to safer speeds.

It's not a very good idea to risk driving long distances or overnight to reach a holiday destination when you are tired, because even if you can cope, there are probably other drivers on the road doing the same thing who can't, and who might drag you into their disasters. In July and August, apart from the French who mostly take to the beaches, and therefore to the roads, in the same few weeks, there are flocks of drivers from northern Europe who have already driven for hours even before they reach France. There are twice as many road accidents in France as in England for about the same number of drivers, and one out of three road deaths are caused by fatigue of this type, so STAY ALERT and TAKE CARE!

Apart from the obvious difference of driving on the right, there are some other important points to keep in mind when you are on the roads in France.

Route planning

If you have a long journey to make you may instinctively choose the *autoroute*, and often this is a good solution. Remember though that especially in July and August hordes of other people will be doing the same thing, especially between Paris and the Midi, so you may spend more time in traffic jams than you save – and once you are in a jam you cannot get out of it, so you risk being stuck in the broiling heat for literally hours. The *routes nationales* may be slower in places but they may save you time overall, and give you more options if you do encounter a problem, or if you come to a place you want to stop at and explore.

In many areas a little map study will reveal comparatively direct country roads which will get you to where you want to be without having to fight the traffic, and which are fun to explore. Beware though on these roads, which are generally well maintained, of oncoming vans and trucks which sometimes hurtle round a corner when you least expect them, and also watch out for crumbly or muddy verges and for ditches if you want to pull off the road or turn round. And look out for your exhaust pipe if you reverse against a rocky bank!

Navigating

Most French towns have a well marked ring road or through road system. On the town outskirts you'll pass the *centres commerciaux*, with *hypermarchés* (many with cafeterias) and chain hotels: Mercure, Novotel (expensive), Ibis, Climat, Campanile (medium), Formule 1 (cheap), etc. (Petrol is cheaper in the supermarket complexes: look out for Auchan, Champion, Continent, Géant, Intermarché, Leclerc, Super-U.)

To get to the town centre follow the signs *CENTRE VILLE*, but if you don't want to stop off (or if you want to get out of town again), stay on the main road following the signs *TOUTES DIRECTIONS* or *AUTRES DIRECTIONS* until you see the name of the town you are heading for next, and follow the signs accordingly (spot the name of the next town at the *bottom* of the sign). Remember that routes are designated *by place names rather than by a route number* (though the number will often be there *above* the sign if you look for it). Thus for a long journey it is a good idea to make a list of the places you plan to go through, so that you can spot the right road to take at an exit or junction, and not miss it because at the crucial moment you are frantically searching all over the map for unfamiliar names.

Essential for exploring in the real countryside are the blue-and-white covered IGN maps, equivalent to the Ordnance Survey, to a scale of 1:25 000, ie 1 cm = 250m. These give you loads of detail - contours, streams, woods, etc - and mark virtually every barn, farm and hamlet, as well as the lanes and tracks connecting them. From all this you can, with a bit of practice, visualise the terrain they represent. On the back roads you'll see signs with the names of the hamlets, villages and farms, from which you can get your bearings and relate where you are to the map.

Things to remember

- TAKE CARE! The accident and mortality rate on French roads is very high, so pay full attention at all times to road signs and to other drivers.

- KNOW THE LAW: Be sure that you know the essentials of the highway code such as the legal speed limits: pleading ignorance of the law will not save you from it! The police are becoming much more strict as part of a major campaign to improve road safety.

- IN THE CAR should be your driving licence, the log book/*carte grise*, insurance certificate and accident declaration form, also a red emergency triangle and a complete set of spare bulbs for your vehicle. You should also have your passport or *carte de séjour*, which you have to carry with you at all times. It's as well to keep some drinking water in the car too.

- SEAT BELTS are obligatory and you can be fined on the spot for not wearing one. Children must be firmly strapped in with the appropriate seat belt, and with a special seat if they are under 3. Children under 10 are only allowed in the front seat if the car has no back seat.

- SPEED LIMITS: on the *autoroute* 130kph (80mph), slowing to 110kph (70mph) in the rain; 110kph on dual carriageways; in built-up areas 50kph (30mph) or as indicated; elsewhere 90/80kph (55/50mph). The beginning of a built-up area is defined by a black and white sign with the name of the place, and the end of it by similar sign with the name crossed through with a black diagonal line. Within these limits you should not overtake either. Remember that speed traps are fairly common, especially on the edges of built-up areas.

- A STOP SIGN at a junction means what it says: you must come to a complete halt behind the white line. If you do not really stop and the police see you, they will give you a hefty fine on the spot and deduct points from your licence.

- THE GIVE WAY sign is an upside down triangle saying *CÉDER LE PASSAGE*. There's usually a similar sign before a roundabout saying *VOUS N'AVEZ PAS LA PRIORITÉ*.

- PRIORITY is often indicated by a sign consisting of a yellow square surrounded by a white band set on its corner like a diamond. This means that the road you are on has priority over others joining it. The same sign with a black diagonal bar across it means you are coming to a junction where you no longer have priority.

- PRIORITY TO THE RIGHT: on minor road junctions with no markings, any car approaching the intersection *from your right* has the right of way. Conversely if the other driver is *on your left*, you have the right of way. Most road intersections now have indications, solid or dotted lines, which show who has priority and reduce the risk of confusion – and collision. But on the back roads and in the countryside take extra care at unmarked junctions.

- TRAFFIC LIGHTS: a flashing yellow light or flashing yellow arrow means you can proceed in the direction indicated as long as there is no other vehicle approaching. It *does not* give you priority.

- THE HORN is only for emergencies, and not for complaining if you get stuck in a queue! It can be useful if you are on a narrow hilly road with blind corners.

- TYRES: keep an eye on them for wear, for your own safety and because they are a favourite target for spot checks by the police, who will not hesitate to give you a hefty fine if yours are unduly worn. Check the pressure too occasionally in the spare tyre (*la roue de secours*).

- TOLLS: the *péages* on the autoroute will usually accept credit cards or even sterling, if you don't want to pay in euros. Some however have a small fixed charge that has to be paid in coins, so you'll need to keep some small change handy.

- ON THE AUTOROUTE make sure you always have enough petrol at least to get to the next service station. If you break down on the *autoroute for any reason* and the police see you, you will be fined. If you break down at night, use your mobile to summon help instead of going to the nearest emergency phone; believe it or not, *the average life expectancy of someone walking along the emergency lane in the dark is 8 minutes!*

Petrol

- Unleaded = *sans plomb* (95/98), diesel = *gasoil/gazole*. Super (*super*) is still available but is being phased out. Prices vary a lot, being much lower at the supermarkets. Diesel is currently still cheaper than unleaded, but the price difference is dwindling. The paying procedure in a self-service garage is slightly different from in the UK: you fill up first, then drive up to the kiosk at the exit to pay, telling them the pump number. The pump won't run until the person who's used it before you has paid.

- Most large supermarket stations (and a few ordinary petrol stations) have a pump which can be activated by a credit card (provided it has a PIN number - though most operate only with a French card). This facility is indicated by a sign of a gas pump and 24H/24H. To operate the pump follow the instructions on the screen, which usually go like this:

Inserez votre carte.	Put your card in the slot.
Veuillez patienter.	Please wait.
Selectionnez votre carburant et validez.	Press the button for the fuel you want then press *valider/oui*.
Tapez votre code et validez.	Tap in your PIN number and press *valider/oui*.
Code bon.	Code OK.
Voulez vous un ticket ? Tapez oui ou non.	Do you want a receipt? Press *valider/oui* = yes or *annuler/non* = no.

Retirez votre carte.	Withdraw your card.
Decrochez et servez vous.	Fill up as you want.
Distribution en cours.	Pump running.
Ticket en cours.	Receipt being printed (though it may never appear).

If it doesn't work first time, press *annuler* and try again. If there's an attendant on hand, you can ask them to put in a specific amount: *"Jusqu'à 25€ s'il vous plaît"*, or to fill it up: *"Faites le plein, s'il vous plait."*

- LPG (GPL in French): This is easier to find on the Continent than in the UK BUT the nozzle connectors are different in each country, so if you are bringing an LPG car over, before you leave you MUST obtain the right connector from your garage *for each country you are planning to visit*. GPL is usually available on the *autoroute* service stations, and increasingly in other places - all major towns, and many minor ones, have at least one garage selling it.

Parking

Street parking may be difficult in major town centres and impossible in towns with ancient narrow streets, but in most places parking areas are provided and clearly signed. Fees are generally reasonable, and over lunchtime, 12-2pm, parking is usually free. A place marked by a yellow rectangle on the road is for deliveries. DO NOT park in an invalid space, remember those who really need it, and that the fine (*l'amende*) for doing so without justification is huge.

If you do get a parking ticket (PV), fill in the relevant sections and send it with a cheque to the address indicated. The fine is lower if you pay it within a month. If you don't have a French cheque, you have to buy a tax stamp at a *tabac* to the value of the fine, stick it on the ticket where indicated, put on an ordinary stamp too and post it. Don't ignore it, it will catch up with you eventually, and be more expensive if you haven't paid promptly.

Other road signs

ACCES INTERDIT = no entry

ACCOTEMENTS DANGEREUX = dangerous verges – or absent, if you are in the mountains

ACCOTEMENTS DESTABILISEES/MEUBLES = soft verges

ALLUMEZ/ETEIGNEZ VOS FEUX = turn on/off your headlights

ATTENTION TRAVAUX = road works

BOUE = mud on the road

CARREFOUR DANGEREUX = dangerous crossroads

CHAUSSEE DEFORMEE = uneven road surface

DEVIATION = diversion

FAUCHAGE = verge and hedge cutting

RAINURAGES = ridged road surface

RALENTIR = slow down

RALENTISSEUR = speed bump

RAPPEL = remember

ROULEZ DOUCEMENT = drive slowly (through village, etc)

ROUTE BARREE = road closed

SANS ISSUE = dead end

SAUF RIVERAINS = residents only

SENS INTERDIT = no entry

SENS UNIQUE = one way

SORTIE DE CAMIONS = lorry exit

SORTIE D'ENGINS = heavy vehicle exit

STATIONNEMENT GENANT = parking forbidden/towing area

STATIONNEMENT INTERDIT = parking forbidden

UTILISER VOTRE FREIN MOTEUR = stay in low gear

VEHICULES LENTS = slow vehicle lane (on uphill gradient)

VERGLAS FREQUENT = ice, danger of skidding

ZONE PIETONNE = pedestrian zone

In case of an accident

In your car you should have a Constat Européen d'Accident or Standard Accident Report. If you get involved in an accident whilst in France it is essential to get this form filled in correctly, otherwise the insurance will not be valid. We sincerely hope you will have no need for this information, but if an accident happens this is what you have to do (more tips on p. 130).

If anyone is injured you must contact the police or the *gendarmerie*. If the only damage is to the vehicles, you simply exchange driver's license and insurance information with the other driver and immediately complete a single *constat*, which requires the following:

- Date.
- Where the accident occurred (town, *département*, etc3.).
- Details of any injuries.
- Details of any damage to the vehicles.
- Name, address and phone of any witnesses.
- The name of the insured party.
- Vehicle identification (registration number).
- Insurance company.
- Driver ID and licence number.

Each party then completes either part A or part B.

- Mark with an arrow the point of initial contact.
- Describe damages.
- Fill in the boxes that describe the circumstances of the accident.
- Make a drawing of the accident.

Each party then takes a copy, checks and signs the other driver's form, and within 5 days must complete their own form and send it to their insurance company.

Useful vocabulary

driver (private)	*le conducteur*	roofrack	*la galerie*
driver (professional)	*le chauffeur*	rubber lead or tube	*la diorite*
passenger	*le passager*	seat	*le siège*
		seatbelt	*la ceinture*
diesel	*le gasoil/gazole*	spare tyre	*le pneu de secours*
leadfree petrol	*le sans plomb*	sparkplug	*la bougie*
LPG	*GPL*	steering wheel	*le volant*
oil	*l'huile* (f)	tailgate	*le hayon*
petrol	*l'essence* (f)	tyre	*le pneu*
[*le pétrole*	crude oil, heating paraffin]	warning light	*le témoin/ le voyant rouge*
super	*le super*	(for radiator, etc)	*(de radiateur, etc)*
2-stroke	*le mélange*	window	*la vitre*
		windscreen	*la parebrise*
accelerator	*l'accélerateur* (m)	windscreen wiper	*l'essuie-glace* (f)
aerial	*l'antenne* (f)		
battery	*la batterie*	breakdown truck	*la dépanneuse*
bodywork	*la carrosserie*	bus	*le bus*
bonnet	*le capot*	coach	*le car*
boot	*le coffre*	car	*la voiture*
brakes	*les freins*	saloon car	*la berline*
bumper	*le pare-choc*	estate car	*le break*
clutch	*l'embrayage* (m)	lorry	*le camion, le poids lourd*
dashboard	*le tableau de bord*	small van	*la camionnette, le fourgon*
dipstick	*la jauge d'huile*	trailer	*la remorque*
distributor belt	*la courroie de distribution*	van	*l'utilitaire* (f)
door	*la porte*	secondhand vehicle	*le véhicule d'occasion*
engine	*le moteur*		
exhaust	*l'échappement* (m)	garage man	*le garagiste*
fanbelt	*la courroie de ventilateur*	mechanic	*le mechanicien*
gearbox	*la boîte de vitesse*	garage doing bodywork	*le carrossier*
handbrake	*le frein à main*		
headlights	*les phares*	service	*la revision générale*
hubcap	*un enjoliveur*	MOT test	*la contrôle technique*
ignition	*l'allumage* (m)	oil change	*le vidange*
indicator	*le clignotant*	repair	*la réparation*
jack	*le cric*		
number plate	*la plaque d'immatriculation*	speed limit	*la limite de vitesse*
petrol cap	*le bouchon du réservoir*	traffic offence	*une infraction, contravention*
petrol tank	*le réservoir d'essence*	fine	*une amende*
pump	*la pompe*	ticket	*le PV (procès-verbal)*
radiator	*le radiateur*		
rear light	*le feu arrière*	to accelerate	*accélerer*
rear view mirror	*le retroviseur*	to be out of petrol	*être en panne d'essence*
rear window	*le vitre arrière*	to brake	*freiner*

to break down	*tomber en panne*	to repair	*réparer*
to change gear	*changer de vitesse*	to reverse	*reculer*
to check	*contrôler*	to skid	*déraper*
to drive	*conduire*	to slow down	*ralentir*
to fill up with petrol	*faire le plein*	to stall	*caler*
to find your way about	*se réperer, s'orienter*	to stop	*s'arrêter, stopper*
to fix	*arranger, réparer*	to take	*prendre*
to follow	*suivre*	to turn	*tourner*
to overtake	*doubler*	to turn round	
to pass	*passer*		*faire demi-tour, rebrousser chemin*
	dépanner quelqu'un	going forwards	*en marche avant*
to rescue someone who has broken down		going backwards	*en marche arrière*

HELP! there's a problem with the car!

Here are some phrases which may be of help in a crisis or if your car has a problem.

There is . . . *Il y a . . .*

a weird noise	*un drôle de bruit*	a vibration, shudder	*une vibration*
a rattle	*un cliquetis*	a leak	*une fuite*
a grinding noise, squeak	*un grincement*	some fumes	*une fumée*

I've run out of petrol. I need some lead-free/diesel.
Je suis en panne d'essence. J'ai besoin du sans plomb/gazole.

I've broken down.
Je suis tombé en panne.

I've got a flat tyre.
J'ai une crevaison.

The motor has stalled and I can't start it again.
Le moteur s'est calé et je n'arrive pas à le redémarrer.

The windscreen has cracked.
Le parebrise s'est fendu.

The radiator has overheated.
Le radiateur est surchauffé.

The handbrake cable has gone.
Le câble du frein à main s'est cassée.

I don't understand what's happened.
Je ne comprends pas ce qui s'est passé.

The XXX has stopped/isn't working any more.
Le/La XXX s'est arrêté(ée)/ne marche plus.

There's been a crash. I've had an accident.
Il y a eu une collision. J'ai eu un accident.

Can you come and help me?/send the breakdown truck?
Est-ce que vous pouvez venir m'aider?/envoyer la dépanneuse?

Here are the details of my insurance company.
Voici les coordonnées de mes assureurs.

At the garage

Can I bring my car in - it needs a full service/oil change, etc.
Est-ce que je peux vous amener ma voiture – elle a besoin d'une révision générale/un vidange.

Please can you check the brake pads/tyres/fan belt/cooling system/oil, etc.
Est-ce que vous pouvez contrôlez les plaquettes/les pneus/la courroie de ventilateur/le système de refroidissement/l'huile …

Will you have to order any parts?
Est-ce qu'il faut commander des pièces?

How long will it take? When shall I come back to collect it?
Combien de temps ça va prendre? À quelle heure je viens la chercher?

Would you have another car that I could use meanwhile?
Est-ce que vous auriez un autre véhicule disponible entretemps?

I brought my car in last week, but it's still got the same problem.
Je vous ai amené ma voiture la semaine dernière, mais le problème est toujours là.

Directions

Useful vocabulary

after	*après*	dead end	*l'impasse* (f)
before	*avant*	dual carraigeway	*la roue à double voie*
behind	*derrière*	gutter	*le caniveau*
beside	*à côté de*	island	*le refuge*
between	*entre*	junction	*le croisement, le carrefour*
beyond	*au-delà de*	lamp post	*le réverbère*
far	*loin*	landmark	*le répère*
in front of	*devant*	(traffic) lane	*la voie*
left	*gauche*	(country) lane	*le chemin*
near	*proche, près de*	layby, rest area	*l'aire* (m)
opposite	*en face de*	motorway exit	*l'échangeur* (m)
right	*droite*	one way	*sens unique*
straight ahead	*tout droit*	parking	*le stationnement*
the first	*le/la premier/ère*	parking meter	*le parcomètre*
the last	*le/la dernier/ière*	pavement	*le trottoir*
the next	*le/la prochain(e)*	petrol pump	*la pompe à essence*
the following	*le/la suivant(e)*	petrol station	*la station service*
the previous	*le/la précédent(e)*	slip road	*la bretelle*
(coming) from	*(en venant) de*	street	*la rue*
(going) towards	*(en allant) vers*	road	*la route*
		road surface	*la chaussée*
barrier	*la barrière*	roundabout	*le rond-point*
bend	*le virage*	sign	*le panneau*
car park	*le parking*	ticket machine	*l'horodateur* (m)
corner	*le coin, l'angle* (m)	traffic lights	*les feux*

Asking the way: 1

(see also Asking for Help, p.147)

A: Excusez– moi, monsieur, est-ce qu'il y a une station service près d'ici?
Excuse me, monsieur, is there a petrol station near here?

B: Oui, bien sûr. Vous continuez tout droit jusqu'au feux puis tournez à gauche et prenez la première rue à droite. C'est au deuxième croisement.
Yes, of course. Carry on straight ahead as far as the lights, then turn left and take the first street on the right. It's at the second intersection.

A: Merci bien.
Thanks very much.

B: De rien, bonne journée. Au revoir!
You're welcome, have a good day. Goodbye!

A: Vous aussi, au revoir!
You too, goodbye!

2

A: S'il vous plaît, vous savez où se trouve la Poste?
Please, do you know where the post office is?

B: Mais oui! Vous voyez le tabac là-bas?
Yes, of course! You see the tobacconist's over there?

A: Juste après le café?
Just after the café?

B: Oui, c'est ça. Vous prenez la rue en face et la poste est sur la droite. Ce n'est pas loin.
Yes, that's it. You take the street opposite and the post office is on the right. It's not far.

A: Merci bien.
Thanks very much.

B: De rien, bonne journée, au revoir!
You're welcome, have a good day. Goodbye!

A: De même, au revoir!
The same to you, goodbye!

3

A: Pardon monsieur, je vais à l'aéroport pour chercher quelqu'un - est-ce que c'est la bonne route par ici?
Excuse me, monsieur, I'm going to the airport to fetch someone – is this the right road?

B: Ah non, madame, vous vous êtes trompée. L'aéroport c'est à l'autre côté de la ville, donc il vous faut faire demi-tour. Vous prenez cette même route mais dans l'autre sens.
Oh no, madame, you've made a mistake. The airport is on the other side of town, so you'll have to turn round. You take this same road but in the opposite direction.

A: Et où est-ce que je peux tourner?
And where can I turn?

B: Au prochain feu prenez à droite, il y a un grand parking de supermarché, donc là vous pouvez le faire. Et au croisement vous verrez les panneaux pour l'autoroute et ensuite pour l'aéroport.
At the next lights turn right, there's a big supermarket car park, so you can turn there. And at the junction you'll see signs for the motorway and then the airport.

A: Un grand merci, monsieur, vous êtes très aimable.
Thank you very much, monsieur, you're very kind.

B: De rien, madame, et bonne route! Au revoir!
Oh it's nothing, madame, have a good journey! Goodbye!

A: Merci, et au revoir!
Thank you, and goodbye!

By air

There is a good network of domestic flights that covers the whole of France, but now that airport security is more rigorous, for a shorter journey it may be quicker and simpler to take the train. It is now possible for instance, if you are travelling via Paris, to board a TGV directly from Charles de Gaulle airport to many major towns. This may be more convenient than an internal flight, since many of these go only through Orly, south of the city. The transfer from CDG to ORL takes about 1½ hrs, by which time the TGV is already halfway to Bordeaux (3hrs) or to Marseille (3hrs 15mins).

Flights out of France usually cost a great deal more than out of England, although there are now cheaper options with easyJet and Ryanair. Both have services to many French towns. Check on their sites for up to date details. Air France of course also serves many towns and cities.

> easyJet GB: 0870 6 000 000 www.easyjet.com.
> Ryanair GB: 0870 1 569 569 www.ryanair.com

By bus and coach

The Eurolines long-distance coach network provides a useful service to many cities in France and in fact all over the Continent. You can get a through ticket (jointly with National Express) from most towns in Britain to Victoria Coach Station, then the Eurolines coach takes you via the Dover–Calais ferry or the Tunnel on to your destination. Reclining seats, toilets (of a sort!) and regular stops for refreshment, etc – no smoking in the bus. In busy periods the scheduling can be erratic, but this is a cheap alternative to the train, both within the country and outside it. Seats are often available at short notice, and you don't have to touch your bags until you arrive.

> Eurolines UK: 08705 143219, 01582 415841. www.eurolines.co.uk
> Eurolines France: 0892 89 90 91. www.eurolines.fr
> Bordeaux: 05 56 92 50 42
> Tours: 02 47 66 45 56

Within France there is unfortunately no national bus network, but all large cities and many larger towns have a bus service. Some are innovative 'green' systems designed to reduce pollution, with buses running on electricity or LPG, and electric trams. The SNCF run buses in certain areas to supplement their train network.

By train

The Eurostar between London and Paris, Brussels and Lille is efficient and generally reliable, and even more attractive now that London to Paris takes only 2hrs 35mins and London to Brussels 2hrs 20mins. But it is very expensive (currently £150 or more for a peak rate single) unless you book 2 weeks in advance, or buy a day return (usually available at weekends). This is much cheaper than a standard single even if you only use the ticket one way. However there are often some good deals available, specially for the over 60s. You can find details of current options and fares on their site www.eurostar.com, where you can download the whole timetable, very conveniently. Further information on www.raileurope.co.uk (for all continental routes) and on www.sncf.com (English option).

The SNCF offers an excellent service, and in spite of occasional hiccups trains usually run on time (and if they are significantly late, your ticket is partly or entirely refunded). There are substantial reductions in fares for under 26s and over 60s, even more generous for the latter if you buy a Carte Senior, valid for a year. The site works well once you understand which boxes to fill in at each stage, but note that they do not always list the cheapest available fares.

For timetables and information in France try phoning your nearest station. (You can find the station number in the Pages Jaunes under *Transports ferroviaires* or else at www.pagesjaunes.fr, then *'gare'* in the box *'activité'* and the name of the town in the box *'localité'*.) They are likely to answer sooner and be easier to deal with than the SNCF information line, and they can explain the considerable choice of fares available. These are grouped according to the period in which you are travelling, your age group, etc. Or else pick up the timetables you need at your local station – but be sure to read all the small print! Tickets are valid for 2 months from the date of purchase. For the TGV express you must reserve a seat, and be *through the gate* at least 20 minutes before it leaves.

When you buy a ticket at the window (*guichet*) you will also be given a printout of your journey times as a reminder. Before going onto the platform you need to *composter* your ticket, ie put it into the orange pillar machine to have it punched (black stripe up – just watch how everyone else does it). This prevents you from using it again, and an inspector will come down the train at some point to check that all tickets have been *compostés*.

When you are boarding a train, check on the display board for your train time and number (marked on the ticket), and watch for the platform number to be posted. At a terminus it's easy, but if you have a seat reserved and are in a through station it's a good idea to look for the display board on the platform showing the train layout, so that you can position yourself at the spot where your carriage will stop. This is advisable especially if you have a lot of luggage as the trains stop for only a few minutes. Carriage numbers are posted on the outside of the train beside the doors.

Sadly very few trains now have any restaurant service, though most have a trolley for snacks and drinks that will eventually reach wherever you are sitting. But there's little choice so for a long trip it's better to supplement with your own rations.

Train information

SNCF *Ligne Directe* (to speak to a person): 0836 35 35 35. Be prepared to wait.

SNCF *Ligne Vocale* (an automated service, press a sequence of buttons): 0836 67 68 69.

For information and booking on line: www.voyages.sncf.com (English option too). In fact if you book and pay for your ticket on line you can now print out the ticket yourself, provided you understand the instructions for doing so.

Booking a train ticket (at the station) *

A: Bonjour, je voudrais réserver un billet pour le trajet Toulouse-Paris, s'il vous plaît.
Hello, I'd like to book a ticket from Toulouse to Paris please.

B: Bien sûr, madame. C'est pour quand?
Of course, madame. When is it for?

---

* This is a sample conversation only, not to be taken as fact.

A: Pour le vendredi 18 ou samedi 19, selon les prix, au tarif senior.
For Friday 18 or Saturday 19, depending on the price – and with the 'senior' discount.

B: Vous avez la Carte Senior?
Do you have a Carte Senior?

A: Non.
No, I haven't.

B: Vous voulez un aller simple ou un aller et retour?
Would you like a single or a return?

A: Un aller et retour, je reviens le weekend suivant.
A return, I'm coming back the following weekend.

B: Un instant s'il vous plaît - donc, si vous partez le vendredi en début d'après-midi en période bleue et revenez la même période le vendredi suivant, ça fait 124€, ou avec la remise senior, 93€. Sinon, le samedi ce serait un peu plus cher – 101€.
One moment please – so if you leave on Friday early afternoon in the 'blue period' and come back the following Friday in the same period, that would be 124€, or with the discount, 93€. Otherwise, Saturday would be a little more expensive– 101€.

A: Je prends le vendredi, alors. Quels sont les horaires de départ?
I'll take the Friday then. What departures are there?

B: Vous avez un départ de Toulouse par TGV à 13.41, arrivée à Paris Gare de Montparnasse à 19 heures, ou bien un départ à 13.54 en train ordinaire, arrivée à Austerlitz à 20.11.
Well, you have a train from Toulouse, the TGV, at 13.41, arriving in Paris at the Gare de Montparnasse at 7pm, or else an ordinary train at 13.54, arriving at Austerlitz at 20.11.

A: Je préfère le TGV. C'est le même prix?
I'd prefer the TGV. Is it the same price?

B: Oui, madame, et c'est plus confortable aussi.
Yes, madame, and it's more comfortable too.

A: Bien sûr! Et pour le retour?
Of course! And for the return?

B: Il y a le TGV qui part de Montparnasse à 14.40, arrivée à Toulouse 20.58, mais il faut changer à Bordeaux. Ou un train direct à 17.20, arrivée à 22.35, si ce n'est pas trop tard pour vous.
There is a TGV that leaves Montparnasse at 14.40, arriving at Toulouse at 20.58, but you have to change at Bordeaux. Or there is a direct train at 17.20, arriving at 22.35, if that isn't too late for you.

A: Non, pas du tout, cela me convient parfaitement.
No, not at all, that suits me perfectly.

B: D'accord. Donc pour le TGV, vous voulez une place fumeur ou non-fumeur?
Fine. Now for the TGV would you like a smoking or non-smoking seat?

A: Non-fumeur s'il vous plaît.
Non-smoking please.

B: D'accord. Vous voulez le payer comment?
Fine. How would you like to pay?

A: Par chèque. C'est combien – vous avez dit 93€?
By cheque. It's how much – did you say 93€?

B: Oui, c'est exact.
Yes, that's it.

A: Voilà.
Here you are.

B: Merci bien madame, voici votre billet avec la réservation. Et voici les horaires aller et retour.
Thank you, madame, here is your ticket with the reservation. And this is the timetable in both directions.

A: Tout est là? C'est tout ce qu'il me faut?
Everything is there? That's all I need?

B: Oui, tout y est.
Yes, that's everything.

A: Merci beaucoup pour votre aide.
Thank you very much for your help.

B: De rien madame, et bon voyage.
You're welcome, madame, have a good journey.

A: Au revoir!
Goodbye!

B: Au revoir!
Goodbye!

Useful vocabulary

carriage	*la voiture*	ticket	*le billet*
connecting train	*la correspondance*	ticket – single	*un billet simple*
corridor	*le couloir*	ticket – return	*un billet aller et retour*
platform	*la voie, le quai*	ticket collector	*le controleur*
seat	*la place*	ticket window	*le guichet*
sleeping berth	*la couchette*	timetable	*l'horaire* (m)

4 Accommodation

As regular visitors will have already noticed, one of the many joys of travelling in France is that hotel accommodation is much cheaper than in GB. Prices quoted are usually per room, with a small supplement for an additional child's bed or cot. The busier hotels and the bigger chain hotels will only keep the room for you if you give them a deposit – by credit card if you book by phone - but many others will simply take your word for it that you will turn up as agreed. A little warning for first-timers: don't march into that imposing-looking building conveniently situated in the centre of town and labelled 'Hôtel de Ville', expecting to find a room - it's the town hall! If the room is cheap, breakfast is comparatively expensive, but now that France is becoming so much more health conscious, this often includes a buffet with juice, cereal, muesli, eggs, cheese, etc, especially in the chain hotels.

The alternatives to staying in a hotel, as you no doubt know, are *chambres d'hôtes* and *gîtes*. The former are the equivalent of a B&B, are usually in someone's house or farm, etc, and are let by the night. Check when you book about bathroom facilities, breakfast, etc. Places that advertise *table d'hôte* serve meals to residents only, usually with a fixed or limited menu but one based on fresh local produce. *Gîtes* are let by the week, include cooking facilities and are often in a separate building.

Another stroke of French genius is the system whereby all self-respecting hotels, *gîtes* and *chambres d'hôte* are registered with their local Office de Tourisme (or Syndicat d'Initiative in smaller towns) which keeps track of room availability, so to find accommodation in an area all you have to do is phone the office, and they will tell you which establishment has the kind of room available that you are looking for. You can then phone the place directly, or in some cases they will phone for you.

Note that being on the local register is not a guarantee of standards, as the places listed are not necessarily inspected unless they are starred hotels or are part of the Gîtes de France, the Bienvenue à la Ferme or similar network. If you want to play safe, stick to one of these – but generally you can count on the French pride in doing things properly to provide the best for their visitors, and most places you go to, even at the lower end of the price scale, will be welcoming and spotlessly clean.

NB: Usually *salle de bains* = bathroom including bath, *salle d'eau* = bathroom with shower, but if it is crucial to your comfort, best check when making your booking.

Useful vocabulary

double bed	*le grand lit*	sheet	*le drap*
single bed	*le lit à une personne*	towel	*la serviette*
bunk beds	*les lits superposés*	coathanger	*le cintre*
cot (often the mesh kind)	*le lit de bébé*	bath	*la baignoire*
child's bed	*le lit d'enfant*	basin	*le lavabo*
spare (folding) bed	*le lit d'appoint*	shower	*la douche*
bedspread	*le couvre-lit*	toilet	*la toilette, le wc* ('vay-say')
blanket	*la couverture*	key	*la clé*
bolster	*le traversin*	lift	*l'ascenseur* (m)
pillow	*l'oreiller* (m)	staircase	*l'escalier* (m)
pillowcase	*la taie d'oreiller*		

Trouver une chambre - Finding a hotel room or *chambre d'hôte*

A: Bonjour/Bonsoir, je suis à la recherche d'une chambre pour ce soir/weekend/ la nuit du 24 avril/etc.
Good morning/evening, I'm looking for a room for tonight/this weekend/the night of 24 April.

B: Bien sûr monsieur, ce serait pour combien de personnes?
Of course, sir – how many people would it be for?

A: On est deux adultes plus un enfant de 12 ans. Une chambre avec wc et baignoire de préférence – est-ce que vous avez quelquechose disponible?
Two adults and a child of 12. A room with a toilet and a bath preferably – do you have anything available?

B: Je regarde – c'est pour une nuit seulement?
Let me see – is it just for one night?

A: Non, pour au moins deux nuits, peut-être même trois.
No, for at least 2 nights, perhaps even 3.

B: Bon . . . je peux vous proposer une chambre avec grand lit plus lit d'enfant, wc et baignoire, pour deux nuits, où bien une autre avec trois lits d'une personne, wc et salle d'eau, pour trois nuits.
Well . . . I can offer you a room with a double bed and a child's bed, toilet and bath, for 2 nights, or else one with 3 single beds, a toilet and bathroom facilities, for 3 nights.

A: C'est à dire avec douche?
You mean with a shower?

B: Oui monsieur, vous avez la douche, le lavabo et le wc bien sûr.
Yes, sir, there is a shower, a washbasin and a toilet, of course.

A: Les chambres sont au même prix?
Are the rooms the same price?

B: Pas tout à fait, monsieur - celle avec la baignoire est à 36€ la nuit, l'autre à 32€.
Not exactly, sir - the one with the bath is 36€ per night, and the other 32€.

A: 32€ par personne?
32€ per person?

B: Ah non, ça c'est le prix de la chambre pour vous tous!
Ah no, that's the price of the room for all of you!

A: Et est-ce que ça comprend le petit-déjeuner?
And does that include breakfast?

B: Non, le petit-déjeuner est en supplément, c'est 5€ par personne.
No, breakfast is extra, it's 5€ per person.

A: Laissez-moi consulter un instant avec ma femme . . .
Just let me check for a moment with my wife . . .

B: Bien sûr!
Of course!

A: Oui, on va prendre la chambre pour les trois nuits – la baignoire on s'en passe.
Yes, we'll take the room that's available for 3 nights – and do without the bath.

B: D'accord, monsieur. C'est à quel nom, s'il vous plaît?
Very well, monsieur. In what name, please?

A: Hansell.

B: Cela s'écrit comment?
How is that spelled?

A: H-A-N-S-E-deux Ls.
H-A-N-S-E-double L.

B: Merci.
Thank you.

A: Est-ce qu'il faut payer quelquechose maintenant?
Do we have to pay something now?

B: Ah non, monsieur, ça va, on ne demande pas d'arrhes sauf en pleine saison.
Oh no, monsieur, that's all right, we don't ask for a deposit except in high season.

A: D'accord. Et pour le repas ce soir, est-ce que vous faites *table d'hôte*/vous avez un restaurant?
Oh fine. And for an evening meal, do you do table d'hôte/do you have a restaurant?

B: Désolé monsieur, on ne fait pas la restauration, mais je peux vous conseiller un bon restaurant à Montmorain, le Lion d'Or.
Sorry, we don't serve meals, but I can recommend a good restaurant in Montmorain, the Golden Lion.

A: Merci bien. Et vous êtes où exactement? C'est facile à trouver?
Thanks very much. And where are you exactly? Is it easy to find?

B: Ah oui, monsieur, ce n'est pas du tout compliqué! Quand vous arrivez au centre du village, vous prenez la route qui part devant l'église vers Montmorain. À 2km à peu près il y a un grand virage vers la droite, et juste après vous verrez un petit chemin sur la gauche – c'est celui-là qu'il faut prendre. Il y a un panneau, c'est indiqué L'Auberge des Bois.
Oh yes, monsieur, it isn't at all complicated. When you get to the middle of the village you take the road opposite the church towards Montmorain. About 2km further there is a big bend to the right, and just after it you'll see a small road to the left – that's the one you should take. There's a sign for the Auberge des Bois.

A: Impeccable, merci bien. Donc on arrive vers 7 heures ce soir.
That's fine, thank you very much. We'll be there at about 7 this evening.

B: D'accord, on vous garde la chambre jusqu'à 19 heures. Si c'est plus tard que ça il vaut mieux nous rappeler.
All right, we'll keep the room for you until 7pm. If you are later than that it would be better to phone us again.

A: Ah oui, je comprends, sans problème.
Oh fine, I understand, no problem.

B: Merci monsieur - à ce soir alors, au revoir!
   Thank you sir - till this evening then, goodbye!

A: Au revoir!
   Goodbye!

Louer un gîte - Renting a *gîte*

A: Bonjour – c'est le Domaine des Vignes?
   Hello, is that the Domaine des Vignes?

B: Oui, bien sûr madame, en quoi je peux vous aider?
   Yes, indeed madame, how can I help you?

A: Je cherche une gîte pour la semaine du 16 au 23 juin – est-ce que vous avez encore quelquechose disponible?
   I'm looking for a gîte for the week of June 16 to 23 – have you got anything still available?

B: Pour combien de personnes?
   How many people is it for?

A: On est quatre, deux couples.
   There are four of us, two couples.

B: Donc vous voulez des grands lits?
   So you'd like double beds?

A: Oui, si possible, et une baignoire, c'est essentiel.
   Yes, if possible, and a bath, that's essential.

B: Un moment s'il vous plaît . . . le mois de juin, vous savez . . . Bon, vous avez de la chance, on a eu une annulation tout récemment, donc il y a effectivement une gîte disponible pour cette semaine. C'est du samedi à samedi, cela vous convient?
   One moment please . . . in June, you know what it's like . . . Well, you're lucky, we've just had a cancellation so in fact there is a gîte available for that week. It's from Saturday to Saturday, does that suit you?

A: Tout à fait! Et est-ce que vous avez une piscine, ou un tennis?
   Absolutely! And do you have a swimming pool, or a tennis court?

B: Désolée, on n'a pas de tennis, mais il y a une belle piscine et un terrain de jeu aussi. Puis il y a un minigolf et trois tennis au centre de loisirs pas loin d'ici.
   I'm afraid we don't have a tennis court but there's a beautiful pool and a games area. Then there's a minigolf and three tennis courts at a leisure centre not far away.

A: Et comment est le gîte? C'est indépendant ou mitoyen?
   And what's the gîte like? Is it a separate building or semi-detached?

B: C'est mitoyen sur un côté mais vous avez une terrasse, et un petit jardin clôturé. Il y a un séjour assez grand avec coin cuisine qui donne sur la

terrasse, et un wc en plus au rez de chaussée, puis les deux chambres et la salle de bains à l'étage.
It's attached on one side, but you have a terrace and a little garden that is screened off. There's a fairly big sitting room with a kitchen area that gives onto the terrace, and there's a toilet too on the ground floor, then there are the two bedrooms and the bathroom on the first floor.

A: Et est-ce qu'on peut laver le linge quelque part?
And is there somewhere to do laundry?

B: Oui, madame. Il y a une buanderie en commun, avec seche-linge, fer à repasser et tout ce qu'il faut.
Yes, madame. There's a laundry room for everyone to use, with a dryer and iron and everything you need.

A: Et c'est combien la semaine?
And how much is it per week?

B: À cette période c'est 320€ pour la semaine.
At that time of the year it's 320€ for the week.

A: Est-ce qu'il y a des charges en plus?
Are there any extra charges?

B: L'éléctricité est gratuite jusqu'à une certaine limite – en été ça vous suffirait largement.
The electricity is free up to a certain limit – in the summer it would be plenty.

A: Et la buanderie?
And the laundry facilities?

B: C'est compris aussi. Il y aura juste le nettoyage à payer quand vous partez, si vous ne voulez pas le faire vous-mêmes.
That's included too. There would just be the cleaning to pay for when you leave, if you don't want to do it yourselves.

A: Et c'est combien?
And how much is that?

B: C'est un forfait de 30€.
It's a fixed charge of 30€.

A: D'accord . . . cela me semble idéal – qu'est-ce qu'il faut faire pour le confirmer? Vous voulez des arrhes?
Fine . . . well, that seems ideal to me - what must we do to confirm it? Do you want a deposit?

B: Oui madame, c'est 15 pour cent, ça fera donc 48€, si vous voulez bien nous envoyer un chèque, libellé au Domaine des Vignes. Vous êtes Madame . . . ?
Yes, madame, it's 15 percent, so that would be 48€, if you would send us a cheque made out to the Domaine de Vignes. And you are Madame . . . ?

A: Madame Martin.

B: D'accord. Vous avez notre adresse sur la brochure, n'est-ce pas?
Fine. You have our address in the brochure, haven't you?

A: Oui, bien sûr, donc je le ferai tout de suite.
Yes of course, so I'll do that right away.

B: Merci, madame. Vous voulez d'autres informations sur la région?
Thank you, madame. Would you like any other information about the area?

A: Je la connais un peu – mais est-ce qu'il y a un golf près de chez vous? Est-ce qu'on peut monter à cheval, faire des sports nautiques?
I know it a little – but is there a golf course near you? Can we go riding, and do some water sports?

B: Ah oui, tout ça, on peut le faire pas loin d'ici, pas de problème.
Oh yes, you can do all that not far from here, there's no problem.

A: Ah oui, une dernière question: si jamais on était obligé d'annuler?
Oh, just one more question: what if we had to cancel?

B: En ce cas-là, nous, on garde les arrhes si c'est un mois avant la date d'arrivée, et si c'est plus tard que ça, vous seriez redevable de la totalité de la réservation.
In that case we retain the deposit if it's a month before the arrival date, and if it's later than that, you would have to pay for the whole booking.

A: Eh oui, je comprends. Mais j'espère bien qu'il n'y aura pas d'empêchement. Je suis très contente de vous avoir trouvé.
Oh, I understand. But I hope nothing will prevent us coming. I'm delighted to have found you.

B: C'est vrai, madame, vous avez de la chance!
It's true, madame, you're very lucky!

A: Alors pour le moment je vous dis au revoir.
Well, goodbye for now.

B: Au revoir, madame, et bonne fin de journée!
Goodbye, madame, and have a good rest of the day!

A: Merci bien madame, à vous aussi, au revoir!
Thank you, madame, the same to you, goodbye!

5 Shopping

Useful vocabulary

Shops - les magasins

baker	*le boulanger*	garden centre	*la jardinerie*
bank	*la banque*	grocer	*l'alimentation, l'épicerie* (f)
bookshop	*la librairie*	hairdresser/barber	*la/le coiffeuse/eur*
[library	*la bibliothèque*]	hardware	*la quincaillerie*
butcher	*la boucherie*	laundrette	*la laverie automatique*
carwash	*le lavage automatique*	laundry	*la blanchisserie*
chemist	*la pharmacie*	newsagent	*la (maison de la) presse*
computer shop	*le magasin informatique*	ready cooked food	*la charcuterie, le traiteur*
department store	*la grande surface*	shoemaker/mender	*le cordonnier*
DIY	*le bricolage/brico*	stationer	*la papéterie*
dressmaker	*la couturière*	supermarket	*le supermarché*
(alterations	*les retouches*)	tobacconist	*le tabac*
dry cleaner's	*le pressing*	wine merchant	*la cave*

Payment - le règlement

balance	*le solde*	deposit	*l'acompte*
banknote	*le billet*	discount/reduction	*la remise*
bargain	*la bonne affaire*	price cut	*le décompte*
bill	*la facture, la note*	purchase	*l'achat*
cash	*les espèces*	receipt	*le reçu/ ticket*
change	*la monnaie*	sales (seasonal)	*les soldes*
cheque	*le chèque*	till	*la caisse*
cheque book	*le chequier*	total	*le total*
cost, price	*le prix*	traveller's cheques	*les chèques de voyage*
credit card	*la carte de crédit*	VAT	*le TVA*

In the shop – dans le magasin

assistant	*le vendeur, la vendeuse*	to buy	*acheter*
department	*le rayon*	to choose	*choisir*
display unit	*le présentoir*	to deliver	*livrer*
model	*le modèle*	to exchange, return	*échanger, rendre*
range	*la gamme*	to go shopping	*faire les courses*
sample, swatch	*l'échantillon* (m)	to look for	*chercher*
shelf	*l'étagère* (f), *le rayon*	to order	*commander*
size	*la taille*	to pay	*payer*
(larger/smaller	*supérieure/inférieure*)	to settle a bill	*régler une facture*
style	*le style*	to send/ship	*envoyer/faire envoyer*
trolley	*le caddy, chariot*	to try on	*essayer*
window	*la vitrine*		

Useful phrases

What time do you close today/on Saturday?
A quelle heure vous fermez aujourd'hui/ samedi?

Are you open on Sunday morning? *Vous êtes ouvert dimanche matin?*
Which day of the week do you close? *Quel jour de la semaine vous fermez?*

> Can I help you/tell you about anything? > *Puis-je vous aider/renseigner?*
Thanks, for the moment I'm just looking. *Merci, pour l'instant je regarde.*
Thanks, I'm already being served. *Merci, on s'occupe de moi déjà.*

Hello, could you help me please? *Bonjour, vous pouvez m'aider s'il vous plaît?*
I'm looking for a/some … *Je suis à la recherche d'un/e …/des…*
I'm looking for something to … *Je suis à la recherche de quelquechose pour …*

Have you something like this but - *Avez-vous quelque chose comme ceci mais -*
  - in a larger/smaller size?   - *dans la taille supérieure/inférieure?*
  - in a lighter/darker colour?   - *dans une couleur plus claire/foncée?*
Have you got this style in size 46? *Avez-vous ce modèle en taille 46?*
May I try it on? *Je peux l'essayer?*
Will you be getting any more of these? *Est-ce que vous en aurez d'autres comme ceux-ci?*
What is it made of? *C'est fait de quoi?*
Does it come from this area? *Est-ce que c'est de la région?*

Thanks, I'll think about it. *Merci, je vais réflechir.*
It's nice, but it's not quite what I want.
C'est bien, mais ce n'est pas tout à fait ce que je cherche.
Good, that's just what I was looking for. *C'est bien, c'est exactement ce que je cherchais.*
Can you gift-wrap it please? *Vous pouvez faire un paquet cadeau, s'il vous plaît?*

How much does that make altogether? *Combien ça fait en tout?*
> How do you wish to pay? > *Comment voulez-vous le régler?*
With a card. In cash. By cheque. *Avec une carte. En espèces. Par chèque.*
Sorry, I don't have any change. *Désolé, je n'ai pas de monnaie.*
Sorry, I don't have anything smaller. *Désolé, je n'ai rein de plus petit.*
Wait, I've got the change, if that helps. *Attendez, j'ai la monnaie, si cela vous arrange.*

Do you have the model no. XX in stock? *Est-ce que vous avez le modèle n° XX en stock?*
Do you have anything similar? *Est-ce que vous avez quelquechose de comparable?*
Is it possible to order one? *C'est possible de le/la commander?*
Do you have an idea when it will arrive? *Vous avez une idée quand il va arriver?*
Can you deliver it? *Vous pouvez le livrer?*
Do we have to pay for the delivery? *Est-ce qu'il faut payer la livraison?*

I need a xxxx suitable for … ing. *J'ai besoin d'un(e) xxxx capable de …*
Would this be effective enough to … *Est-ce que celui-ci serait assez performant pour …*
Is it the latest model? *Est-ce que c'est le modèle le plus récent?*
Is there a more powerful model? *Est-ce qu'il y a un modèle plus puissant?*

What kind of guarantee does it have? *Qu'est-ce qu'il a comme garantie?*
Do you service this kind of thing? *Est-ce que vous faites l'entretien de ce genre d'appareil?*
Can you supply the spare parts? *Vous pouvez fournir les pièces détachées?*
Do you do the repairs on the spot? *Vous effectuez les reparations sur place?*

Au marché - At the market 1

A: Bonjour madame, je voudrais un kilo de ces pommes de terre, s'il vous plaît, et un demi-kilo de courgettes.
Hello, I'd like a kilo of these potatoes please, and half a kilo of courgettes.

B: Et avec ça?
Anything else?

A: Quelques tomates, et des pêches bien mûres.
Some tomatoes, and some really ripe peaches.

B: Combien voulez-vous?
How many do you want?

A: Six pêches et une bonne livre de tomates, les tomates de vigne là-bas.
Six peaches and a good pound of tomatoes, the vine tomatoes over there.

B: Ce sera tout?
Will that be all?

A: Ah non, j'ai besoin d'une belle salade aussi.
Oh no, I need a nice lettuce too.

B: Voilà – alors ça fait sept euros cinquante en tout.
Here it is – so that makes 7.50€ in all.

A: Voilà, merci bien.
Here you are, thank you very much.

B: Merci à vous, et bonne journée.
Thank you, and have a good day.

A: Merci, vous de même, au revoir!
Thanks, the same to you, goodbye!

B: Au revoir!
Goodbye!

Au marché - At the market 2

A: Bonjour, monsieur, est-ce que je peux goûter ces saucissons?
Good morning, could I taste these sausages?

B: Bien sûr – ceci est très bon, c'est du chevreuil.
Of course – this one is really good, it's venison.

A: Et celui-là?
And that one?

B: C'est du sanglier, c'est bon aussi, et un peu plus fort.
It's wild boar, it's very good too, and a bit stronger.

A: Vous avez raison, ils sont très bons tous les deux. Je prends un peu de chacun.
You're right, they are both very good. I'll take a little of each.

B: Combien je vous en mets?
How much shall I give you?

A: Une moitié de chacun. Combien je vous dois pour tout ça?
A half of each one. How much do I owe you for all that?

B: Ça vous fait 4.80€ en tout. Vous voulez essayer autre chose?
That makes 4.80€ in all. Would you like to try anything else?

A: Non merci, ça suffit. Attendez, je crois que j'ai la monnaie . . . c'est bon?
No thank you, that's enough. Wait, I think I've got the change . . . is that right?

B: C'est exacte, monsieur. Merci bien, et au revoir!
That's it exactly, monsieur. Thank you very much, and goodbye!

A: Merci à vous, au revoir!
Thank you, goodbye!

A la boulangerie - At the bakery

A: Bonjour madame, je voudrais six croissants comme ceux-ci, s'il vous plaît, et trois petits gâteaux comme ceux-là.
Hello, I'd like 6 croissants like these, please, and 3 little cakes like those ones.

B: Ceux-ci, madame?
These ones, madame?

A: Oui, exactement.
Yes, exactly.

B: Ce sera tout?
Will that be all?

A: Non, je veux un pain de campagne aussi. C'est combien, le plus grand?
No, I'd like a campagne loaf too. How much is the larger one?

B: Trois euros soixante.
3.60€.

A: Et le plus petit?
And the smaller one?

B: Deux euros quatre-vingt.
2.80€.

A: Je prends le plus grand s'il vous plaît.
I'll take the larger one please.

B: Et avec ça?
And anything else?

A: Oui, je voudrais commander douze croissants pour dimanche.
Yes, I'd like to order 12 croissants for Sunday.

B: Bien sûr, madame, à quel nom?
Of course, madame, in what name?

A: Gilbert.

B: Vous voulez des croissants au beurre?
Would you like the croissants made with butter?

A: Bien sûr, ils sont tellement bons!
Of course, they're so good!

B: Très bien madame, c'est noté.
Very good madame, it's noted.

A: Avez-vous de vos quiches aux poireaux aujourd'hui?
Have you got any of your leek quiches today?

B: Non, madame, on les fait seulement le weekend.
No, madame, we make them only at the weekend.

A: Quel dommage! Alors, ça fait combien en tout?
What a pity! So that makes how much altogether?

B: Treize euros quatre-vingt.
13.80€.

A: Désolée, je n'ai pas de monnaie.
Sorry, I don't have any change.

B: Ce n'est pas grave . . . voilà!
That's not a problem . . . here you are!

A: Merci bien.
Thank you very much.

B: Au revoir et bonne journée!
Goodbye, and have a good day!

A: Vous de même, au revoir!
The same to you, goodbye!

Faire les courses - Going shopping

A: Bonjour, monsieur, je peux vous aider?
Hello monsieur, can I help you?

B: Bonjour, je cherche . . . /un guide avec des bonnes photos de la ville.
Hello, I'm looking for . . . /a guidebook with some good photos of the town.

/un pull en taille 44.
/a sweater in size 44.

/un bon foie gras de la région.
/a good local foie gras.

A: Quelque chose comme ceci?/ce modèle?
Something like this?/this style?

- Je vous conseille celui-ci.
I recommend this one.

B: Non, je ne l'aime pas beaucoup.
No, I don't like it much.

- Ce n'est pas vraiment ce que je cherchais.
  It's not really what I was looking for.

- C'est trop grand/petit/clair/foncé.
  It's too big /small /pale /dark.

- C'est bien mais c'est un peu cher.
  It's nice but it's a bit expensive.

Je préfère quelque chose plus coloré/plus petit/plus artisanal/moins cher.
I'd prefer something brighter /smaller /more handmade /less expensive.

Je peux voir celui-la dans la vitrine?/sur le présentoir?
Can I see that one in the window? /on the display?

A: Bien sûr. Cela vous convient mieux?
Of course. Does that suit you better?

B: Oui, ça me plaît beaucoup. C'est combien?
Yes, I like it very much. How much is it?

A: (price) Comment voulez-vous le régler?
How do you wish to pay?

B: Vous acceptez les cartes Diners' Club?
Do you take Diners' Club cards?

A: Désolé, on n'accepte que les cartes Visa ou des espèces.
Sorry, we only take Visa cards or cash.

B: D'accord, donc en espèces . . . désolé, je n'ai rien de plus petit.
Fine, in cash then . . . sorry, I don't have anything smaller.

A: Ce n'est pas grave, pas de problème. Voici votre monnaie.
That doesn't matter, no problem. Here's your change.

B: Merci.
Thank you.

A: C'est pour offrir? Vous voulez un paquet cadeau?
Is it for a present? Would you like it gift-wrapped?

B: Ah oui, effectivement, c'est pour l'anniversaire d'un ami.
Oh yes, actually it's for a friend's birthday.

A: Voilà, monsieur!
Here you are!

B: Merci, c'est très joli.
Thanks, it's very pretty.

A: Avec plaisir, monsieur. Au revoir!
It's a pleasure, monsieur. Goodbye!

B: Au revoir!
Goodbye!

Passer une commande – Placing an order

A: Bonjour, monsieur, j'ai vu dans votre catalogue un lave-vaisselle de la marque Ignis, le modèle numéro xxxx. Est-ce que vous en avez encore en stock?
Hello, I've seen in your catalogue an Ignis brand dishwasher, model no. xxxx. Do you still have any in stock?

B: Désolé monsieur, ils sont tous vendus. À ce prix-là, vous savez . . .
Sorry, sir, they're all sold. At that price, you know . . .

A: Justement, c'est le prix qui m'intéresse! Est-ce que vous en aurez d'autres dans les jours qui viennent?
Exactly, it's the price that interests me! Will you have any more in the next few days?

B: C'est bien probable, au moins dans une quinzaine.
It's very probable, at least in a couple of weeks.

A: Et au même prix?
And at the same price?

B: Oui, monsieur.
Yes sir.

A: Bon, je veux en commander un si possible.
Good, I'd like to order one if possible.

B: Bien sûr. Vous me donnez vos coordonnées?
Of course. If you give me your name and address?

A: Oui, c'est Monsieur Ferris, à . . . (address).
Yes, it's Mr Ferris, at . . .

B: Merci. Et votre numéro?
Thank you. And your phone number?

A: C'est le 05 01 02 03 04. Est-ce qu'il faut payer quelquechose en acompte?
It's 05 01 02 03 04. Do I have to pay anything as a deposit?

B: Non, monsieur, ce n'est pas nécessaire. Dès qu'on a la livraison on vous appellera, et vous pouvez venir chercher votre appareil.
No, sir there's no need. As soon as we have the delivery we'll phone you, and you can come and collect your appliance.

A: C'est possible de le faire livrer? Il y a des frais pour cela?
Is it possible to have it delivered? Is there a charge for that?

B: Oui, c'est un forfait de vingt-cinq euros - mais vous savez, c'est assez volumineux, mais ce n'est pas très lourd. Nous, on peut vous aider à le charger.
Yes, it's a fixed charge of 25€ - but you know, it's quite bulky but it's not very heavy. We can help you load it.

A: Oui, vous avez raison. Et je trouverai quelqu'un ici pour me donner un coup de main et le décharger. Et pour la garantie et tout ça?
Yes, you're right. And I'll find someone here to give me a hand to unload it. And for the guarantee and all that?

B: C'est garanti d'office pour deux ans, et on vous fournit tout ce qu'il faut comme documentation avec le reçu.
It's guaranteed automatically for 2 years, and you'll be given all the paperwork you need with the receipt.

A: C'est rassurant. Donc vous me tenez au courant?
That's reassuring. So you'll let me know what's happening?

B: Bien sûr, monsieur, vous pouvez compter sur moi.
Of course, sir, you can count on me.

A: Merci bien, et au revoir.
Thank you very much, and good-bye.

B: Au revoir.
Good-bye.

Going shopping

As regular visitors to France will already know, the French score pretty high in their devotion to the modern religion of consumerism, even if this has not yet supplanted more orthodox faiths by opening all its temples to its devotees on Sundays to the extent that this happens in the UK. Those places of business which are traditionally open on Sunday mornings (but never in the afternoon) are devoted to another faith vital to the French: the shrines to quality food, in the often portly shape of the bakers, *pâtissiers*, butchers and *traiteurs* who are relied on to provide worthy ingredients for the ceremonial Sunday lunch.

Alas, this devotion to quality is crumbling, in France as everywhere else, in the face of the onslaught of commercialism with its mesmerising brainwash of ads, sales gimmicks and pressure to buy and be seen in or with the biggest, shiniest, recentest model of superfluous widgetry. But though they are great fashion followers, the French are not that easily duped, and generally have a keen eye for a fair price and a bargain. Hence the hysteria over the sales (*les soldes*), held by law in the same weeks in January throughout the country, and more or less simultaneously in the summer.

Supermarkets

Hence also the growth of the massive *supermarchés* which blot the landscape in and on the edges of so many towns. But however much one deplores their appearance, let alone their effects on killing off other trades and traders, it is hard to live without them, since they offer an amazing range of goods of reasonable quality at very keen prices. Bottom of the range in price, but not always in quality, are the cut-price chains such as Lidl and Leader Price (which was surely meant to be called Price Leader!), then come Atac and Super-U. In the middle are Leclerc, Intermarché, Champion, Casino/Géant (the pioneer of supermarket chains), and so on, and at the top, for choice and quality, Auchan and Carrefour. In fact many of these chains are all part of the same group, but have kept a slight difference in identity. Since they are franchises, even within one chain you will not necessarily find identical goods at identical prices.

As for the way they operate, it is pretty self evident, but for those who haven't yet discovered them, here are a few pointers. Detach your trolley from the row by putting in a 1€ coin, and off you go round the race track of endless aisles. If you can't find what you want, you can ask:

"S'il vous plait, où se trouve le lait frais/les oeufs/le pain?"
"Please, where is the fresh milk/the eggs/the bread?"

Many supermarkets now bake their own bread on the premises, and produce a good choice: wholemeal (*complet*), wheatgerm (*au son*), mixed grains (*aux céréales*), rye (*au seigle*), with bacon bits (*aux lardons*), walnuts (*au noix*), etc. These all have more taste and last longer than the whiter kinds. Many local bakers now make these variety breads too. Some chains (eg Carrefour) have a fair choice of organic produce (*produits biologiques*) including packaged goods, milk, egg and fruit juices. Milk is mostly the UHT variety in cartons but if you look in the chilled or dairy section you'll find fresh milk, and sometimes even unpasteurised should you want it.

As for fresh foods, there are usually well stocked cheese and deli counters, and a variable range of meat and of fresh fish depending on the size of the establishment. The bigger ones often have a system with numbered tickets so that people are served in the order of their arrival. The fruit and veg, on the other hand, may disappoint you, as there is not such a wide range as in a big UK supermarket. Moreover the things that are there are often very tired and look as if they have been weeks on the road, which indeed they may well have been. And some of those that aren't wilting only look better because they've been irradiated. So for fruit and veg, you'll find much better quality in your local market, even if there's less choice.

In a way this is a reminder to live and eat more according to the seasons, and to what the farmers in the region have to offer. After all, do we really need Kenyan green beans in January, or Chilean apples in July? But that's the tail of a very fat rat, the complex question of who really benefits from all this international trading and airlifting. One can't help suspecting that it doesn't do a lot for the average Kenyan or Chilean.

But to return *à nos oignons*: note that in larger produce departments there are scales on which you weigh (*peser*) your purchases yourself. There is a touch screen above the scales with symbols for each type of fruit and veg, so put the bag of whatever you have bought on the scales, press the appropriate symbol and the machine will spit out a ticket which you stick on the bag. If you can't see any scales anywhere, don't worry, that means your purchases will be weighed for you at the checkout.

Many supermarkets also have an excellent choice of wines, at prices which will startle you until you get used to them. Once they get above 5€ you are already getting into quality drinking! And usually you'll find a range of significantly good wines between 10€ and 20€. Remember though that strong neon lighting damages the inner workings of the wine process, so if you want the best, look for the supermarkets that have dimmed or non-neon lights in their wine department (eg many Leclercs, Champions, Carrefours).

Many larger establishments have ATMs on the premises, and they all accept credit cards, even for comparatively small amounts. For carrying away your purchases, most now have heavy duty plastic bags which cost 1€ and are replaced free when they wear out. Also useful in hot weather are the insulated bags sold for frozen foods, which are good to take with you to the market to keep cool your chosen cheeses, fish, etc.

Apart from their food ranges, these mega-temples (*les grandes surfaces*) sell thousands of other things, and also have services such as dry cleaning, photocopying, photo printing, key cutting, etc. They often have excellent ranges of household linens and towels, and an assortment of hardware and of equipment for making preserves. You'll notice too a dazzling array of cleaning products, for second only to the French enthusiasm for acquiring things is their passion for keeping them clean and shiny. Hence the range of sprays and potions for cleaning every conceivable kind of material and surface. Sad to think that these *produits* themselves probably do far more damage to the environment in general than the dirt they were designed to chase away in the first place, but for the average French housewife that realisation is still a long way off.

But needless to say the directors of *la grande distribution*, as it's called, are aware that the gilt of mass buying is wearing off the gingerbread of mass production, and are acknowledging the shift in the public psyche towards wanting goods of greater individuality and better quality. Thus you will find, alongside their mass produced ranges, other products (often with cottage-industry style packaging) which are local or from other identified regions of the country, and even from that strange place, abroad - witness the rows of oriental ingredients, curries, Tex Mex, etc, which are fairly recent arrivals on the shelves.

Markets

However for real flavour and colour there is nothing to match the local market. And along with the social and visual pleasures it provides, there's the added satisfaction of knowing that by going to it you are supporting the health of the local economy, and your own health too. There's no doubt that the fruit and vegetables produced by the local market gardeners, who are usually sparing in their use of chemicals (for financial reasons as much as anything else), do far more for one's health than the wilting or over-bright and samey rows of produce in the supermarket. Of course they are a little more expensive, but unless you are buying mountains of them the extra cost is hardly significant, and the extra benefit to all concerned is well worth the slight difference. In many markets there are now serious organic producers, with a good range of packaged as well as fresh foods. Look for the green AB logo, which is only granted under the strictest conditions, so you know you are getting the real thing.

As shopping at the market is as much an art as it is an experience, we offer a few tips to help you enjoy it:

- Get there soon enough! The stallholders arrive any time from 7am and are generally in business by 8.30 or so, then they start packing up by noon. So to get a parking place nearby, to savour the ambience and to catch the lettuces at their freshest, it's worth a prompt start to your morning.

- Take a straw shopping basket with you; not only will it help you 'go local', but it will prevent your fingers being sliced off by plastic bag handles. During hot weather it's a good idea to take an insulated bag too for keeping cheese, fish, etc, cool till you get home.

- Do a quick tour of the market to get your bearings before buying anything, then go round again to select the best of what you've seen.

- The tiny stall with just a few items and a weathered *paysan* - or *paysanne* - behind it will be a local smallholder; the vegetables are home grown without artificial help, the eggs have golden yolks, the chicken comes complete with head and feet instead of a plastic overcoat, but the taste will be honest and fresh, even if it may all look rather rustic. Don't touch anything, they will serve you – often using a hand held beam scale, as introduced by the Romans.

- Next to them you may find a bigger stall where several people are serving, the choice of produce is large, the vegetables are uniformly shaped and unblemished, and the prices are cheaper. The majority of what's on offer is grown with a bit of technological help and purchased by the market vendor at wholesale distribution centres. Help yourself to the plastic bags on the stall and select what you want.

- Between the two you may also find a large stall with a good selection of produce locally grown, often manned by a family who work on a professional scale. Most of what they sell will be their own production of which they are rightly proud, and they often have extras such as fresh herbs and unusual vegetables.

- And of course there are the specialists, their stall piled high with a mound of *tresses* of garlic, of strawberries or melons or sausages or mushrooms just gathered from the woods.

- Don't be afraid to ask questions of the vendors on how to prepare an unfamiliar vegetable, or if you can sample the olives or the strawberries. Ask to taste the cheese, *foie gras*, *saucisson* or wines before you buy; most vendors will be happy to oblige and to explain the finer points of what they have on offer.

- Above all, observe the locals; watch where they shop for their huge variety of crusty breads, their cheeses, their *charcuterie*, their fruit. Remember, they've been there before.

By now, it should be nearly noon; time to find a seat on the nearest terrace for a coffee or a cooling drink, to watch the passing parade, and to dream of the delights you are going to create with your purchases.

DIY

For those who live here, the other favourite rendezvous for shopping, especially in the first year of residence, is the nearest DIY or *bricolage - le brico*. Like the supermarkets, they are stocked with a huge variety of goods of all shapes and sizes, so it's as well before you go to list exactly what you need, down to the last millimetre – literally! Anything you don't see on the shelves you can ask for at the reception desk (*l'accueil*). In the larger ones it's possible to order timber, hardboard, beadings, picture framing, glass, etc, cut to size. And usually they will deliver anything bulky or very heavy – sand, bags of cement, tiling, paving slabs, etc - for free if you live nearby, for a reasonable charge if you are further away. The bigger places will also deliver ready mixed concrete.

Of course if you have a builder on your premises they will advise you where to go and indicate where they have an account. Otherwise it's easy enough to open an account yourself, probably worth it if you are planning to do a lot of work on your property as you'll just have one monthly bill to settle. See the Renovating your House section (pp. 94ff.) for more on this engrossing topic and the relevant vocabulary.

Quality shopping

But however useful the mega-temples may be, there are good reasons for making a point now and again of taking your custom to some of the smaller specialist shops and boutiques that are such a joy to behold and explore, and which do so much to create the special interest and individual flavour of even the average French town. Often such places have an exquisitely done window display and you can see at a glance that the people who run the establishment are rightly proud of what they produce and/or present. This comes across in the way they serve their customers too, in the greetings and goodbyes, and in the trouble they take to package or even gift-wrap what has been bought. Prices of course are a little bit higher, but, as with market purchases, the few extra euros one spends are going towards upholding a whole way of doing things which it would be tragic to lose.

To imagine life without it, one only has to think – but not for too long! – of the average uniformised UK high street, so full of chain stores that nowadays you can hardly tell one town centre from another. Thank the gods, and those stubborn Gauls, that the French are much too individualist to let such steamrollering happen to them and to their towns. And if it's not too impertinent to say so, let us as incomers do our bit to keep up the style, the quality and the variety we have come here to enjoy!

Opening times

Generally shops open some time between 8 and 9 in the morning, with the smaller local shops and *tabacs* at the beginning and larger ones at the end of this period, except for the bakers who are usually open by 6.30 or even earlier. Post offices open at 8.30, banks at 9 or 9.30. Then beware the lunch break! One of the few difficult things to get used to over here in the rhythm of daily life – especially if your usual day begins with a lingering breakfast – is that EVERYTHING CLOSES at 12, or 12.30 in the case of some food shops. Only in the height of summer do the supermarkets stay open all day (*sans interruption*), though some of them may do so out of season on Saturdays, rarely during the week. (The mega *hypermarchés* and *centres commerciaux* don't close at midday.) Everyone opens again by 2 or 2.30 (many *Postes* open at 1.30), and stays open until 6, or often later. In the cities these times are more elastic, and many *alimentations* or *épiceries* (local grocery shops) are open all hours of the day, night and weekend.

Most places (except the *Poste*) are open on Saturday afternoon; bakers, butchers, *charcuteries* and florists open on Sunday morning in order to provide the wherewithal for the strict observance of Sunday lunch, then on Monday most shops, garages, hairdressers, etc, are closed. Banks are too (except in those few towns where there is a Monday market), as are many offices – *notaires*, insurance brokers, etc. Note that on the numerous bank holidays in the French calendar, all offices and most shops *close all day*, with the exception of the bigger supermarkets, who often insist on steamrollering the competition by staying open on bank holiday mornings. On Mondays the supermarkets are in business as usual, and on Sunday mornings in June, July and August they are usually open till 12. When a bank holiday falls on a Tuesday or a Thursday many people take the chance to *faire le pont* ('make the bridge'), ie stay away from work on the intervening Monday or Friday and have an extra long weekend.

Advertising

One less than lovely aspect of French commercial life is the unending bilge of leaflets and brochures put out by local shops and businesses which come and clog up the letterbox with maddening persistence. You can stop them being delivered by putting a sign on your box saying *'pas de publicité'*. But then you might miss out on that one leaflet that tells you about something you did really want to know about . . . for instance the visit of the van that sells tools and household stuff. These *bricos* on wheels tour the country regularly and before their arrival send out catalogues of their current stock which also tell you when they are next coming to a town near you. The vehicles in question are the size of large removal vans and packed with a huge range of stock, and there are some real bargains to be had. If you want to buy, bee-line to the designated rendezvous, queue up behind your neighbours, fill in the order form in the catalogue and hand it to the driver/salesman, who will dive into his Aladdin's cave and reappear with what you've asked for.

Significantly less welcome are the thick brochures sent out every couple of weeks by the big supermarket chains, detailing their current offers. These are printed on semi-gloss paper which can't be recycled satisfactorily, and they really constitute a significant crime in the waste of resources. A whisper of this heresy has their devotees up in arms, protesting that without them they'd never know which weekly bargains to go for. And they're not any happier when it's pointed out that if the supermarkets weren't regularly spending this humungous amount of money and paper on printing enough copies to reach virtually every household in the country, *everything* on the shelves could be very much cheaper *every* week! A rumour was heard a while ago about an environmental tax being stuck on these monstrosities and on the rest of the bumpf that usually goes straight in the bin – we shall see . . .

Then there are the catalogues, from major chains such as 3 Suisses, La Redoute, etc, and any number of smaller ones. The major ones are on sale in the newsagents. If you live in the sticks they are specially useful as they have an incredible range of clothes and of household things, computers and hifi etc, plus outdoor stuff in the summer. Most also have, in addition to the normal home delivery service, a 24 hour service that delivers your order to a local shop which serves as a depot (also for returns). Most have very good sites as well so you can order on line, and their own payment/credit cards (which, be warned, charge an extortionate rate of interest). However they often have fantastic giveaways, and do their best to keep you interested by giving ever increasing discounts through the season. The only downside – apart from having to pay for all those tempting things – is that once you are on their mailing list, whatever they promise to the contrary, loads more bumpf will appear in the letter box from other companies and catalogues who have mysteriously heard about you.

6 Money

Useful vocabulary

Money	L'argent (le fric, les sous, les ronds, le blé, l'oseille, les tartines . . .)		
banknote	le billet	expenses	les dépenses (f), les frais (m)
cash	les espèces (f)	fixed charge	le forfait
coin	la pièce	income	le revenu , les rentrées d'argent (f)
a 50c coin	une pièce de 50 centimes	instalments	les versements échelonnés (m),
small change	la monnaie		les cotisations (f)
cash machine	le distributeur (de billets)	purchase	l'achat (m)
currency	les devises (f)	receipt	le reçu
exchange rate	le taux de change	sale	la vente
traveller's cheque	les chèques de voyage (m)	sales (seasonal)	les soldes (m)
amount	la somme, le montant	to pay	payer, régler
amount due	la somme dûe	to pay in cash	payer en liquide/espèces
balance	le solde	- in instalments	
bill (for smaller amounts)	la note		- en plusieurs fois/ par tranches
bill, invoice	la facture	- monthly	- par mensualités
charges	les charges (f), les agios, les frais (m)		
deposit (eg for house)	le déposit	HT (hors taxes)	excluding taxes
deposit (eg for car rental)	la caution	TTC (toutes taxes comprises)	
down payment	l'acompte (f)		including all taxes
discount	la remise	TVA	VAT

At the bank

bank	la banque	funds available	la trésorerie
bank account	le compte bancaire	overdraft	le découvert
current account	le compte courant	signature, signing	la signature
savings account	le compte d'épargne	transfer	le virement
bank statement	le rélevé de compte	withdrawal	le retrait
bank transfer	le virement		
branch	l'agence (f)	to be in credit	être en credit
cheque	le chèque	to be overdrawn	être en découvert/déficit
cheque book	le chèquier, carnet de chèques	to fill in a cheque	remplir un chèque
credit card	la carte de crédit	to make out a cheque to	libeller un chèque à
credit	le crédit	to cancel a cheque	annuler un chèque
debit	le débit	to cash a cheque	encaisser un chèque
deposit (paid in)	le versement	to pay into an account	verser sur un compte
direct debit	le prélèvement automatique	to make a transfer	faire un virement
figures	les chiffres (f)	to withdraw from it	retirer d'un compte

Finance

accountant	l'expert comptable (m)	accounts	les comptes (m)
accounts (department)	la comptabilité	allowance	la pension

balance sheet	le bilan	loss of earnings	la manque à gagner
borrowing	l'emprunt (m)	minimum wage	le salaire minimum
cost price	le prix coûtant	mortgage	l'hypothèque (f)
date due	l'échéance (f)	pay	la paie
debt	la dette	pay slip	le bulletin de salaire/la fiche de paie
funds	les fonds (m)	profit	la bénéfice
gain	le gain	retirement pension	la (pension de) retraite
income	le revenu	salary	le salaire
investment	l'investissement, le placement(m)	shares	les parts, les actions (f)
liable (eg for tax)	redevable	taxable income	le revenu imposable
loan (for property)	le prêt (immobilier)	taxes	les impôts (m)
loss	la perte	turnover	le chiffre d'affaire

Money, money, money . . .

Where to start on the prickly subject of money? Except to say that if you are moving here and doing up a house you will need lots of it! Of course mortgages and loans are available, and in fact banks and money-lending organisations are falling over themselves to persuade the French to borrow more and to spend more, in an effort to keep the consumerist merry-go-round turning. This is a complete reversal of their traditional attitude, which was that they were doing their customers a favour by holding onto their money for them, and that anyone who dared to be overdrawn even 20 francs – literally – deserved to be *interdit*, ie struck off their books and forbidden to darken the doors of any banking establishment for the next 10 years.

Nowadays, having realised that they make much more profit by allowing and charging for overdrafts, most banks are very ready to provide them, but even so one needs to be careful not to overstep the limit agreed. There is still a risk of being declared *interdit bancaire* if you write a cheque for which you do not have enough funds or authorised credit on your account (*un chèque sans provision*).

As a result of this system, any cheque you write will be accepted as valid and does not need a bank card to prove it, though if it is for a large amount you may be asked for proof of your identity. The only downside is that if you lose your cheque book anyone can sign and use your cheques, so keep it safely - the more so since stopping a cheque is expensive. In fact you can only do this if the book is lost or stolen, not if you just change your mind about buying something for which you have already handed over a cheque.

Credit cards are accepted for payment almost everywhere (except in markets or very small places), even for fairly small amounts. Note though that French cards operate with a PIN code only, whereas the UK ones have to be swiped, so you must be sure to have – and remember! – your PIN code.

Bank accounts

Apart from the strictness about overdrafts explained above, these operate much as you'd expect, with the welcome difference that there are no charges as yet (April 2004) on cheques. However this may change in the near future. The other difference you may notice when you go into a bank, once you've got through the door system which often works with a bell or a card swipe, is that there's a much more relaxed atmosphere and even a more open layout, marking the absence of the siege mentality which has alas become necessary in less ruly places. On the contrary, much is still done on the basis of mutual trust and openness. Long may it last.

Practically speaking, the bank will provide you with a cheque book, debit or credit card depending on your assets, regular statements and all the usual services. As mentioned above, they will also probably be ready to help you with a loan for purchase or *travaux*, or indeed for any other project. Most banks have some e-banking facilities which vary with the establishment chosen. The Poste also offers reliable, up to date and moderately priced banking services (see the comments on this on p. 72-3), and is in fact the largest banking establishment in the country. One of its best points is its e-banking facilities.

Your name and address will be printed on your cheques so this is a useful extra proof of your address. To fill in the cheque, put the money amount, in words, on the line *'payez contre ce cheque . . .'* , the name of the payee on the long line *'à'* or *'à l'ordre de . . .'*, and just above your signature, the name of the place where you are writing the cheque on the short *'à'* line and the date on the *'le'* line. An important detail to remember, to write a figure 7 with a horizontal line through it, otherwise it will be read as a 1.

You will also find a couple of pages in your cheque book (or a coupon that is part of your statement) marked *relevé d'identité bancaire* (RIB) on which are printed your name and address, along with the bank and branch codes and your account number (*vos coordonnées bancaires*). This information will be required for setting up direct debit arrangements, and sometimes an actual RIB will be asked for as well. Ask your bank for extra copies if you need them. There will also be a form for ordering your next cheque book, or you can arrange for this to be posted to you automatically.

Before you pay a cheque into your account you have to sign it on the back, and add your account number if you send it in by post. Note that even a French euro cheque often takes 5 days or so to clear, and a euro cheque from another country will take a couple of weeks and *carry the same charges* as a cheque in a foreign currency.

It is illegal to write a cheque that is post-dated. Which brings us to another topic, that of requesting credit or extra time to pay a large or unexpected bill if you have a glitch in a transfer of funds or whatever. If for instance you are faced with an unexpectedly hefty bill from the garage or have to replace an expensive appliance, you can ask if you can split the amount into two or more payments:

"Est-ce que c'est possible de payer en deux/plusieurs fois?"
"Is it possible to pay in two/several instalments?"

People will usually say yes, in which case you write all the necessary cheques then and there, with the actual date, and agree with the person you are paying when they will present them to your bank. Once you have written the cheques they are legally binding so you must be sure to have the funds available by the dates agreed. To spread the cost of a France Telecom or EDF/GDF bill, you can send in a cheque as part payment and then send the balance later, but you must arrange this with the accounts department in advance.

The simplest method of paying of course is by monthly direct debit, *le prélèvement automatique*, and all the phone, utilities, insurance companies, etc, offer this option. To set this up they will send you a form – of course! – to fill in with your personal and bank details, and they may ask for a RIB and a cancelled cheque (*un chèque annulé*) as well. Regular bills that arrive by post have a coupon at the bottom (*un TIP*), ready printed with your address, bank reference, etc, which you can use for payment *instead of* sending a cheque. All you have to do is sign and date it where indicated and return it in the envelope provided. You can pay these over the counter too at the Poste. If you have an account with the Poste you can pay many bills on line.

If you expect to be transferring major amounts of money from sterling to euros or vice versa, you may want to arrange an account with a bank branch in Jersey or Guernsey, thus minimising exchange charges. Another possibility is to transfer a major amount into a savings account here on which you can draw as necessary, thus avoiding some charges and earning a little something at the same time. Otherwise the cheapest way to access your sterling funds in smaller amounts is simply to make withdrawals with your cash card. A reminder that many larger post offices change money, without charging any commission.

Values

Like every other country France has its share of rogues, thieves and pickpockets (some of the most skilled being young East Europeans operating on the RER trains between central Paris and CDG airport, just to warn you!), but naturally enough they tend to congregate in the cities, leaving most of the countryside in comparative peace. And among the country locals the traditional ethos of courtesy, hospitality and fair dealing is still very much alive, along with a personal pride in doing the best and the most for friends, neighbours and customers, rather than the grudging minimum that is all too familiar in other places we won't mention.

However this generosity and readiness to help has nothing to do with being naive or tolerating being cheated or taken advantage of. They are as quick as anyone else to notice if they do not receive the same respect in return, or for instance are underpaid for services rendered. Showing your gratitude to a neighbour who does something for you may be tricky, as they may refuse actual money, so this is the cue to use your imagination and produce a thank you in the form of a bottle of something interesting, a pretty pot plant, cuttings or fruit from your garden, good photos of their kids or pets, or whatever you think will mean something to them and show your appreciation for the attitudes they are keeping alive. And this is one way of helping a tradition that the UK has sadly lost, to survive and to flourish.

The LETS system

Those of you who are familiar with the LETS system (the Local Economy and Trade System) may be interested to know that various species of LETS networks flourish in different parts of France. Here it is called the SEL (Système d'Echanges Locaux), and the addresses of groups in each *département* can be found at www.transversel.apinc. org. More general info on the system and on several interesting publications at www.asso.francenet.fr/sel. For those who haven't yet heard of it: the LETS system has developed as a modern version of the barter system, but with the inspired difference that exchanges in kind, skills, services, etc, do not have to be a straight swap between two people, but can be made with anyone in the network.

The services offered are given a value in the 'currency' of the group, and each member can 'earn' by selling goods or services to anyone else. Each transaction is priced by agreement between the members concerned, which provides flexibility, and the currency can be 'earned', 'saved' or 'spent' as if it were money. Groups have their own systems of accounting and their own cheques or notes representing the currency.

It works as follows: Anna babysits for Barbara, who earns back what she has paid out for the babysitting by walking the dog for Charlie, who earns what he has paid out, plus a bit more, by painting a ceiling for Denis, who services a car for Elisabeth, who has saved up almost enough to 'pay' for the job and earns the rest by helping Fred sort out a computer problem, then Fred earns back what he has paid to Elisabeth by 'selling' some vegs from his garden to Georgina, who babysits for Anna . . . and it works! Most groups hold regular markets too, selling produce, crafts, etc, payable in their own 'currency'.

The system started in Australia and now functions in many parts of the world. In some Australian communities you can even pay your local taxes this way. The French version of course involves lots of meetings and ardent discussions on deeper principles which generate significant quantities of hot air – but if you are interested in alternatives this is a great gateway into the colourful realm of like-minded souls.

Gîtes and chambres d'hôtes

No review of the money question in France would be complete without a few comments on an activity that may appeal as a way of making some. But if you are hoping to set up or take over gîtes and/or chambres d'hôtes, be warned that this is now a very competitive market with lots of places on offer and an increasingly choosy clientele. Naturally the demand for them is the greatest in and around the tourist hotspots, and just as naturally this is where suitable properties cost the most to buy.

The most important factor to keep in mind is that the normal letting season is short, more or less limited to July and August, which is lemming time for the French as they all head for their grandes vacances, and school hols time for neighbouring nationalities as well. In fact from 15 July to 15 August you could probably let your space three times over, but to attract people before and after this you need to offer something special.

It goes without saying that you need a pool, if it's heated so much the better. Also perfect plumbing, child-safe grounds, and for spring and autumn, optional heating. But perhaps the most important factor is to be in the right area, where there is plenty to do and a choice of towny or country and sporty options, and plenty of interest for children, as families with young are frequent clients for gîtes in the summer. If you go for an area with tourist activity then it is worth getting on the books of the local Office de Tourisme who will send you clients (after lots of form filling), and in some cases advertise your property on line (for a noticeable fee). But to merit this and to make the most of the system, the accommodation you offer has to be top quality and ideally to have some distinguishing feature that makes it stand out from the rest.

Unless you take over a going concern and therefore inherit a client base, it can take a long time to build up your bookings, and in any case it is not realistic to think you'll be able to live solely from this source unless you have a property special enough to merit bookings more or less year-round. We have actually met people who have come over with the rosy hope of buying some spacious pile and converting it instantly into an adequate income for an entire family with growing children . . . don't even go there! It can't be done! Quite apart from having to buy an exceptional property, you'd need to have enough capital to live on for a couple of years if not more while building up your clientèle, and that's not counting any renovation costs. And even if you are only updating existing gîtes it can still swallow up a minor mountain of cash.

However there are rewards and pleasures - social, financial and aesthetic - to be had from providing a place where people can enjoy their holidays, if you can afford to do things well and provide the extra touches that make your guests want to come back and to tell their friends about you. Among other advantages, it may enable you to live somewhere larger and more spacious than you could otherwise afford.

But it is definitely *not* something that can be done as a shoestring operation. Apart from paying for publicity, there are always unexpected costs and things to fix, extra charges and taxes to pay (such as the *taxe de séjour*, due for each night spent by each client on your premises), grounds to keep in order, safety and insurance factors to consider, etc, etc. And incidentally, running *gîtes*, etc, rates pretty high on the acid-test-of-a-relationship scale! For more about the nitty gritty of all this, see the hints in the Appendix (p. 154), contributed by friends who have a beautiful *domaine* with space for 20 visitors.

More vocabulary

un prix/une somme . . .	*a xxx price/a xxx sum . . .*
modique	*modest*
correct(e)	*fair, reasonable*
abordable	*affordable*
intéressant(e)	*keen, worth investigating*
important(e)	*substantial*
onéreuse	*high, large*
élevé (prix)	*high*
exagéré (prix)	*inflated*
exorbitant(e)	*exorbitant*
global(e)	*inclusive, overall*

bon marché	*cheap*
cher	*expensive*
une baisse des prix	*a drop in prices*
une hausse des prix	*a price rise*
un faible rendement	*a low return*
un rendement satisfaisant	*a satisfactory return*

un pécule	*a nest-egg*
une pactole, une coquette somme	*a tidy sum*
un pourboire	*a tip*

111€ pile/tout rond	*111€ exactly*
999€ et poussière	*999€ and a few centimes*

être fauché	*to be broke*
avoir les moyens de payer/faire quelquechose	*to have the means to pay/do something*
être en mesure de . . .	*to be in a position to . . .*

faire un bilan	*to draw up a balance sheet, make an assessment*
faire un devis	*to provide a quote*
chiffrer quelquechose	*to calculate the cost of something*
estimer quelquechose	*to estimate something*

Voulez-vous que je vous le chiffre?
Would you like me to work out the approximate price?

Voulez-vous que je vous fasse un devis?
Would you like me to give you a quote?

7 ⚘ Services and Utilities

Post

Surely one of the magnets that draws people to this wonderful country is that along with all the riches of tradition and history, there are numerous wonders of the modern world that work extremely well. One of these is the postal service, La Poste. There are post offices everywhere, and though in most towns there is only one central *poste*, even many large villages have their own office. The idea of sub-post offices is also gradually catching on, and in some places there is a post office counter in the village shop.

Apart from the convenience of the usual postal services, the Poste also runs a very efficient banking service (it's the largest banking organisation in the country), so if you have an account with them you can access it almost anywhere. Handy if you live in one of the many villages which have a Poste but don't yet have an ATM. Most larger post offices have ATMs, on the Cirrus, Plus and all the usual networks.

Sending post

Post offices (*les bureaux de poste*) in towns are generally open from 8.30am to 12 noon, and from 1.30/2pm to 5/5.30 except on Saturdays. The hours for village post offices vary, and in fact sadly the hours are being reduced in many others too. Stamps (*les timbres*) can also be bought in *tabacs* (tobacconists - look for the red lozenge symbol above the door), and in many places that sell postcards, if you ask them nicely. Letter boxes are rectangular and yellow, usually attached to a wall somewhere fairly obvious, and the time of collection (*la levée*) is shown on them. Except in major towns there is only one collection from the central Poste, just at closing time. It usually takes 48 hours for first class post to reach its destination in France, or in the UK.

Postal rates and services

There are a number of different rates and services: for letters and small parcels abroad, first class is *prioritaire*, second class *économique*. Within the country the choice is *lettre* for first class or *économique*. Put one of the appropriate stickers on whatever you are posting (there are rolls of them on or near the counter) or write it on. If you want pretty stamps – and there are always new series being issued - ask for *timbres de collection*. In many post offices there are efficient self-serve coin-operated franking machines with a touch screen, which have an English language option. Worth trying if there is a queue.

Registered post is *recommandé*, and you can also request a proof of delivery (*un accusé de reception*). In this case a copy of the original receipt (*le récépissé*) will be returned to you, with your usual post, when the item has been delivered. There's also an option of *la lettre suivie*: a sticker with number and bar code is put on your letter and you can then check its progress either by phone or on the Internet, until it reaches the *destinataire*.

For posting larger items you can buy mailing boxes in sizes S, M, L or XL – yes really! – or bottle-sized, which are ready stamped (*un carton préaffranchi, prétimbré*). They are fairly expensive but the postage is included and they are very tough, and convenient to use. Delivery is within 48 hours, and as with the *lettre suivie*, you can follow their progress. You can also buy in the post office tough pre-stamped mailing envelopes which are cheaper and very practical. For urgent documents or smaller items there is a Chronopost service, which guarantees delivery anywhere in France (and in some other neighbouring countries) in 24hrs. This is expensive but you get a refund if it takes longer than promised, so keep the receipt carefully in case there is a problem and you want to claim (*faire une réclamation*). When you send a parcel (*un colis*) or packet (*un paquet*) you need to put your own address on the back crossed through, labelled *expéditeur* (sender).

Another very useful service that has been mentioned, many of the larger post offices have an exchange service (*change*) that *does not charge any commission*. Some are in the Western Union network too, which organises rapid and safe international cash transfers. Many post offices have photocopy machines (*une photocopieuse*), and an Internet facility (*une borne Internet*). To use this you buy a card at the counter which gives you a certain amount of time online, and slot it into the machine. One of the staff will help you get going if necessary. It's also possible to pay France Telecom and EDF/GDF bills over the counter. Apart from these services La Poste is always adding to its range in order to keep its customers happy.

Receiving post

For delivery (*la livraison*) you need to have your own letterbox (*une boîte à lettres*) by your front gate (or in the entrance hall if you have an apartment) as the post person (*le facteur, la postière*) will only come to your door if there is something to sign for. If your house doesn't have one already, you can buy a regulation box at the post office or in a *brico*, with a key which the *facteur* has a duplicate of. There is a slot on the front of the box into which you put a label with your name, in legible letters! Since the French don't usually give their houses individual names and houses don't always have numbers, this label is the only way for the postman – or anyone else – to know which house in the road or village is yours.

The time the post is delivered varies of course according to how far you are from the nearest sorting centre, but it is usually mid to late morning. It's worth knowing that if you live somewhere rural, the postman will collect your letters from your own box as well as deliver. If you don't have stamps handy, leave some change with the letters and the postman will stamp them for you.

Most post offices have a post box (*une boîte postale*) system, and there is also a *poste restante* service at many larger offices. To sign on for a box, you have to prove your identity and that you live in the postal area (*la circonscription*) covered by that office. The fee covers 6 or 12 months, and gives you your own BP address. The said BP may be an actual locker (*un casier*) in the post office to which you have your own key, or in a smaller place it's as likely to be a section in an accordion file kept behind the counter. There is also a forwarding system, which works automatically with printed address labels. Ask for the forms *pour faire suivre le courrier* a couple of weeks before you want the change of address to take effect. The fee will pay for a year's forwarding, or more if you are lucky.

I was once the proud owner of the BP3 in a village post office of the accordion file variety, where naturally my name and face soon became known. When I moved on my letters were forwarded for the statutory year, and even two years later, occasional missives would still arrive, readdressed in the careful hand of the unfailingly helpful and courteous postmaster.

Banking with La Poste

This works well as there is the minimum of fuss when opening an account and there are minimal charges. (Presumably this is because the Poste do not rely for their profits exclusively on their banking services.) The Poste's investment plans regularly score high in the league tables of attractive and reliable returns. They will also arrange loans for house purchase or other projects.

To open an account you need to make an appointment with the *conseiller financier* at the nearest post office that has one (usually in a largeish town). As with most other banks, once you've filled in the forms you will be issued with a debit card (Visa), and with a cheque book when you have a minimum amount of cash paid into the account. You have the option of a credit card also when your credit rating is established. Once the account is functioning you can withdraw or pay in funds, pay in cheques, etc, in *any* post office.

To keep track of it all, you can check your balance and recent transactions via an automatic answering service on the phone, or on the Net. On the Net you can also carry out numerous transactions, pay bills, manage your share portfolio, etc. The Poste is the only banking service that does not charge its customers for withdrawing money from a cash machine belonging to a different establishment.

See the previous chapter on Money for more on this topic.

Telephone

As we've commented above, one of the joys of France is the happy cohabitation of the picturesque, the historic and the still living past, alongside the latest gadgetry and conveniences of modern life. Not least among these latter is the very efficient telephone system and all that pertains thereto.

The phone system is managed and basically run by France Telecom, who are responsible for the lines and installation, though they no longer have the monopoly of usage. For the purposes of the phone system France is divided into 5 regions, each with its area code:

01 = Paris and the Ile de France	04 = southeast France (inc. Provence)
02 = northwest France (inc. Normandy)	05 = southwest France (inc. Aquitaine)
03 = northeast France	06 = mobile phone numbers

- To make a call within the country, even if it's just down the road, you have to dial the area code (or the 06) as well as the 8 digit number.

- For dialling abroad, dial 00 + the country code, then the area code *without the 0*, then the number. (Unless you're calling Italy, in which case include the 0.)

Public phones

The only drawback of the system is that the old coin phones disappeared along with the franc, so to use any public phone, you need a phone card (though phones which take an ordinary credit card are becoming more common in big cities). You can buy a phone card (*une télécarte*), encoded with either 50 or 100 units (*cinquante/cent unités*), at a post office or *tabac* and in some bars that are licensed to sell tobacco. *Télécartes* are also available from vending machines in many airports.

The digital display on the phone will lead you through these steps:

1. *Décrocher*	Lift the receiver.
2. *Introduire carte ou composer Numéro Vert*	Insert your *télécarte* or dial a toll-free number.
3. *Patienter*	Wait a minute.
4. *Numéroter*	Dial your number.
5. *Raccrocher*	Hang up the receiver.

The phone will beep if you leave your *télécarte* in the slot. To make a second call without hanging up, push the white button quickly instead of replacing the receiver. You should then be prompted for the *Numéroter* (Dial) instruction again.

"Call me back"

All pay phones have their number marked in the booth and accept incoming calls. If you don't have enough card credit to talk for long, you can make a quick call, give the number to the other person, hang up and wait for them to call back. This can be handy when calling overseas, since a call from France may cost more than a call going the other way.

Point Phones

Point Phones are little cream-coloured pay phones commonly found in bars, restaurants and hotel lobbies. They cost a little more than standard street pay phones, and they too accept phone cards only. As another option, many hotels and bars have phones in the lobby hooked up to a meter. After your call they'll check the meter and tell you how much you owe. Very convenient but beware, they usually mark up the charges about 50%.

Mobile phones

Needless to say, in a country where one of the main national sports is talking, the mobile phone (*le portable, le téléphone mobile*), which enables people to practise the sport whenever the fancy takes them, is an imperative part of most people's life equipment. The latest reckoning indicates that 70% of the population have one, and the merest glance around the average group of passers–by will prove the point, also that the phones in question are rarely idle for long. Glance at the drivers too, you'll come to the same conclusion – but PLEASE NOTE that there are now hefty fines for using a mobile phone while at the wheel.

There are many different mobile networks offering all kinds of deals which it would be impossible to detail here, not least because under the pressure of competition they are continually being updated, and adding to the range of services and widgetry that they try to convince their customers to use. One of the most useful of these is the *facture détaillée*, the itemised bill. And of course with the latest phones there are the fancier options of taking and transmitting photos, even video clips, etc.

Alternative networks

The same is also true of the alternative fixed line networks, of which there are now several, most of them significantly cheaper, most of the time, than France Telecom, particularly for phoning abroad. No need to make any changes to your number or phone, you just dial a prefix for each call. Joining them is a simple matter of a phone call; here are the relevant numbers and sites:

One.Tel:		www.onetel.fr
Primus:	0800 333 999	www.primustelecom.fr
Tele2:	0805 04 11 25	www.tele2.fr
9telecom:	0811 00 10 09	www.9telecom.fr

The only thing they don't tell you is that they charge each call from the time you start dialling, so you have to pay something for every call even if you don't get through. But it's often only a fraction of a centime, so your overall costs will still probably be much lower. These networks now offer Internet access too, at very competitive rates. One network you are strongly advised to avoid is Tiscali. Horror stories abound of their inefficiency, both in the functioning of the network itself and especially in their tendency to continue direct debiting clients who have said they want to cancel.

You can in theory subscribe to several of these alternative networks and use the cheapest one for the type of call you wish to make. However this gets complicated as the rates are chiselled a little further every few months, so it is probably easier to stick to one of them. They each offer a preselection option so that all your calls go through their system automatically. This saves you remembering to dial their prefix, but it also means that they have the right to cut you off if you neglect their bill.

In any case the installation itself and the line remains with France Telecom, to whom the line charges are paid. And in fact their call charges are also dropping rapidly, so once you are actually in residence and have your line functioning, you can review the current call rates and make your choice.

Opening a France Telecom account

Opening an account is easy. Go to your nearest Telecom office (address in the Pages Jaunes) with proof of your identity (*une pièce d'identité*) and your address (*un justificatif de domicile*), your bank details (*les coordonnées bancaires*) and the name of the previous subscriber if any (not essential but if you have it they'll trace your number more quickly in their system). If it is a new house and you don't yet have another utility bill as proof of your address, any official letter with your name and the address on it will do. The line will normally be functional within 48 hours.

The charge for opening an account where there is a line already installed is currently 46€. The cost of a new line with a new installation depends on the circumstances, ie how far your property is from the nearest functioning line. This amount will be added to your first bill which will arrive in 2 months' time. Be sure to tell them if you want the bills sent to a UK or other address. There is also a direct debit option (*le prélèvement automatique*), a good idea if you are not resident all the time as the line may be cut off if you lose track of the bill. On the bill you will see a coupon at the bottom, a TIP, with your bank info, etc, which works like a cheque, so to pay the bill *all you have to do* is date and sign the TIP and post it in the envelope provided (cf p. 67). The first bill will have a TIP and ask you to return it with a RIB – are you getting the picture?! – so that they have your bank details.

When you sign up with France Telecom you will also be given the choice of having an itemised bill (*une facture détaillée*) listing every call (which is free), and numerous other options (which aren't), such as the Top Message answering service, automatic redial of engaged numbers, display of the number of an incoming call, conference calls, etc, all of which are too complex to go into here and are always being updated. As part of their strategy to stay on the cutting edge of communications technology, France Telecom also provides a broad-band Internet access (*une ligne haut-débit*) in many parts of the country. Currently the basic connection costs 30€ per month. More details from your local Telecom office or on www.francetelecom.com.

On the phone

Useful vocabulary

(land) line	*la ligne (fixe)*	switchboard	*le standard*
portable/mobile	*le portable/mobile*	answering machine	*le répondeur*
cordless phone	*le sans fil*	answering service	*la messagerie*
network	*le réseau*	phone book	*l'annuaire* (f)
phone set	*l'appareil, la poste*	directory enquiries	*les renseignements*
plug/socket	*la prise*		
receiver	*le récepteur*	to connect, plug in	*brancher*
dialing tone	*la tonalité*	to ring	*sonner*
ringing tone	*la sonnerie*	to dial	*faire le numéro, numéroter*
buttons	*les touches*	to pick up the phone	*décrocher*
* button	*la touche étoile*	to hang up	*raccrocher*
# button	*la touche dièse*	to phone	*appeler*
phone number	*le numéro*	to ring back	*rappeler*
phone call	*un appel*		

Useful phrases

C'est Janine/Henri à l'appareil, est-ce que je peux parler à Jean-Pierre/Suzanne?
This is Janine/Henri (on the phone), please can I speak to Jean-Pierre/Suzanne?

C'est moi./Lui-même. (m)/Elle-même. (f) *Speaking.*
Je vous la/le passe. *Here s/he is. /I'm putting you through to her/him.*
Désolé(e), elle/il n'est pas là en ce moment. *Sorry, s/he's not here at the moment.*
Sa ligne est occupée. *His/her line is busy.*
Ne quittez pas. *Please hold.*
Je vous écoute./J'écoute. *I'm listening (= Please go ahead.)*
Désolé(e), ce n'est pas le bon numéro. *Sorry, you've got the wrong number.*
Désolé(e), je me suis trompé(e) de numéro. *Sorry, I've dialled the wrong number.*
Un moment s'il vous plaît. *One moment please.*
Merci de patienter quelques instants. *Please wait a moment.*
Appuyez sur la touche étoile/dièse. *Press the */# button.*

Veuillez rappeler plus tard./Veuillez renouveler votre appel ultérieurement.
Please ring back later.

Veuillez laisser votre message après le bip sonore.
Please leave your message after the beep.

Le numéro que vous demandez n'est pas attribué.
The number you have dialled is not listed. (or you've misdialled)

La ligne de votre correspondant est momentanément indisponible.
The number you are calling has been temporarily suspended.

On se rappelle. *Let's ring each other later.*

Je te passe un coup de fil demain. *I'll give you a buzz tomorrow.*

Ansaphone message

Bonjour, vous êtes bien chez Suzanne et Jack Harrison. Merci de laisser votre message, on vous rappelera dès que possible/dès notre retour. À bientôt.
Hello, this is the number for Suzanne and Jack Harrison. Please leave your message, we'll call you back as soon as possible/when we return. Goodbye.

Leaving a message

A: Bonjour, je voudrais parler à M. Chavanne s'il est disponible.
   Hello, I'd like to speak to M. Chavanne if he's available.

B: Désolé, madame, il n'est pas là en ce moment.
   I'm sorry, madame, he is not here at the moment.

A: Vous pouvez me dire à quel moment je pourrais le joindre?
   Can you tell me when I could reach him?

B: En effet il est en déplacement, il ne revient que mardi prochain.
   Actually he's away on a trip, he won't be back until next Tuesday.

A: Alors . . . je peux lui laisser un message?
   Well then . . can I leave a message?

B: Bien sûr, madame, c'est de la part de qui?
   Of course, madame, who's speaking?

A: Madame Freeman. C'est pour lui dire que nous avons bien reçu son courrier, mais il reste encore quelques détails à préciser. Donc s'il pourrait nous rappeler à son retour?
   Mrs Freeman. It's to say that we've received his letter, but there are still a few points to clarify. So if he could ring us when he gets back?

B: D'accord, madame, je ferai la commission.
   All right, madame, I'll give him your message.

A: Merci bien, au revoir.
   Thank you very much, goodbye.

B: Au revoir, madame, et bonne journée.
   Goodbye, madame, and good day.

Finding phone numbers

Phone directories for each *département* come in two chunks, the ordinary alphabetical one and the Yellow Pages, the Pages Jaunes. The latter gets delivered free but for the white one, or if there aren't any in your house, you have to go to the nearest Telecom office. The catch is that the lists are divided into communes, so when you want to find someone's number you have to know before you start which commune they live in. For the Pages Jaunes trade numbers this isn't really a problem, but for personal numbers, or for the numbers of organisations where you have the name but not their address, it can be frustrating.

The good news is that you can find the information more easily on the Pages Jaunes site www.pagesjaunes.fr. (In English on www.englishpagesjaunes.fr.) On the Pages Jaunes table, type in the kind of business you are looking for – *garage*, *plombier*, *gare* - in the *'activité'* box, and the town in the *'localité'* box. If you don't want to or can't specify the town then you can just put in the *département* name or number in the *'département'* box. On the answer page there is usually a map option, so click on *'carte'* if you want one, and when it comes up you can zoom to get various levels of detail.

To find a number when you already have a name, go to the Pages Blanches page and type the name in the top *'nom'* box. If you know the town, put that in, but if you don't, just put in the name or number of the *département* and wait for the answer. This is useful for finding the addresses and numbers of organisations, for instance the nearest office for health service refunds (CPAM), the nearest EDF office, etc.

For directory enquiries (*les renseignements*) you can dial 12, but very unhelpfully the machine now asks you first if you want to be put through (*mise en relation*) to your number directly, in which case you have to say *"oui"*, or if you want an operator, in which case you have to say *"opérateur"*. Inevitably the machine has a hard time recognising accents, so you may have to go through this routine more than once. The operators are very helpful once you reach them. If you ask them to put you through directly you are still told the number.

For international enquiries dial 00 33 12 + the code of the country you want.

Phone problems

If you have a problem with your phone line, dial 1013 (the call is free) and you will be put through to the Telecom service department (*service après-vente* or *SAV*). This is an automatic answering system with the usual maddening series of options and buttons to press. If you want to talk to a real person, *don't start on the button pressing routine*, just wait, and you will eventually hear the welcome tones of a real voice! Once you have managed to explain your problem, it is usually dealt with very promptly. If you have a query about your bill, dial 1014 for the *service client*, also free, and if you want to ask about adding a new line, dial 1016.

Notifying a problem with the phone

A: Bonjour, je vous appelle pour signaler un dysfonctionnement sur notre ligne. Je vous donne le numéro – c'est le 0X.XX.XX.XX.XX.
Hello, I'm calling to notify a problem on our line. I'll give you the number – it's 0X.XX.XX. XX.XX.

B: C'est Monsieur B--? . . . à (*your address*)?
That's Mr B--? . . . at (your address)?

A: Oui, c'est ça.
Yes, that's it.

B: Quel est le problème exactement?
What's the problem exactly?

A: - Depuis ce matin il n'y a aucune tonalité.
Since this morning there's no dial tone.

- Il y a un drôle de bruit sur la ligne.
There's an odd noise on the line.

- On peut recevoir les appels mais on ne peut pas les faire.
We can take calls but we can't make them.

- Quand on fait le numéro, la tonalité ne change pas.
When we dial, the dialling tone doesn't change.

B: D'accord, monsieur, je vous demande de patienter un moment, je vais le tester pour savoir si la faute est sur la ligne ou sur l'installation . . . C'est bien sur le réseau – donc ne vous inquiétez pas, ce sera réparé dans les plus brefs délais.
All right, I'll just ask you to wait a minute while I run a test to see if the fault is on the line or in the installation . . . It's on the line, so don't worry, we'll get it repaired as quickly as possible.

A: C'est rassurant - vous imaginez bien qu'on s'en sert tout le temps, donc c'est urgent.
That's reassuring - you can imagine, we use it all the time, so it's urgent.

B: Bien sûr, on fera le nécessaire le plus rapidement possible.
Of course, we'll deal with it as soon as possible.

A: Merci bien, et au revoir.
Thank you very much, goodbye.

B: Au revoir!
Goodbye!

Electricity

At the time of writing the EDF/GDF (Electricité/Gaz de France) still has a monopoly on supplying electricity and mains gas, though this may change in the future. It is easy to open an account with them. As with France Telecom, you go to the nearest agency with the proof of your identity and address, your bank details and name of the previous subscriber (*le propriétaire précédent*) if there is one. If it is a new house your builder will probably have opened an account for it already in his own name, so if you have the details from him it is easy to change this to your name. Bills can be paid by fixed monthly instalments, or every 2 or every 6 months depending on the circumstances. For how to pay the bills, see the comments above on paying the phone bill, p. 75. The bill will indicate whether it is based on an estimate (*une estimation*) or on an actual reading (*un relevé*).

The electricity tariffs (*les tarifs*) available for a private house boil down to the following choices:

Tarif Bleu: this has two options, first the *tarif de base*, with which your electricity costs the same all day and all year round, ie more than necessary, considering that you also have the option of the *tarif heures creuses*. With this one, electricity is cheaper during certain hours (*les heures creuses*) than in others (*les heures pleines*). Usually the *heures creuses* are from 1.30-7am and 1.30-3pm. If you want to minimise costs you can buy a 24hr timer (available in most *bricos*) which can be adjusted to run your dishwasher or washing machine during these times, or you can ask the EDF to install a special connection on which the current functions only during these hours, to which the appliances can be connected. If you have an electric water heater it will normally be set to run only during these periods, but it is worth checking this.

The standing charge for this tariff is higher than for the *tarif de base*, but your overall bill will probably be less if your house is occupied more than half the year. Your meter will have a dial showing the consumption in each period, and the two totals (marked HP and HC) will be shown on your bill. The other deciding factor in your choice of tariff is whether your house is occupied during the winter or not. To find out why, read on!

The most popular EDF tariff, the Tempo, has 3 cost levels: cheap during *heures creuses*, moderate during *heures pleines* and extortionate on 22 selected days during the winter. These 'red' days are chosen according to the weather, which means that on the coldest days of the year the electricity is at its most expensive. However this system is not as hard-hearted as it sounds. For one thing the EDF are not allowed to have red days at the weekend, nor to have more than three consecutively. And if you choose this tariff they will install for you beside your fuse panel a little box (*un boîtier*) that tells you from about 8 in the evening what rate is going to be charged for the following day. So provided you remember to check it, you will be warned ahead of time, and if there's a red day coming up you can plan accordingly to make your *pot au feu*, huddle round your wood burner, or go out for some bracing exercise!

On the whole the occasional inconvenience is more than compensated for by the savings the rest of the year. Of course if you're not planning to be there in the depths of winter anyway, you can sign up for this option without a qualm. Note however that the standing charge for this tariff is now much higher than for the *tarif bleu*, so it is only worth getting involved with if you use a lot of electricity for hot water, cooking, some of your heating, etc. If you ask them the EDF will send a consultant to talk to you at home and give you free on the spot advice as to the tariff most suitable for your circumstances and pattern of usage.

Storm hazards and fuses

In many parts of France, especially in hilly country, the summer heat builds up and creates electrical charges that result in dramatic storms with lots of thunder and lightning. Modern electrical systems here are designed to cut out immediately as soon as there is a surge of current, so the first thunderclap or lightning flash may well plunge your home, or your *gîte,* into darkness. However this is easily remedied, provided you know where to find the mains breaker (*le disjoncteur*) and which button or lever to push on the fuse board (*le panneau éléctrique*). Usually there are two separate ones. In principle all fuses and levers are working when the switches are in the UP position and the rectangular black button on the control box is IN. *Be sure to ask when you arrive or take possession* where to find the relevant controls in case there is a blackout (*une coupure de courant*).

It's advisable to protect any sensitive electrical equipment - computers, TV, etc – with a special insulating plug (*une prise anti-foudre*) which you can buy in any *brico* or big supermarket. However these are not infallible, and in view of the extreme weather conditions we have experienced in recent years, it's best to unplug the equipment anyway when storms are forecast to be on the safe side. (NB: If you are having an induction hob fitted in your kitchen, ask the electrician to put it on a separate socket (*une prise indépendante*) so that you can unplug it if a storm is imminent. If it is wired in directly, it is liable to be burned out by the lightning, as happened recently to a neighbour who had just had her kitchen refitted at vast expense.) The electrics may also cut out if there are any frayed or loose wires in switches or plugs, dodgy light bulbs, etc, so if you have an unexplained blackout, check any possible culprits of this kind before sending for the electrician.

Gas

If you live in town or an area with mains gas, the procedure for joining the system is as above for the EDF and it can be done at the same time in the same office. Otherwise, you will have the joy of using butane or propane gas in bottles (*une bonbonne*) or cylinders, which you can buy from all the big supermarkets and many village stores and garages. (It does come in tankfuls too but these hold far more than you'd need for normal domestic use unless it's providing year-round heating.) You pay a rental fee (*la consigne*) for the first one plus the refill fee (*le recharge*), then only for the refill as and when needed. When the bottle is empty you take it to anywhere that sells the same type of gas (indicated by the colour of the bottle), and swap it for a full one. (Be sure to take its metal collar with it too.) Watch out, a full one is very heavy!

On a new bottle the outlet is sealed by a small blue plastic cover which you pull off – if you can! Then fit the nut on the end of the gas feed onto the screw outlet on the bottle, and turn it *anti-clockwise* to tighten it (you may need a spanner to make it really tight). Then unscrew the knob on top of the bottle a turn, and you're in business. The gas pressure is pretty high, so there's no need to open it all the way.

Though the bottles are very safe it is always advisable, if you have a choice in the matter, to have them installed so they are parked outside the house with a lead through the wall into the kitchen. This saves space in the kitchen too, as a bottle takes up a whole cupboard. In this case there will be a sort of safety valve on the gas conduit inside the kitchen which locks automatically when you close off the gas bottle to change it. Once you have fitted and opened the new bottle, give the valve control a half turn and back again, and the gas from the new supply will come through. If you are leaving the premises empty for any length of time it's a good idea to shut off the gas bottle by screwing down the knob on top of it.

If you expect to use a lot of gas you can buy the tall cylinders which hold double the amount of the normal short fat ones – and weigh twice as much! It is a good idea to have a system with connections for two bottles so that you can keep one full one in reserve. Though a bottle will last 3 months or so with normal small family use, it will invariably run out just when you have invited friends for Sunday lunch, when you are knee deep in jam, or at some other really convenient moment. Often it makes a strong gas smell a day or so before it expires. However if it does so and you don't have a back-up, don't panic. Many small garages or even bars in the country sell gas and are open on Sunday mornings – ask your neighbours where the nearest one is, if you haven't already located it.

Water

There is no monopoly in France for water supply so you will have to check with the people you are buying from, or your builder, which water board operates in the area you are going to. (Or check in the Pages Jaunes under *'eaux'*.) Remember that water is metered, so you will be charged according to the quantity you use. The rates are generally double those in the UK, so it's advisable to check your meter from time to time if you are running a pool or watering the garden a lot. It is worth having an efficient shower installation with a thermostatic tap which avoids wasting water - and time - while you adjust the temperature, and also having a dual control toilet flush, something else that saves a significant amount of water.

The meter (*le compteur*) is usually under an inspection cover on the mains near the house. The water board is responsible for the pipes before the meter but you are responsible for them after the meter, so check occasionally that there are no leaks – if there is a leak (*une fuite*) on your side you have to pay for the water lost. In winter it's a good idea to put some insulation for the mains into the inspection pit to prevent it freezing. In many parts of central and southern France the water is very hard (*calcaire*), so you may want to invest in one of the many water softening systems (*pour l'adoucissement de l'eau*) on the market. The jug-type filters for drinking water are also becoming more and more widely available.

The French are now becoming much more concerned about the pollution of their water resources, which sadly is considerable, especially in areas of intensive agricultural activity like parts of Brittany and the Beauce area west and south of Paris where traces of dozens of chemicals and pesticides are found in the groundwater. Communes are required to have the local water supply tested regularly and to publish the results (*les analyses d'eau*), so this is something else to check on especially if there are young children in your household. As of 2003 it is illegal to have any lead piping in the water system, so houses being sold now have to be certified lead-free. It is the vendor's responsibility to have this checked and to replace any pipes that are still in lead. In general this is only a problem in older town housing.

Cancellations

When you leave your property definitively, it is an easy matter to cancel (*résilier*) your *abonnements* for the phone and EDF/GDF. Inform the offices concerned about 2 weeks ahead of time that you wish to cancel, and if you don't have a direct debit arrangement, give them your forwarding address for the final bill. They'll probably ask you to ring again nearer the time to confirm when you actually leave. If you live somewhere accessible the EDF/GDF may come to do a meter reading (*faire rélever le compteur*) just before you leave, but if you live out in the sticks they will ask you to do the meter reading yourself and phone them with the numbers (*le rélevé*). The water boards function differently, and with some of them you cannot cancel your *abonnement* until there is a new owner (or tenant) to take it over. Thus if you are selling your property you have to go on paying the standing charges, even if the house is empty, until the sale is completed and the new owners take over the responsibility for the water bill.

Refuse

Along with their growing concern about other environmental matters, the French have over the last few years become more careful about recycling (*le recyclage*). Some *départements* are more conscientious than others about dealing with the end product, but in most areas there are bottle banks all over the place and facilities for collecting everything that can be recycled. The collection (*le collecte*) of refuse (*les ordures menagères*) is the responsibility of each commune, and generally it happens at least once a week, more often in the hot summer season.

If you have elected to live in a town then all you have to do is put your bin (*la poubelle*) out on the pavement on the relevant day. If you have chosen to be in the country, you will see in your village, or at strategic points along the road, groups of large rectangular bins into which you put your rubbish. The bins come in different colours, brown ones for general rubbish and a green one for anything that can be recycled *(les recyclables)*, excluding glass. Note that *les recyclables* include *all* paper, plastic, packaging, containers, cans, metal, etc, which you should rinse out if necessary and dump loose *(en vrac)* into the green bin. Everything else *(les autres déchets)* should be tied up in a proper bin bag and dumped into a brown one. If you have larger things to get rid of, you can ask the neighbours or at the *mairie* for the whereabouts of the nearest rubbish dump, *la déchetterie.*

8 ✿ Houses

Acquiring your house

The house hunt

As in any context, the process of finding a house that suits you can be very lengthy, or it can be sudden and short. You will no doubt have already put together from previous experience your personal checklist of things to look out for in the choosing process, and of features you do and don't want. Very rarely is a house ideal in every respect and there are bound to be a few downside factors, the essential thing being to differentiate between those you can do something about and those that you cannot. (You'll notice once you start looking that properties in France are often classified by the number of square metres of living space they provide, a useful guideline once you've calculated what your requirements are.)

Once you start looking you'll soon realise that there are more properties for sale in France than you could even visit in a lifetime, so it makes sense to narrow the field as much as possible. No doubt you've already found your favourite corners of this wonderful country, but remember that a place that's ideal for a couple of summer weeks may be less so longer term. It may be wise to rent a place for a while in an area that appeals to you, so that you can discover what it's like year round. You can never do too much homework and research – into climate, local architecture, places to go and things to see and enjoy, transport and travel options – before making your choice of an area in which to concentrate your search. Nowadays of course with the Net and other sources such as the property magazines, you can do much of this research from your own front room, and then spend actual hunting time on your next trip with maximum effectiveness.

In fact you may well find out more from these sources than you can on the ground, since local estate agents are often very cagey about the details of the houses they have on offer, and the particulars (*la notice*) are usually very vague. This is partly to prevent clients from identifying the houses for themselves and making their own deals with the owners. However once you've convinced an agent that you are really serious they will give you the addresses of the houses you have chosen from their portfolio and want to visit, which you can go and look at first from the outside on your own. As a precaution they will ask you to sign a *bon de visite*, a promise that you won't make any offers without going through them. Then if you like any of the places you've seen, they will arrange an appointment to visit them properly, and will go with you.

If you are the romantic type you may well fall for a gem of a house that you discover draped in June roses at the end of a lush and winding lane, and have instant visions of your nearest and dearest coming to join you in all this peace and beauty. Yes, sometimes it works, and one does meet people who have bought a house on impulse and never regretted it. But sadly they are not in the majority, so you'd do better to take a close look at what it is the roses are draped over - specially if it's part of the roof! - and picture the luscious lane aslurp in November mud . . .

Practicalities

First thing to check in any rural house is the state of the roof (*la toiture*), since the most popular and picturesque parts of the country tend to have picturesque, historic and expensive-to-repair roofs, of magnificent timbers (*la charpente*) and eventually friable tiles (*les tuiles*). Then the foundations (*les fondations*), if any - many traditional stone houses are built directly on a broad trench of rubble – and possibilities for damp (*l'humidité*) or water seepage (*les infiltrations*). Many farms of course have their own well or spring, useful to know about. If the house has not been modernised at all, you'll need to check where the nearest water mains, electricity and phone lines are (*les alimentations d'eau, d'éléctricité, la ligne téléphonique les/la plus près*), as charges for installing these services can be very high.

Unless the house is recent or has been recently converted you may need to have it rewired, and the standards for electrical installations (*l'installation éléctrique*) are now very strict. (The current is compatible with UK appliances if you want to bring them over.) You'll probably want to redo some of the plumbing (*la plomberie*) too. But the rude stories about French plumbing are now out of date and the modern version is just as efficient as the UK variety, if not more so. Most country houses have their own drainage, ie a septic tank (*une fosse septique*), and provided this has been installed correctly it looks after itself and only needs emptying every four years. (More details on this phenomenon on pp. 100-101.)

A great many properties on the market are advertised as partially renovated, ie the *travaux* have been started but not finished (*travaux/rénovations/aménagements à terminer* or something similar), and if this is the case with the house you are considering, it may be wise to ask the agent what still needs to be done, and to find out if you can whether the vendors encountered any insoluble problems – other than running out of cash, that is. Many particulars claim the property has its '*gros oeuvre en bon état*' ('major structure in good condition') but sadly this vague and optimistic phrase doesn't signify a lot. It should mean that at least the roof isn't about to collapse, but don't count on it! And be aware that anything that claims to be '*habitable*' may be so for owls or chickens, but is unlikely to be so for humans until a considerable amount of devoted work has been done. ('*Habitable de suite*' is more encouraging.) '*Beaux volumes*' usually translates as, 'well, there's plenty of space . . . but not much in it'. Curiously enough, in a country where so many old houses change hands, professional surveyors, who would in theory find out the truth of the matter, are not that easy to find. See the comments on Surveys (p. 92) for more on this topic.

One of the first questions to spring to the UK buyer's mind is, what about the heating (*le chaffauge*)? Yes, in most parts of the country it will be needed for three or four winter months (mid-November to mid-February or March), but unless you feel the cold extremely, most of the year you will need it only rarely, and in the summer months you'll probably be more concerned with keeping cool than with getting warmer. See comments below on the types of heating system available.

Points to check outdoors and on the *terrain*: the general lie of the land, aspect relative to the sun and wind, natural drainage, soil type (if you are planning to dig it up for a garden or excavate for a pool), proximity of high-power electric lines (*les lignes de haute tension*) which are to be avoided at all costs as they are a major health hazard. Other points to clarify: are the boundaries clear (*les limites*), are there any disputes about them with the neighbours, any access problems, are there any footpaths (*sentiers*) or public rights of way (*servitudes*), are there any obvious sources of noise or nuisance (eg farmyard smells). The estate agent should be able too to tell you if there are any local planning regulations that might prevent you doing what you want in terms of putting in a pool and/or pool house, adding extensions, planting trees, etc. (See the Gardens and Pools chapter for hints on landscaping issues.) And of course it's as well to check the exact location and condition of the water mains, junction boxes (*les compteurs*), *fosse* and soakaway, etc – if any . . .

Further homework

Apart from the property itself, you'll naturally want to check obvious things like access and transport options, nearest services, shops, etc, local medical facilities, maybe schools, sports and general things to see and do. We suggest that in addition, if peace and privacy are important to you, you also do a little research in the neighbourhood to find out how busy it is in the summer - for instance how much traffic is there (*la circulation estivale*), are there any campsites (*les campings*) within earshot (ie 3-4km) - and whether there are any new housing developments (*lotissements*) or roads planned nearby. Many rural *communes* are now offering cheap building land in order to attract new residents, and you may or may not want to find one mushrooming on your doorstep. And we know of one French couple whose farm property was expropriated to make room for a motorway, not once but *three* times. To paraphrase Lady Bracknell, to suffer this once may be a misfortune, but three times does seem to smack somewhat of carelessness!

Another factor to consider carefully, which is becoming increasingly relevant with every month that passes, is whether you wish to be in a neighbourhood with other British families. In many ways having a few of one's compatriots not too far away can provide lots of extra pleasure, plus the security of having people around who speak the same language, literally and figuratively. And you can hope that if they have chosen to live in the place you've chosen, you will have a certain amount in common. However if you plan to come to France because you like it for being French, you may want to avoid villages or towns where the British (and/or Dutch or Germans) form a major part of the population – and there are increasingly many of these.

For instance a hill village near Montpellier of 400 inhabitants, who include 20 British families – or a village in a choice part of the Lot where the Remembrance Day service saw turnout of 12 French families and 18 British ones – or chunks of Brittany where one house in three is being bought by Brits – or Sarlat, the gem of the Dordogne, where a major building firm sells one house in four to the British (and almost as many to the Dutch) – and the list could go on and on. To say nothing of a notorious town south of Bergerac with a majority Anglo population, complete with pub and cricket team, where the minority language is French. According to 2004 statistics there are at least 1,00,000 British property owners in France. No wonder that increasingly one hears, even out of season, ringing tones of English echoing across a village square or down the aisles of the supermarket.

Inevitably the locals hear them too, and are not always entirely thrilled. I've heard recently of houses for sale being bought up by the commune in order to prevent them going to more foreigners. This isn't from any personal objection, but in an effort to keep a balance in the community. After all, one can understand the ill feeling caused when houses, specially those in prime positions, are bought by people who then leave them empty much of the year, even more so when these second homes change hands at prices that the locals who want a first one, and who want to stay in the area, cannot aspire to. And in many small towns and villages in conservation areas there isn't any scope for building additional cheaper houses for younger families. Thus there is a real danger, especially in some choice country areas, of the incomers, like tourists everywhere when they become too many, destroying the atmosphere and even the very fabric of the picturesque local life they have in theory come to enjoy.

Hence this word of caution if you are looking for a living French community to become part of eventually. When you are making your choice it is worth finding out about the local *mairie*, and whether they welcome foreign buyers or not. Generally they do, especially if the buyers are planning to renovate a house or farm that would otherwise be left to rack and ruin, but it is as well to check this since the local mayor, who carries out many functions in the administrative system, will be a vital factor in your life, especially if you need building or planning permission.

As your neighbours also will probably be, if you have any near by, so it may be worth a few discreet enquiries about them too. Stories about the welcomingness and generosity of French neighbours abound – even if in some communities the welcome may be wearing a bit thin - so you need have no fears on this account, but in any case it is important to start off relations on the right foot. Hence the hints on doing so in the chapters on Meeting and Greeting and on People.

Ask at the *mairie* too, if the estate agent hasn't already provided it, for a copy of the relevant section of the *cadastre*, the equivalent of a large scale Ordnance Survey map which details every property in a commune and the boundaries of each plot (*parcelle*). In many places the inheritance laws, designed to re-divide property with every passing generation, have created a hotchpotch of *parcelles* that has little logic to it, so you may need to do some homework with the *cadastre* and check on the ground exactly which plots are included in your potential purchase (they are numbered on the map) and where their boundaries are.

One important point to clarify, probably with the help of your agent, is the question of which fixtures and fittings (*les installations fixes et accessoires*) the vendors are going to leave in the house, in the outbuildings if any, and in the grounds, and which they are taking away with them. It is not unknown for a proud new owner to walk in to their new home and then into the kitchen, for instance, only to find gaping holes instead of the things that were there before, electric wires dangling forlornly and dangerously from the ceilings, and even sawn off bits of radiator pipe sticking out of the wall.

So get a list in writing if you can of the items that are to be left (*un inventaire, un état des lieux*), and have it included in the contract. If the vendors are leaving the house some time before completion, it may be worth arranging a visit to the property before signing to make sure that everything has been left as agreed. On the other hand any furniture you arrange to buy from the vendors should be dealt with and paid for separately (or should be specified in the sale contract if it has been included in the price) so that it does not confuse the assessment of your tax liability on the sale.

Taxes and all that

Another issue for a couple to consider carefully before buying is the question of single or joint ownership, and linked to this is the question of inheritance (*la succession*). This is a thorny subject on which you must consult a *notaire*, or the consulate if you prefer to discuss the matter in English. By French law, when one parent dies their property is automatically divided up equally between all their children, including those from any previous marriage. The widow (or widower) has the right to continue occupying the family home and to keep a proportion of the total value of the estate, but at their death this too passes automatically to the children in the same way. This law was instituted by Napoleon as a deliberate tactic to break up the wealth of the aristocracy, and it was not one of his better ideas.

If you become resident in France, ie spend more than six months of the year here, you automatically become part of the French system and therefore subject to this particular law. However various arrangements can be made to circumvent it, the commonest being the setting up of a private property company (*une société civile immobilière* or SCI) which then has the right to dispose of the property as its directors (of which there must be at least two) deem fit. Note though that, in addition to initial costs which are scaled to the value of the place, the company then becomes liable for annual taxes.

There is the possibility also of making a contract called a *donation entre époux*. Under this arrangement, at the death of one partner, the surviving one retains the full ownership of the property and the right to remain in it, though at their death it passes to the children, if any, as described above. This arrangement can be set up after the actual purchase is completed, whether or not this has been made in both names.

Note that if you are a resident these inheritance laws apply to all your assets, estate and possessions in France or abroad, whereas if you are a non-resident, they apply to the building(s) and land in France only, not to the contents of the house or other capital or assets held abroad. Obviously it is essential to obtain professional advice on these matters before taking any steps towards an actual purchase, even more so if you are planning any money-earning activity on the premises such as *chambres d'hôtes*.

Another law to which residents automatically become subject governs the ownership of a couple's property. Whereas under UK law a couple who marry each retain possession of their own property unless they decide otherwise, in France it's the opposite; signing on the dotted line of the marriage certificate puts the property of each partner into joint ownership (*le communauté de biens*), unless they make an agreement to the contrary. A couple who become resident here are entitled if they wish to make a contract maintaining their separate ownership (*la séparation de biens*). This is a simple matter and can be done free of charge. If your *notaire* asks for information about your *régime matrimoniale* this is what they are talking about.

Something else that's advisable to do before you leap is to check the tax liability relating to the property. Two types of tax are levied annually on property: the *taxe foncière*, assessed principally on the land owned, and the *taxe d'habitation*, payable on the buildings. Their levels vary according to the situation and quality of the property. The former tax is payable in the autumn by whoever was the owner on the previous 1 January. If the property changes hands during the year then it is common practice for the amount due to be shared proportionately between the vendor and the buyer.

The *taxe foncière* now includes a charge for rubbish collection, the rate depending on the *commune* but generally modest compared with UK equivalents. (If you are on mains drainage there will be a charge for this to pay to the commune, proportionate to the amount of water going through your meter.)

Similarly the *taxe d'habitation* is payable in the autumn by whoever was living in the house on the previous 1 January, so if the property is let then the tenant is liable (*redevable*). If you are selling a property and it is empty on 1 January while awaiting completion, then you can apply to have your liability for this tax waived (*un dégrèvement*). You need to ask the *mairie* to provide a letter certifying that the house is vacant on this date, and they will send someone round to *faire une constatation*, ie check that it is really empty. A copy of your remover's bill will help to clinch the point and convince the tax office when you receive their demand that you are no longer liable.

Then of course there is the obligation for residents to pay income tax, which is assessed on the calendar year, and you will be sent a substantial form to fill in for this purpose (*un avis d'imposition*) in spring of the following year, with a deadline for payment usually on the last day of March. The forms are notoriously complex and confusing (even though somewhat simplified of late), so you may need to call on the services of an accountant (*un expert comptable*) or to visit your local tax office, who will help you understand what information you have to provide where. It is essential to complete all the paperwork by the due date, otherwise a heavy penalty may be imposed, and also to keep all the related paperwork for the next three years. The actual tax can be paid in three instalments spread over the year, or even monthly.

You will no doubt want to take professional advice too in order to sort out your tax liability in France in relation to any liability abroad, in order to avoid being taxed twice. The Inland Revenue will provide the form required for avoiding double taxation on your income, in English and in French, for you to complete and send to the offices concerned. When you come to sell your property, you will be liable for capital gains tax (*les impôts sur les plus-values*) if it is a second home, but not if it is your main residence.

The purchase

The process of buying a property in one's own country is fraught enough, and when doing so in another country you will inevitably be confronted by a number of unfamiliar hurdles. What follows here does not claim to be an exhaustive study of the subject, nor is it a substitute for up to date legal advice. However it does outline the main stages of buying a property in France, and highlights some of the factors to watch out for.

Note that there is no obligation for the sale to be made through an estate agent, so if you find the property you want by your own efforts or through other people you know, and if it is being sold privately, as many houses are, the sale can be handled entirely by a *notaire*, thus saving the agency fee, which is in the 6-7% range. Little enough consolation when you have to pay a hefty 7-10% of the purchase price (nearer 3-4% for a recent house) to the *notaire* anyway, but it helps! The *notaire* may also have details of property to sell, but check if the prices quoted include all the fees or not. Of course the route of the private sale is only feasible if you have a good command of the language. If you don't, you'll no doubt need an agent to hold your hand, answer your questions about the area and steer you through the rest of the process. In the more popular areas many estate agents have a working knowledge of the relevant English.

In these areas too it is not unknown for unqualified and unauthorised individuals, often ex-pats, to pose as estate agents and offer properties for sale which they have heard of from private vendors or *notaires*. The prices they offer may seem attractive but beware, they can charge on top whatever fees they like as they are not under any professional control, and the 'client' will have no proof of these charges to deduct from their eventual capital gains liability. Moreover since they are not registered they have no right to hold deposits, nor do their 'clients' have any recourse if they run off with same - it does happen! - or if there is a problem of any kind with the subsequent finances of the transaction or with the property itself.

What these characters lack in legal credibility they often try to make up for by being very pally. Any so-called 'agent' who makes a song and dance about helping you find the place of your dreams but who does not have a proper office to take you to, is obviously to be treated with caution! If you have any doubts you can ask to see their accreditation. The French equivalent of this role is the *marchand de biens*, a dealer in property, who may be entirely authentic but, as above, it's best not to tangle unless they can prove it and you can follow and dispute the small print.

You may be surprised to find that the vendors (and the agent) will expect you to use the same *notaire* as they do, so that the same person handles the sale (*la vente*) and the purchase (*l'achat*). This situation is very common in France, and it usually works out smoothly since the code of conduct for a *notaire* is very strict. (A *notaire* in fact is a public functionary, and is not on the side of an individual client.) However you are under no obligation to do this, and if you engage your own *notaire* you do not have to pay anything extra, your *notaire* and the vendor's will divide the fee between them.

Note that behind every property transaction trails a long line of charges and fees, some payable by the vendor, others by the buyer, so, unless your pockets are very deep, you are strongly advised to find out before committing yourself exactly which ones you will be liable for. They usually add up to a significant percentage – 15% is not unusual - of the price quoted in the first place, which has to be added to it.

The buying process

Once you have survived the ups and downs of finding the property that fits your expectations and your budget, the actual buying process comes in two stages. The first stage is the joint signature by vendor and buyer in the presence of a *notaire* of a *compromis de vente* (or *promesse de vente*), a document which constitutes a commitment by both parties to complete the sale (also called *le sous seing*). At this juncture the buyer is obliged to pay a deposit (*un déposit*) amounting to 10% of the agreed price, which is paid into an account at the *notaire's* and handed over to the vendor when the sale is completed.

At this second stage, which takes place once the necessary documents have been assembled, the final contract (*l'acte définitif*) is signed and the rest of the purchase price is paid. Sounds easy, doesn't it?! (Some estate agents are authorised to complete the *compromis* and hold deposits, so if yours does so, ask for an authorised receipt, and be sure the *notaire* is aware that the deposit has been paid before they send you the bill for completion.)

After signing the *compromis*, the vendor cannot change their mind about selling, but the purchaser has seven days in which to reconsider their decision to buy (*un délai de rétractation*) and to withdraw if they wish to. Even after this there are three further conditions in which the sale can be cancelled: first, if the buyer requires a loan (*un prêt immobilier*) to complete the purchase, and fails to obtain it; second, if they wish to make changes to the property which require planning permission (*un permis de construire*), and this is not granted. The *compromis* should include a get-out clause (*une clause suspensive*) covering each of these situations (in some cases there may be others). The third condition takes a little longer to explain.

If the property in question includes more than 2,500m² of land (about half an acre) then it is considered to have agricultural potential, and an organisation called the SAFER, which interests itself in rural matters, is automatically offered the first option to purchase. As a rule they only exercise this option if the land is of good quality, so in most cases this procedure is only a formality. The only catch is that it usually takes at least two months for the pieces of paper to make their way from pillar to post and back again, though if you are in a hurry you can pay a fee for them to be shoved along more speedily. The upshot is a declaration from said organisation that they are not interested in the property you are interested in, which frankly a little common sense could have told everyone in the first place . . . but then what would all those bureaucrats do if the system worked on common sense?

A number of other documents have to accompany the *compromis*. The *notaire* will provide a copy of the relevant *cadastre* indicating the buildings (*bâtiments*) and the *parcelles* included in the sale. You are advised to check carefully that each of these, with their correct numbers, is included in writing in the contract. Then both vendor and purchaser must supply proof of identity and address, and birth certificate and marriage ditto if applicable. These have to be translated into French, by a certified translator. (The nearest British Consulate will do this for you, for a modest fee.) In theory the originals have to be supplied too, but the *notaire* may be prepared to photocopy them, and even to accept them in English, so it is worth checking this beforehand. The vendor must provide proof of their title to the property and that there is no outstanding mortgage, and certificates to prove that it is free of termites, asbestos and lead. If there are any uncertainties about the boundaries around the property, documents clarifying these may be required too.

The last stage of finalising the sale is usually set for 60 days from signing the *compromis*. This is not obligatory, but unless you are very lucky or have a *notaire* on your side with some dynamite up their sleeve, it is very unlikely to take less time than this to collect all the documents and complete all the procedures. If you are not able to be present at the final signing then you can easily arrange with the *notaire* a power of attorney (*une procuration*) which entitles someone else to sign on your behalf. (This can be arranged if you are buying or if you are selling.)

A few days before the completion day the *notaire* will send you a copy of the contract (*le projet de l'acte*) to study and check, with the details of the remaining sum required for completion. They will probably ask for this to be paid with a bank draft (*un chèque de banque*), so check beforehand with your bank what the procedure is – it may take a couple of days for this to be issued, and you will probably have to order it and collect it *in person* from the branch where your account is held. If this is not feasible then the *notaire* may accept a bank transfer of the funds (*un virement*), but this too has to be set up with a couple of days' notice to make sure the money arrives in time for the signing.

Another option which may be useful if time is short, is for the *notaire*'s office to request the transfer from the bank directly, which they can do by fax if they have all the necessary details on your account, etc. The bank will then contact you for another fax confirming your authority for the transaction. Doing it this way may save a few precious days. As well as checking the arithmetic in the contract, this is the moment to check that the numbers of the *parcelles* listed are accurate.

When the great day of the final signing comes, all the documents have to be checked and read aloud by the *notaire* to everyone, then signed as in the first round: both parties initial each page of the sale document, and sign the last one. (As mentioned earlier, a married woman signs the documents in her maiden name.) Then the cheque for the remainder of the purchase price has to be handed over (if the funds aren't already there), in exchange for the keys for the property. Don't leave the *notaire's* office without them – thereby hangs an incredible tale!

A now local couple, who'd reappeared from the UK all ready to sign on the dotted line and move in to their new house, went through the rigmarole on the designated day as required, all i's dotted and all t's crossed and all moneys duly handed over. But they rashly left the *notaire's* office without asking for the keys from the vendor – who as it transpired had not finished moving out his furniture, hadn't arranged anywhere else to sleep for that night, was heart-broken at the prospect of leaving his childhood home, and insisted on staying in the house two more days and nights! Even a warning letter from the *notaire* didn't budge him, and he only left the premises three days later when his mates turned up with a van to cart away the last of his belongings, and to drag him off too. So it is as well to make sure, among all the other things to make sure of, that your dream home comes with guaranteed vacant possession!

All this may sound dauntingly complex, but don't despair, others have survived the process! Herewith are some words useful to know as you embark on your house hunt.

Useful vocabulary 1

une agence immobilière	*estate agency*	un bungalow	*holiday bungalow*
un agent immobilier	*estate agent* (m/f)	un atelier	*workshop*
le/la propriétaire	*the owner* (m/f)	une cabane	*holiday cabin, (garden) shed*
le vendeur	*the seller* (m/f)	un abri (de jardin)	*(garden) shed*
[la vendeuse	*female shop assistant*]	un débarras, une remise	*shed, storeroom*
l'acheteur	*the buyer* (m/f)	une buanderie	*laundry/utility room*
les (petites) annonces	*(classified) ads*	une cave, un cellier	*cellar*
la notice	*house particulars*	un grenier, les combles	*attic*
les dimensions	*measurements*	une chambre d'amis	*a spare room*
les directions	*directions*		
le plan d'accès	*access map*	les dépendances	*outbuildings*
l'état des lieux	*inventory*	une grange	*barn*
le contrat	*contract*	un hangar	*open-sided barn*
l'acte sous seing privé	*preliminary contract*	un auvent	*lean-to*
l'acte authentique/définitif		une étable	*stable, shed for animals*
	final sale contract	une porcherie	*pigsty*
		une bergerie	*sheep shed, barn*
une maison principale	*main house/home*	un four à pain	*bread oven*
- sécondaire	*second/holiday house*	un garage	*garage*
- de vacances	*holiday house*		
- indépendante	*detached house*	terrain constructible	*building land*
- mitoyenne sur un côté		une parcelle	*plot of land*
	semi-detached house	une limite	*boundary*
- mitoyenne, en terrasse	*terraced house*	une borne	*boundary marker*
- de plan pied	*with ground floor only*		
- de maître	*semi-grand formal house*	l'entrée	*entrance, drive*
- d'amis	*guest house*	une haie	*hedge*
- à louer	*house to rent*	une clôture	*fence, fencing*
		un grillage	*chain-link fence*
un immeuble	*apartment block*	une balustrade	*railings*
un appartement	*flat*	une barrière	*barrier, fence, farm gate*
un studio	*bedsit* (also *a studio*)	un portail	*(garden) gate*

Surveys

Strangely enough in a country where so much of the property that changes hands is old, the French are not in the habit of having a survey done on a house they are considering buying. If there are obvious things to check, such as an evident source of damp or a wavering roof line, they will probably arrange to visit the premises with a competent *artisan* to advise them, but they don't often go through the expensive rigmarole of a full survey, nor is this required for a mortgage.

Needless to say, horror stories abound of dire problems discovered as soon as the new owner opens the nearest cupboard, or lifts the first floorboard . . . Indeed this optimism may seem to a Brit very short-sighted, and when you come to buy you will no doubt want to have a proper health check done on your property before you sign on the dotted line.

That being said, since 2003 several aspects of a property being sold do have to be checked by a specialist, and usually one firm will do all of them. These items are the presence of termites in the woodwork (a scourge introduced via certain ports from imported timber which is gradually spreading all over the country), the presence of asbestos, and of lead, for instance in old pipework or paint. The vendor is responsible for having these checked, for dealing with any problems that are discovered, and for providing a certificate to the *notaire* proving that the property is free of them (*une expertise parasite/amiante/plomb*). If you are selling, look under *traitement des bois* in the Pages Jaunes to find an agent near you, or try www.best-termites.com.fr. (The lead factor is not relevant in houses built after 1945, and many eastern areas are still termite-free.)

Perhaps in the wake of this legislation, there has appeared on the market a super specialist who will do a complete check for the above items, plus for damp, faulty wiring, problems in the roof and a number of other potential ills. However such beings are as yet comparatively rare, and if you can't find one, you can ask your agent to locate an *expert immobilier* to do the structural survey (*un bilan de santé immobilier*). This will probably cost 200-500€ but is a good investment if the property is not a recent one.

An alternative is to find a general builder (*un entrepreneur, un maître d'oeuvre*) who is knowledgeable enough to give you an accurate assessment, or to ask individual artisans to come and advise you on specifics: a *maçon* if there is stonework to consider, a *menuisier* for carpentry and staircases, a *couvreur* for a check on the roof, an *éléctricien* to check on the wiring (for which the *normes* - regulations - are becoming more and more strict), a *chauffagiste* (heating engineer) or *plombier* (plumber) to check out an old heating system.

You should explain when you contact them that you are not yet the owner, and make it clear whether you are asking for advice (*un conseil*), a full report (*une étude*), or for a quote (*un devis*) for actual work, and unless it's the latter, that you will pay them a fee (*une honoraire*) for their visit. Of course if you are considering major works you may have decided to call on the services of an architect, who will do the survey as well as quoting for the work. Some architects will do just the survey, for whatever fee they choose to charge - there is no standard scale.

Another area where you may want professional advice is the matter of the boundaries around your chosen - or about to be chosen - property. As Robert Frost has reminded us, "Good fences make good neighbours." In town the boundaries (*les limites*) between neighbouring properties are usually obvious enough, but not necessarily so in the country. For this problem a specialist does exist, called an *expert géomètre*, ie a land surveyor, and many is the generations-old feud they have been called upon to settle. Starting from the *cadastre*, the *géomètre* will carry out an *arpentage*, ie check and redefine if necessary the exact alignment of the intended boundaries in relation to the present position of walls, fences, etc. They will put markers (*bornes*) along any poorly defined sections and will send the results of their deliberations to the owners concerned.

As a buyer you are under no obligation to have this *bornage* done, but in fact it is advisable to clarify all aspects of the boundaries and access if there is any shadow of doubt in the matter or on the ground, such as a shared driveway (*un accès partagé*) or a stretch of boundary wall that has disappeared into the undergrowth. It would be naive to leave any future settlement of such a question to the goodwill of neighbours whom you do not yet know. This becomes even more important if you expect to have major work done, or even a pool put in, which may mean diggers, heavy lorries, etc, coming and going.

If you do call in the *géomètre*, the documents from them, signed by all parties concerned, will be required by the *notaire* before the sale can be completed. If there is an obvious area of confusion the vendor may agree to pay the fee for this survey themselves, or may at least share it.

There is the related question of who is responsible for the maintenance of the said boundary walls, etc. The rule is that if the ground is the same level on each side of the wall, the wall is *mitoyen*, ie it belongs half and half to each neighbour and both are equally responsible for its maintenance. However if the ground is higher on one side, it is deemed to be a retaining wall (*un mur de rétènement*) and is therefore the property and the responsibility of the owner on the uphill side.

Renovating your house

There are so many wonderful and picturesque houses in France, especially in the countryside, waiting to be loved and rescued, and you would have to be very hard-hearted indeed not to be seduced by one or other of them into a flight of romantic fantasy, imagining how this splendid pile, though slightly crumbling round the edges, could be transformed into the home of a thousand dreams.

Well yes, maybe it could – if you have the money, the determination and the patience, and preferably the complete range of building skills and equipment at your command. For one reason why so many of these characterful places are in such a sad state is because it is extraordinarily difficult in most areas to find the artisans who will do the necessary work. A few pertinent enquiries in the bars or *mairie* of your chosen neighbourhood, or among property owners you may already know locally, will produce the phone numbers of any amount of talented carpenters, plumbers, roofers and what have you, and if you ring them often enough they will come and cheerfully look over your potentially dream home and will even within a month or so, if you ring them often enough, produce quotes in duplicate of all the jobs and materials required to carry out the transformation. So far so good, apart from the phone bill.

That is the easy part. What follows is months if not years - literally - of chasing them to come and do the work they have promised, and moreover to come in the right order, so that the tiler comes after the roofer and not before, and the electrician and plumber do their usual double act, taking turns to put connections in the walls and then attach them to the relevant objects, the while waiting for the tiler to come back again and do his bit. Of course there will be fewer headaches of this kind if you have taken on a general builder who will be in charge of coordinating his troops, but even so you will doubtless have to do some chivvying. Similarly, if you are doing things in the grand manner and entrusting it all to an architect, he will in theory keep the work up to speed, but you will probably have to pay fairly heavily for the privilege.

Terrible tales abound of workmen who promise sincerely to come and get on with the job, do a day or two's work, then disappear completely for months on end. Don't take it personally, it happens to French clients too, so be prepared! In fairness it should be said that when they do turn up, the local craftsmen and builders work hard through the day from 8am to 5pm, apart from the religious observance of lunch break from 12 to 2. This may seem excessive but is essential in hot weather. And though they may gratefully accept a cool beer at the end of the day, they do not, like some builders we might mention, need to be refuelled every hour on the hour with teas or coffees.

If you do decide to take the plunge into doing *travaux*, you should reckon that the work will take at least twice as long as they tell you at the beginning, and if it's only twice you are very lucky. But all that being said, if you take a few precautions you will probably find that in the end the work is done well. There are of course rogue builders in this country as in all others, but more in the town than in the countryside, where generally builders are keen to nourish their reputation, and where they know you will probably summon them to fix or redo anything that is not satisfactory. Sadly most rogue builders one hears about are British ones, who misuse their supposedly privileged position among their newly arrived fellow countrymen who can't manage the language and who assume that life will be easier with a builder who speaks and thinks English. It ain't necessarily so. And if said builder is not officially registered, you have no comeback if any problems do arise. If in doubt, ask to see their papers.

Three useful rules

Three golden rules to achieve a happy ending:

First rule: Make clear exactly what you want done! Of course you may have to modify your ideas as the work progresses, but it is essential to start out with a clearly specified plan in writing, *un cahier des charges*, which you and the builders can agree on and refer to in case of doubt or confusion. And since a picture is worth a thousand words, it's a good idea to provide also clear drawings (*les dessins*) or sketches (*les croquis*) of significant changes – eg new floor layout, new doors or windows (*les ouvertures*), etc - to be agreed by both parties.

Second rule: Spend time studying the quotes you are given and make sure they are explicit and detailed enough, that they match the points listed in the *cahier* and that you understand the technicalities, eg that you know your *plinthes* from your *solives* (see below). Clarify anything you are not sure of with the builder concerned *before* they start. Don't assume they will do things the way a British builder would; for instance don't be surprised if they don't put underfelt on the roof. In many areas it isn't used because the wide variation in temperature between day and night in spring and autumn creates lots of humidity which would get trapped in it.

Third rule: Make sure that both you and the builder sign both copies of his quote (*le devis*), and keep yours carefully. It must be on headed paper with the registration (Siret) number of the company, specifying the type of materials to be used and the detailed prices, without and with taxes (HT and TTC). Once signed it is legally binding, and it is your main weapon if you have to make a complaint. The price quoted is also legally binding, provided you ask for the work to be started within 3 months (or 6 – it should be specified on the quote). On the other hand, a random piece of paper with a few figures on it and a name squiggled at the bottom is of no use at all if it comes to a dispute.

The proper *devis* also provides the basis for agreement if you want the builder to alter anything once the work is finished. If this is because he has not done what is specified in the *devis* then obviously it's his responsibility to make the necessary changes. However if he's followed the agreed plan but you don't like the result, then it's just as obviously up to you to pay for anything you want redone.

Another good reason for keeping all the quotes and all the receipts for materials, bought by the builders or yourself, if it is a *maison sécondaire*: when you come to sell, the cost of work done on the property can be deducted from the profit you make on the sale - assuming there is one! - and this will reduce the amount of capital gains tax you will have to pay. (If it's your *résidence principale* then you don't pay this tax.)

Planning permission

Of course all this is assuming that you have overcome the major hurdle of obtaining planning permission. After decades of not bothering too much what was built where, the French are now much more careful of their environment and have created a complex planning system, which is particularly stringent if you live in a conservation area (*un site classé*), eg in a *quartier ancien* in a town, in sight of a listed historic building or in a specially sensitive landscape. Most of the Dordogne valley, for example, is a conservation area where planning rules are generally strict. This means that in addition to being passed by the local authority, plans have to be approved by the architect from the Bâtiments de France (Monuments Historiques) in the *département*.

If you are planning to build, you first need to obtain, or make sure that there is, a *certificat d'urbanistation* or CU (the equivalent of a building permit), which classifies a particular plot as building land. If this permission is granted it is valid for a year, renewable for 2 more years, within which time plans for the intended building must be submitted. If they are not, then the CU lapses and has to be applied for again. The building plans must be at least approved and stamped by an architect, even if they are drawn up by the builder who is going to do the work.

The situation is a little simpler if you are renovating rather than building entirely new. The kind of permit you need depends on the extent and outward visibility of the work you intend to do, as well as on the site and surroundings of the house. An extension, for instance, requires permission if it is going to add more than a certain percentage to the original volume of the building. In a conservation area you need permission for changing windows or roofs, or for any externally visible alteration such adding as a veranda, even for building a greenhouse, and there is a limited choice of traditional colours that can be used for exterior paintwork.

It goes without saying that it is ESSENTIAL to check all these requirements carefully, with the advice of an experienced builder or architect, before you start to do anything, even if - or especially if - you are going to do some of the work yourself. It is not unheard of for buildings that have not been approved to be knocked down again by the local authority. The plans, for building work of any kind, go first to your local *mairie*, who will of course be ready to advise you. Needless to say all the paperwork involved takes time to chug its way through the frequently clogged up system. Some types of work need approval from the *mairie* but not from anyone higher up, and in this case you can submit an application for 'non-planning' permission (*une déclaration de travaux*), which has slightly fewer bends to get round.

And it cannot be repeated often enough, that you need to keep ALL the relevant paperwork very carefully for the foreseeable future, as you may need to produce it to interested officials, for insurance, tax matters, etc, and of course if you ever sell your property again. In fact even if you are thinking of putting up a smart garden shed, the first step is to buy a large filing cabinet for said paperwork . . . I exaggerate, of course – but not much.

Costs

It goes without saying that any kind of renovation will cost substantial amounts of money. You can reckon that for a medium sized (4-bed) house that needs a fair amount of work, the *travaux* will cost the equivalent of the purchase price – and that's without a hand-whittled kitchen or gold-plated taps! If it's smaller (eg a barn) but needs major work, then the works will cost more proportionately. And if it's big and old and needs major work – then the sky's the limit for the final cost. And don't forget to include in your reckoning the costs of any work on the grounds, which on a larger property can soon add up: clearing undergrowth, trimming trees, putting in a driveable entrance, levelling and *terrassement*, and of course a pool.

One considerable advantage of having a new house built, apart from the luxury of arranging things in it as you want, is that the pricing is predictable. The builder will detail everything that goes into it, leaving you the choice of finishes and fittings such as tiles, flooring, bathroom fittings, and kitchen units and appliances, all of which gives you control over what you spend. (Another plus, new houses have a builder's guarantee on the building and fittings, valid for 10 years.) It may be a reasonable trade-off to go for new and sacrifice some picturesqueness, if the house is mainly for holidays and you are not going to be on the spot to manage and oversee a saga of renovation. However carefully you explain what you want done, it is unlikely to be carried out as you expect in your absence – and the worst of it is that you don't discover what the builder *didn't* understand until you come back and see that he's done something different from what you thought you were asking him to do!

Also it is a not negligible factor that a new or newish house is easier to sell than a renovated old one. The French usually go for newer properties, and any serious British, Dutch or other foreign buyers, to whom older properties usually appeal, may prefer to buy something unrenovated and do the conversion to their own taste. There's no avoiding the fact that, as in almost any property market nowadays, it is virtually impossible to recoup the total cost of a large renovated property if you have to sell it again even in the medium term, let alone the short term; while something more modest, of medium age and medium size, may be more readily re-saleable. However if you are in a position to take it on and to throw caution to the winds, there is nothing like the thrill and eventual satisfaction of planning, dreaming, hovering, sweating, grovelling, slaving and slogging to carry out the transformation of a place you have fallen in love with and can finally bring to life.

Usually a builder will ask for one third (*un tiers*) of the total price quoted for a job to be paid at the beginning of the work (*en acompte*), to finance the materials and some of the costs, then one third at a stage to be agreed, and the last third when the work is completed. Builders are of course not averse to being paid partly in cash, but avoid anyone who asks you to pay this way, and beware anyone who asks you to pay for the whole job up front. Above all, don't part with *any* money until you have a legally binding *devis* in your hands!

Some technical points

Well, if all this has not deterred you and you still want to realise your dream, here are some points to keep in mind when you embark on *travaux*:

You may plan to bring materials over from the UK, where they are often cheaper and of course more familiar. With **paint** this is a good idea, as the French excuse for paint (*la peinture*) is absurdly expensive and woefully inadequate in covering whatever it is you want to cover. **Wallpaper** (*le papier peint*) you might want to bring too unless you are really keen to be disguised as a local. Looking over the wallpaper ranges on offer in most DIY places prompts the reflection that while the French are capable of creating the ultimate in elegance, they are also capable of producing the direst trash.

Electrics. Don't. The regulations (*les normes*) for electrical installations are becoming more and more strict each year, thanks to Brussels, and are more so in France than in the UK. If you use UK wiring in a French house and then want to insure it, you will have to take all the wires out again and replace them with Euro-standard ones. There is *no alternative* to having the work done by a fully qualified electrician. However the actual current is the same so you can use UK appliances with local plugs – which it should be said in passing come in various weird configurations and can be something of a challenge to fit.

Plumbing. Pipework (*la tuyauterie*) is of a comparable standard, but don't forget that you may get confused between metric and imperial measurements - and if you have to replace or add anything locally, it will of course be in metric. There are many more pipe sizes available in France, each destined for a particular function. Taps (*la robinetterie*) are an important matter because the water supply in a French house comes straight off the mains and is therefore at a higher and a variable pressure (though it is possible to have a widget fitted that will regulate it). The cheaper ranges of taps will not stand the strain and will start leaking after a few months, but the more expensive ranges will be adequate. All French plumbers are now sold on installing single mixer taps everywhere, and if you want anything different you will have to stand over them to make sure they do what you want - but given the statutory very high temperature of the hot water, a tap of this kind is actually safer. (Many of these taps have a lever incorporated at the *back* to operate the plug, so if the plumber produces one, make sure the basin is fitted with enough space behind to get at it.)

Plaster. If you are going to do any of it yourself, bring some from the UK. The local variety sets as soon as you blink at it and requires generations of practice to get a decent result.

Tiles. Don't bother, unless you desperately want something colour matched and custom made that you have found already. There is a huge choice of tiling (*le carrelage*) available here in most builder's merchants at very good prices. Don't forget that your future home is on the same continent as all the master ceramicists of France, Spain and Italy, so it's a bit silly to drag tons of tiles back across the Channel.

Roofing and all the heavier materials are obviously better bought over here. Apart from the hassles of transport, in most areas there are strict regulations about roofing materials and styles. Aside from insurance issues (see above), it's unreasonable to expect a local builder to work with unfamiliar materials when there is plenty of choice on the local market, especially in wood and of course in local stone.

And then what is the point in committing oneself to living in another country and then expecting to do everything as in the UK? There are already too many ex-pat houses over here where you can walk in and feel just as if you were in deepest Surrey – is that really what you want to achieve? There's also the respect due to the generations of local builders - carpenters and stonemasons in particular - who have created these wonderful buildings that fit in so harmoniously with the landscape. So in a word, go local as much as possible. You will be happier with the end result, and you will be on better terms with your neighbours and with the local community.

Insurance

Insuring the site (*le chantier*) and the building in progress is the responsibility of the builder, until the moment when the *charpente* (the roof frame) is in place. At this point the building becomes officially a house, and it is up to its owner to have it insured. Finding an adequate policy may take a little effort on your part since there is a considerable choice on the market. It's advisable to study the fine print of each policy you are considering, since insurers are notorious for including some little loophole small enough to escape the notice of the average client before they sign, but just big enough for them to wriggle out of when it comes to meeting a claim.

Look specially at the terms covering damage from the weather, which as we have all noticed has been more than a little crazy of late. (*Les intempéries* = bad weather, *dégâts des eaux* = water damage, *inondations* = flooding, *foudre* = lightning, *catastrophes naturelles*). As for house contents, as usual you will need to declare any special items and provide proof of their value. The policy will automatically include cover for public liability (*la responsabilité civile*), which is obligatory for all house owners.

Heating systems

It may seem strange to sun-starved Brits that the French have not yet realised how lucky they are when it comes to possibilities for heating their houses, and how much money and pollution they could save by using solar panels (*les panneaux solaires*). Of course there may be difficulties in a conservation area with slapping solar panels all over your roof, but in most places they can be installed discreetly enough to provide heating at least for a pool and/or some of your domestic water. Useful information is available on the site www.energy-shop.info/france, a multi-language site for the Dutch manufacturers Mastervolt, a market leader.

Another very effective, economical and environment-friendly system, feasible for a new or mostly gutted house, is the use of geothermal heating (*le chauffage géothermique*), which takes advantage of the natural warmth of the earth. For those not familiar with this idea: it works like under-floor heating but is laid under the earth at a depth of about 60cm, with a grid of water pipes that collect the heat in the soil and transfer it into a pipe system in the house. This is also laid under the floors, so you don't have to bother with radiators, though these can be included if preferred. The pipes are laid over an area 100-120% that of the house itself. Another great advantage is that the system can be switched over to keep the house cool in summer.

A key factor of course is the terrain you are building on, and whether it can be excavated to the necessary depth. This is the messy and expensive part, but the overall installation costs are only about 8-10% higher than those for a standard oil-fired system, and once it is installed the running costs are *virtually nil* as it keeps itself going by gravity feed. There are no tanks to refill, no fumes to send into the atmosphere, and nothing to run out of. It's possible to link in a booster system for extra hot water for any occasion when you might need it. As with the solar systems, you may have to do the research on this yourself and then convince your architect or builder to adopt it. France is in fact a pioneer in this technique, though most installations to date are in cities and in public buildings. More information at the site www.avenir-energie.com (English option), or else at www.geothermal-heating.com, which provides details of the system and addresses of agents in France (click on Thermatis Technologies SA).

Other options for heating are oil (*le mazout* or *fioul*), or gas (*le gaz* - from the EDF/GDF). Both of course need a large storage tank (*une cuve*), refilled by a regular delivery, which needs to be sited close enough to the road for access. The supplier for *mazout* or *fioul* (in the Pages Jaunes under *combustibles*) will tell you the maximum distance they can deal with, which in fact is usually quite a lot, 30m or so. Note that an oil tank can be installed in a cellar or outbuilding if you have one big enough, whereas a gas tank has to be outside, under or above ground, and a statutory distance from the house and other inhabited buildings.

Then of course there is the electric option, with night storage heaters and/or wall radiators, and an immersion heater (*un ballon/chauffe-eau éléctrique*). These may be useful for bathrooms or to give any other system a boost, but in general they are much more expensive than other heating methods. But for a warm-weather-only house this may be adequate and convenient, so if you want to check it out, an EDF consultant will come to give you a free assessment of your heating needs, and will quote for a suitable installation. Whichever system you choose, the thermostat for the hot water will be set at 50°C or more, a legal requirement in order to ward off the bacteria that cause legionnaire's disease.

Fireplaces

The traditional heating method in the country of course is the open fireplace, with a vast chimney which lets in at least as much cold as the heat it is supposed to give out. Very picturesque, but efficient it is not . . . hence the welcome appearance of the cast-iron wood burning stove, which uses the same flue but keeps the heat in, and in fact radiates it very satisfactorily to its surroundings. These *poêles* come in two kinds, the freestanding type which can go into a wide open fireplace (with the rest of the flue closed in), or the *insert* which is set into a purpose built fireplace. These don't radiate as much, though they usually have extra vents to circulate the hot air produced. Both kinds can have a glass door so that you can enjoy the look of the fire without the smoke and without losing the heat. (You'll find in the supermarket or *brico* a *produit décapant* made specially for keeping the inside of the glass clean.)

Even if you aren't counting on it for heating, you'll probably want a fireplace anyway. To obtain the wood you need, ask in the neighbourhood or look in the small ads for *bois de chauffage*. The best is oak (*chêne*), second choice hornbeam (*charme*) or chestnut (*châtaigner*), and it should be really dry – 2 years old – so that it does not gum up the chimney with soot. Check this with your supplier, though no reputable one would sell you anything younger. It is sold by the cubic metre (*une stère*), and when you order, remember to specify what size you need it cut to.

NB: You must keep the flue cleaned, either by a sweep (*un ramoneur*) or by using a special cleaning kit (*une bûche de ramonage*) which you can buy in the supermarket or *brico*. This consists of a set of composite 'logs' which you burn at intervals to keep the soot from forming. Your house insurers will probably require proof annually that you have kept the flue clean, either a receipt from a *ramoneur* or the certificate included in the 'log' kit.

The septic tank

To those unfamiliar with the notion of having a septic tank (*une fosse septique*) at the bottom of the garden it may seem rather medieval, but in fact this method of waste disposal works perfectly well, and provided the *fosse* has been installed correctly, it is unlikely to give any trouble and you can more or less forget about it. However having one installed is quite a business as it requires the digging of two very large holes. First of all the plumber or builder will decide on the siting of the *fosse* to provide the best drainage, and will advise you on the appropriate size, which will depend of course on how many people you expect to be living in the house, and how much time they will be there. It's best to over-estimate rather than under, as the cost of the tank is the least of your worries, and you never know what the future may bring, in terms of friends who want to visit, expanding family and/or paying guests.

The main headache may well be getting the hole dug, especially if you are on stony ground. The tank itself is a hollow and seamless concrete cube affair which will be delivered and dropped into said hole by a suitably equipped digger or lorry. A second slightly less huge hole has to be dug on the downhill side of it for the soakaway, a filtering pit of statutory dimensions filled with sand. Below this, the more or less clean water (*les eaux grises*) drains away into the ground. A modern *fosse toutes eaux* will collect all the waste water (*les eaux usées*) from the house including the kitchen, but in an older system you may find a smaller receptacle fitted on the kitchen drain, the *bac à graisse*, which filters off the worst of the kitchen gunge. This has an inspection cover (*un regard*) and needs to be cleaned out every few months. The *fosse* will have the same, so that it can be cleaned out when necessary. Don't worry, there are professionals who do this unlovely job with the minimum of fuss, and in any case it only needs to be done every four years. (Rumour has it - April 2004 - that a more complex model of *fosse* is will soon become obligatory for new installations.)

Otherwise the only maintenance required for the *fosse* is the addition once a month or so of an enzyme accelerator in the form of a sachet of powder (or liquid) which you simply tip into any toilet and send off down the drain. Look in the *supermarché* or *brico* for Eparcyl or an equivalent (and for the appropriate *fosse*-friendly loo cleaner). But you must be sure NOT to put any other stray items down the toilet other than what goes there naturally and the toilet paper. Make sure your guests realise this too.

Well, if you are not daunted by the prospect and are still prepared to launch into your *travaux*, here is a second dose of relevant vocabulary to help you on your way.

Useful vocabulary 2

wall	*le mur, la paroi*	exposed stone	*la pierre apparente*
low garden wall	*le muret*	dressed stone	*la pierre taillée*
internal wall	*le cloison*	dry stone	*la pierre sèche*
ceiling	*le plafond*	cornerstone	*la pierre d'angle*
floor	*le plancher*	keystone	*la pierre/clé de voûte*
staircase	*l'escalier* (m)	lintel	*le linteau*
landing	*le palier*		
step	*la marche*	breeze block	*le parpaing*
		cement	*le ciment*
chimney	*la cheminée*	concrete	*le beton*
roofing	*la toiture*	reinforced concrete	*le beton armé*
roof	*le toit*	render	*le crépi*
roof frame	*la charpente*	mortar	*le mortier*
gable	*le faîtage*	rough plaster	*l'enduit* (m)
Roman/Provençal tile		plaster	*le plâtre*
	la tuile canal/ romaine	grout	*le mastic*
ridged tile	*la tuile mécanique*	screed	*la chape*
flat tile	*la tuile plate*		
tiling (on floor or wall)	*le carrelage*	beam	*la poutre, poutrelle*
floor tiling or slabs	*le dallage*	joist	*la solive*

lath	la latte	shower head	la pomme de douche
plank	la planche	bath	la baignoire
beading, moulding	la moulure	tap	le robinet
skirting board	la plinthe	mixer tap (two taps, one spout)	le mixeur
parquet	le parquet	mixer tap (with single tap lever)	le mitigeur
panel	le panneau	plug	la bonde
hardboard	le contre plaqué	plug hole	le trou d'écoulement
plaster board	la plaque au plâtre	toilet tank	le réservoir
wall/floor covering	le revêtement	toilet bowl	la cuve
rock wool	la laine de roche	toilet flush	la chasse d'eau
glass wool	la laine de verre	toilet seat	la lunette
insulation	l'isolation (f)		
air conditioning	la climatisation	shutter	le volet
central heating	le chauffage central	window/door frame	le cadre
		window	la fenêtre
gutter	la gouttière	window sill	la bordure de fenêtre
downpipe	la déscente de gouttière	dormer window	la lucarne
pipe	le tuyau, la canalisation	window panes	les carreaux
drains	les évacuations	glass	le verre
sewer/drain	l'égout (m)	strengthened glass	le verre trempé
mains drainage	tout à l'égout	reinforced glass	le verre armé
septic tank	la fosse septique	putty	le mastic
septic tank (all waste water)		curtain rail	la tringle
	la fosse toutes eaux	awning, blind	le store
grease trap (on kitchen drain)		double glazing	le double vitrage
	le bac à graisse		
inspection cover	le regard	threshold	le seuil
		front door	la porte d'entrée
tank	le bac, la cuve	glass door	la porte vitrée
boiler	la chaudière	sliding door	la porte coulissante
hot water tank	le chauffe-eau, le ballon	hinge	la charnière, le gond
washer	le joint, le clapet	door fittings	les huisseries (f)
(control) valve	la vanne	(door) handle	la poignée
		lock	la serrure
sink	l'évier (m)	key	la clé/clef
worktop	le plan de travail	bolt	le verrou
cupboard	le placard	padlock	le cadenas
storage unit	l'unité de rangement (m)		
shelf	l'étagère (f)	fusebox	le panneau éléctrique
cooker hood	la hotte	fuse	le fusible
extractor fan	l'extracteur (m)	mains breaker	le disjoncteur
electric fan	le ventilateur	control box	le boîtier
		socket	la prise (de courant)
washbasin	le lavabo	plug (on appliance)	la fiche
shower	la douche	switch	l'intérrupteur (m)
shower tray	le bac à douche	wire	le fil

cable	le câble	spirit level	le niveau
tubing for wires	la gaine	(tape) measure	le mètre
		string	la ficelle
light bulb	l'ampoule (f)	rope	la corde
light fitting	le luminaire, lustre	strap	le cingle/sangle
wall light	l'applique (f)	hook	le crochet
lampshade	l'abat-jour (m)	inspection lamp	la baladeuse
lighting	l'éclairage (m)	extension lead	la rallonge
security light	l'éclairage de sécurité	plug board	la rallonge multi-prises
		ladder	l'échelle (f)
paint	le peinture	stepladder	l'escabeau (m)
wallpaper	le papier peint	tarpaulin, plastic sheet	la bâche
glue	la colle	acrow, support	l'étai (m)
varnish	le vernis, la glazure	scaffolding	l'échaffaudage (m)
coat, layer	la couche	crowbar	le lévier, le pied de biche
undercoat	la sous-couche		

		entreprise de construction	building company
paintbrush	le pinceau	entrepreneur	builder
roller	le rouleau	maître d'oeuvre	building boss, site/works manager
trowel	la trouelle		
screwdriver	le tournevis	artisan	craftsman, worker in skilled trade
pliers	la pince	carreleur	tiler (except for the roof)
spanner	la clef	charpentier	carpenter for roofs
saw	la scie	chauffagiste	heating engineer
drill	la perceuse	couvreur	roofer
drill bit	la mèche	ébeniste	joiner, furniture maker
sander	la ponceuse	électricien	electrician
hammer	le marteau	maçon	stonemason, builder (unspecified)
nail	le clou	ménuisier	general carpenter
screw	le vis	ouvrier	worker, employee of artisan
rawlplug, peg	la cheville	peintre	painter
bolt	le boulon	plâtrier	plasterer
nut	l'écrou (m)	plombier	plumber

HELP, there's a problem in the house!

We've got a problem with . . . /There is . . .
On a un problème avec . . . /Il y a . . .

something wrong	une anomalie	a leak	une fuite
a breakdown	une panne	a crack	une fissure
a failure/weakness	une défaillance	a hole	un trou

Explaining the problem

The boiler has broken down.
La chaudière est en panne.

It won't start/stop.
Il a du mal à démarrer/à s'arrêter.

I can't get it to work.
Je n'arrive pas à le faire marcher.

I've followed the instructions, but the machine still doesn't work.
J'ai suivi la notice, mais l'appareil ne marche toujours pas.

It worked all right for a while, then it stopped.
Ça marchait correctement un certain temps, puis il s'est arrêté.

I can't understand the assembly instructions.
J'ai du mal à suivre la notice du montage.

It's leaking around the tap.
Il fuit autour du robinet.

The seal isn't watertight.
Le joint n'est pas étanche.

The plug has come loose from the wall.
La prise s'est détachée du mur.

The light switch doesn't work.
L'interrupteur ne fonctionne pas.

The radiator/heating isn't effective enough.
Le radiateur/chauffage n'est pas assez performant.

The chimney doesn't draw very well.
La cheminée ne tire pas très bien.

The door has dropped, so it doesn't shut properly.
La porte s'est affaissée, donc il ne ferme pas correctement.

The shutter/window has warped, it's hard to close it.
Le volet /La fenêtre s'est deformé/ée, c'est difficile de le/la fermer.

There is a draught around the door.
Il y a un courant d'air autour de la porte.

There's a crack in the ceiling.
Il y a une fissure au plafond.

Some of the roof tiles are cracked.
Quelques tuiles se sont fendues.

Some of the floor tiles have come loose.
Quelques carrelages/dallages se sont détachés.

The damp is getting into the cellar.
L'humidité s'infiltre dans la cave.

Possible diagnosis

It isn't connected properly.
Ce n'est branché/raccordé correctement.

It wasn't put together/installed correctly.
Ce n'était pas monté/ installé correctement.

It's just a loose connection.
Ce n'est que la connection.

The washer has worn out.
Le joint s'est usé.

There's a part missing.
Il manque une pièce.

Maybe there is a faulty part//a manufacturing fault.
Il y a peut-être une pièce défectueuse/défaillante.//une vice de fabrication.

Possible remedies

You'll have to XXX it . . .
Il faut le/la XXX . . .

- fix	*remédier*	- block up	*boucher*
- change/alter	*modifier*	- unblock	*déboucher*
- replace	*remplacer*	- seal	*sceller*
- exchange	*(é)changer*	- even out/smooth off	*aplanir*
- send it back to the manufacturer/supplier		*renvoyer au fabricant/au fournisseur*	

At the DIY - Au Brico

I'm looking for something to use for XXX – what do you recommend?
Je cherche un produit pour XXX – qu'est-ce que vous recommandez?

- sealing the joint around the bath
  sceller le joint autour de la baignoire

- preventing mould under the sink
  empêcher les moissisures sous l'évier

- unblocking the drains
  déboucher les canalisations

- stripping parquet/beams
  décaper le parquet/ les poutres

- removing paint spots from stonework
  enlever les taches de peinture sur des pierres apparentes

- treating the woodworm in an antique cupboard
  traiter les vers de bois dans une armoire ancienne

- insulating the attic
  isoler le grenier

- removing the moss from the paving around the pool
  traiter la mousse sur la plage de la piscine

- killing off brambles/a tree stump
  tuer les ronces/une souche d'arbre

9 Gardens and Pools

Gardening in France[1]

After centuries of assuming that a garden should be part of an architectural design and therefore that plants should be controlled and shaped to fit into a ready made pattern, the French have begun to discover that actually nature does things rather well on its own, and that if left to themselves, trees, shrubs and flowers turn into something quite wonderful with their own style and individuality. No doubt there are profound conclusions to be drawn from this in terms of shifts in the national psyche, but that's a topic for others to elaborate on. Left more or less to themselves, it should be said, since as anyone who's tried it knows, a garden that looks artlessly natural is the result of inspiration, careful planning and hours of discriminating weeding!

It's intriguing to see that the model for this new 'natural' approach is the *jardin à l'anglaise*, and that the latest garden feature the serious French gardener aspires to is *le mixed border*. Most garden magazines include photos if not entire articles of and about gardens in the UK, and not only the grand gardens, the more informal and rustic ones too. Rioting roses, carpets of bulbs nodding in the spring breezes, tree-high rhododendrons, billowing borders, and most sacrilegious of all, patches of waving meadow starred with wild flowers where the velvet lawn used to be . . . whatever next? Where are the clipped box hedges of *autrefois*? But that's a little unfair; France does have its cottage garden tradition in the *jardin de curé* ('the vicar's garden') which is also rising in fashionability, and there are many wonderful gardens in this country that combine the best of both worlds, with some spaces that are classically formal and others that are riotously natural.

Some thoughts on garden planning

Most of the people recently arrived here with whom I have talked about gardening come into one of two categories. Either they are already keen gardeners and longing to start again in a different and more generous climate, even though they are not too sure what will grow and what won't; or else they have limited gardening experience based on a patch significantly smaller than the property they have bought, and are somewhat daunted by the prospect of having to manage a much larger area. And generally all of them are wondering how much they want to recreate an English style garden and how much they want to do something different which will possibly look better in the new context.

Everyone can recognise the classic French style garden with its formal layout, its jigsaw geometry and lots of box hedges to clip. This style derives from the Italians, and it starts from a preconceived pattern to be imposed on Nature, since the gardens and terraces are designed as a continuation of the grand spaces and the decorative curlicues within. Whereas the English principle is to start with what Nature has designed, and then to arrange and correlate the plants into a whole that looks more harmonious than anything Nature could have managed by itself; or else, at the opposite extreme from the classic approach, to let Nature do it all and leave the plants to seed themselves where they will.

---

[1] Most of these comments are based on experience in the southwest of France, so should be adapted in the direction of lower temperatures if you are in the north, and even higher ones if you are in the southeast. However most of them are relevant for anywhere south of the Loire except in the higher hill country.

In my experience the gardens that work best combine some elements of each approach. Especially in a large area, some structure and overall planning is essential; in fact I would say that the larger the space, the more important it is to decide what you are going to do with it overall before you start. Of course you may decide to plant only a small proportion of the whole, and your plan may be in stages to be realised over several years; but it saves work, money and tears to start with one rather than without. When you arrive it is tempting to start digging up a bit here and putting in a couple of shrubs there just to get things going, which is entirely understandable but not necessarily the best move if you want eventually to have a garden that is coherent and satisfying. On the other hand it would be a mistake to launch into anything grandiose until you have a clear idea of the factors you and your plants will be dealing with.

The most obvious of these are the aspect, the microclimate, the soil quality, the natural water supply if any, the prevailing winds, the maximum summer heat and the minimum winter cold. Perhaps less obvious to those thrilled to escape from gloomy northern skies is the need for shade. However if you want to have a range of plants and to keep some of the familiar English ones then shade is essential – and it's very welcome for people too once the sunny season gets going! Best are high deciduous trees which give light shade but don't smother, so if you have any on your *terrain* that seem superfluous, don't be in a hurry to chop them down until you have considered your overall layout and have worked out whether you can make use of the shade they already provide. Of course more shade can be imported in the shape of mature trees, which are available at a price, or younger quick-growing ones (see the suggestions for shade trees below).

Established trees also provide a ready-made support for vigorous climbers such as the species clematis (*montana, viticella*, etc), rambler roses like New Dawn, and, if they are tall enough, rampantly climbing roses such as Wedding Day, Kiftsgate *et al*. Deciduous shade also provides an ideal situation for naturalising bulbs, if this appeals. In several places near my home there are literally acres of wild snowdrops, violets, daffodils, wood anemones and lily of the valley, but all growing in light woodland where they stay cool in the summer. And one of the more exotic gardens nearby has clumps of white pointy *viridiflora* tulips planted here and there in its open grassy woodland, to entirely magical effect as the pearly white green-streaked flowers come out in perfect synchrony with the new bright green foliage on the trees.

Which brings us to another essential factor in garden design, the use of colour. As most experienced gardeners know, it can work wonders in creating interest and coherence, on a small or a large scale. The basic principle is to group similar colours together, with the cooler blues, pinks and mauves in one part of the design and the hotter reds, oranges and yellows in another. Some colours go with both groups and can act as a link between them, such as the lime green of *alchemilla mollis* or the purple/dark red foliage of purple sage, heuchera Palace Purple, the dark leaved euphorbias, etc, and of course white. Contrasts also work, for instance lemon yellow with lavender blue or golden yellow with royal blue, and if you choose the right ones, some strong pinks and cerises look great with orange and scarlet. (Personally I always avoid cerise with yellow, which to my mind never works.)

Confining one colour group or main colour accent to one area makes for a more restful effect and for more interest, also for a challenge to find plants of the colour group that you want. I discovered this when creating a white border, inspired like so many others by the white garden at Sissinghurst, and scoured the nurseries and the catalogues for everything with white flowers: roses, peonies, lavender, irises, poppies, cranesbills, etc. All set off by contrasts of silver and grey foliage, and a few inky purples – *geranium phaeum*, black parrot tulips, dark violas and few others.

These highlights are what make it all work. And in fact you can get away with creating colour contrasts in plants which would clash horribly on a flat surface, since a living flower colour is actually made up of thousands of varying hues that our eye cannot distinguish but which resonate with each other to create surprising harmonies. So even if you have allocated distinct colour areas, you may want to have one or two signature or theme plants, which look good with any colour group and can seed themselves where they like or be tucked in as your fancy takes you; more discreet ones such as the geranium Johnson's Blue, hearts'ease pansies, annual larkspurs, white flowered annuals; or more eye-catching ones like the alchemilla already mentioned, the mixed colour escholtzia (California poppies), *lychnis coronaria* (white or cerise flowers and grey leaves), or the striking dark red *phormium tenax* or its relatives.

Foliage of course is also a vital part of the garden texture, and as well as being the background for all this colour drama, it can provide lots of nuances and interest in itself. Variegated plants appear on the market in ever greater numbers, and though too many together tend to look messy, they make wonderful accent plants. Some, like the periwinkles and ajuga, are specially useful to brighten dry shade under trees or odd corners where nothing much else will grow. Many otherwise not very remarkable shrubs, such as euonymus, come into their own with glowing autumn colours and berries, and others with red or bronze tinted foliage, like photinia and *abelia grandiflora*, provide welcome contrasts even when not in flower. Bronze fennel is another of my favourites, though it seeds itself rather too generously. The coloured sages I find excellent for this max-and-match, and ready to flourish in this not so easy climate - *salvia purpurea, tricolor, aurea* (gold-tinged), etc - and all the more welcome for being present all year and keeping their colours alive even through the winter.

Another vital organising factor is shape: shape in individual plants and in the overall plan. Here we come back to the classic-or-not question, to which my answer is always, yes – in small doses! Though to me an entirely formal garden with miles of topiary is very much less than thrilling, one that is entirely random becomes all too easily messy and non-restful. So even if it wasn't part of the French tradition, I would always vote for having some part of the garden in a recognisably structured and formal style. This can be achieved with hard landscaping, and also with using plants which have a definite profile: phormiums, achillea, sedums, iris, etc.

Probably you will have, actually or in your mind's eye, a terrace of some kind, and this makes a logical starting point for some structure in layout and planting, as it is the practical and visual link between the shapes of the house and the unshaped grounds around it. Keep in mind that a terrace too will need its shade, and that a wide expanse of solid stone or concrete paving will become a glaring oven under the summer sun, so it's a good idea to incorporate a pergola or loggia of some kind, either built out from the house or independent. The same is true around the swimming pool.

The *maçons* will probably try to argue you out of it, but if you are having a new terrace laid, keep some spaces boxed out for access to the ground beneath (or a deep enough planting hole with drainage) so that you can plant some climbers which will have more than a pot to grow out of and can clothe the structure, as well as some carpeting aromatic plants to soften the expanse of stone. If you plan borders around the terrace or against the wall of the house, remember there too to make the planting spaces broad and deep enough to prevent them from drying out and getting baked.

By definition, most of those parts of the country which the British consider picturesque tend to go up and down somewhat, so the odds are that you will have a few slopes to incorporate in your planting plans. And a great asset they are, provided they are not too steep or too close to the house. If you have a major slope that is fairly steep but you want to plant interesting things in it, you may be better to call in a bulldozer (see below) and have it split into definite terraces with a wall to retain each level. Expensive to begin with but much more satisfactory for planting choice. Don't forget that when the weather is not baking hot it sometimes rains very hard, so the terracing will also prevent soil getting washed downhill.

It's worth giving the same treatment and defining the levels even on a smaller bank, but as with building a rockery, it's important to build in properly the rocks or whatever you are using as retainer, and not just to stick them on the surface and hope they will stay there. It's possible to get old railway sleepers (*les traverses de chemin de fer*) which can be used for this purpose. They also make good steps, either used on their own or as fronts for a flight of steps back-filled in stone (or with gravel – these are cheaper but not so safe as the gravel easily gets washed or trodden out).

Having these different levels to play with is a great asset, specially if there is some shade. There are many plants with dangling flowers which benefit from being seen closer to eye level - hellebores, dicentras, aquilegias, fuchsias, hemerocallis - and lots that look good flopping over a wall: rock roses, some cranesbills, The Fairy rose, alchemilla, gypsophila, smaller cistuses, prostrate rosemary, *teucrium fruticans*, etc.

Then there's the matter of shape within a planting area. Here too you have the choice of tidy or random, depending on the context. If you have a smaller scale border along a wall or as part of a formally laid out area, it will probably look better to keep a restrained and logical slope effect with taller things at the back, middles in the middle and lower ones, like teacher's pet, at the front. You can always prevent this from looking boring by the use of colour and contrasting textures. But for a border on a larger scale it may be more fun to think of a rocky coastline rather than a tidy slope, and to have 'headlands' of larger plants and shrubs alternating with 'coves' of lower ones, and the occasional sentinel clump of taller or spiky plants towards the front, like rocks jutting up from the waterline.

If you want to include some early flowering plants in the border, the instinct is to put them at the front where they will be seen as soon as they peep out in spring. However you then have to watch them wilt and keel over, which is not so thrilling. So I find it best to keep lower ones near the front but to put taller daffs, etc, in the middle or towards the back, where they will still show up before everything else gets going, and when it does, they can fade out gracefully into the surrounding cover.

Apart from the geometric shapes of the terrace, there may be other parts of the garden which lend themselves to being a focal point, with a paved area, a pergola, some seating, a path, a group of plants in formal tubs or matching pots, and so on. The scale of these features will depend of course on the overall scale of your garden, but they always add interest, both in themselves and by creating a contrast with more random and natural planting. If your acreage, imagination and pocket can manage it, there is plenty of fun to be had creating *allées*, *tonnelles*, water features, fountains and so forth. Unfortunately in France there are not so many gardens to visit as in the UK, and those that are open tend to be the very grand ones, but there are plenty of ideas to be gleaned from the gardens featured in the magazines if you don't already have a garden dream of your own that you have been longing to create.

Gardening in French conditions

The main difference between gardening here and in the UK is that in most of the country, except of course in the mountains or in other extreme conditions, the growing season is significantly longer, and many trees and shrubs that you plant or inherit will increase in size at a very satisfactory rate. This means that it is possible to create an established looking garden in a comparatively short time. It also means however that when planning your planting you need to allow more space than you would normally, especially around major subjects, and to avoid putting smaller herbaceous or ground cover plants very close to larger shrubs or trees, or indeed to each other.

With ground cover you'll notice this specially. As a plant-raising friend once pointed out, people usually want ground coverers to grow quickly to carpet a certain area, and then to stop. But unfortunately the plants don't know this, and will carry on regardless over flowerbeds and into neighbouring shrubs or whatever, if they have the chance. So choose your ground cover plants with discretion and plant them more sparsely than the UK normal. (No lamiums or variegated ground elder unless you have a woodland acre to fill!)

Ditto with climbers, especially wisteria, campsis, etc. The former will grow a mile a minute once established, and needs a solid framework for support – it will twist even a metal railing out of shape unless this is really thick. And even the usually manageable Virginia creeper should be placed with care, since here it will, once established, produce a blanketing thicket. Handy if you have a medium sized ruin to disguise, but otherwise it may become a bit much! The same goes for the passion flower vine, which once established will produce a thicket of rampant climbing and twining stems - but that's a nicer problem to have.

Then there are a few other rampant spreaders such as *macleaya cordata* and the older varieties of hypericum that I would also advise against unless you have a significant part of an acre to spare, and if you are a devotee of the bamboo and *graminae* brigade, I strongly suggest you choose *only the less or non rampant* kinds. In warmer areas the more aggressive bamboos are unstoppable, and I've seen established ones sucker and spread to a radius of 15 feet and more in just one season. In theory they can be restrained by being planted in a concrete-lined hole – with drainage of course – but even then they are quite capable of finding an escape route and causing havoc with a major invasion of more genteel neighbours. And once they have got out, there's nothing you can do about it, they are indestructible.

Another factor to remember is that the height of this longer season is largely made up of much hotter days, and especially with the extreme summer temperatures of late, any walls exposed to the sun get very hot. Even in my fairly breezy hilltop garden the west facing house wall registered 38°C/100°F+ for several hours a day for several weeks in July and August. So don't plant anything in this sort of situation that cannot stand getting roasted, and don't plant whatever you choose right against the wall (or under the roof drip if there is no gutter). And even for those that can stand the heat, shade their base with lighter planting and give the roots a good drink every few days.

One beautiful climber that survives in these conditions is *trachelospermum jasminoides*, a long name for a lovely plant with glossy oval evergreen leaves and fragrant white jasmine-type flowers through the summer. It is also content with semi-shade. Campsis is happy too in the heat, with its flamboyant orange or yellowy trumpets and vigorous greenery (both of these are hardy), as are the various forms of *solanum jasminoides* (semi-hardy), plumbago (ditto, pale blue phlox-type flowers) and of bougainvillea in its many dazzling hues (alas not hardy except in the southeast). Note that the campsis (or bignonia) has suckers like ivy so it will attach itself to its support. The others mentioned need training on trellis or wire.

Other reliable summer flowerers, apart from the familiar ones, are lantanas, oleanders, hibiscus (the shrubby *syriacus* type), agapanthus and canna lilies. The first of these need to come in for winter (unless you are in a very sheltered warm spot) and the others need protection against a possible spell of severe cold. There is also a very useful and pretty range of flowering sages of the *salvia microphylla* clan, semi-shrubs with silvery-green foliage and a delicate appearance that belies their toughness in the face of drought. Their small flowers come in bright shades from white and cream to scarlet, crimson, magenta, sky blue (*this* sky blue!) and deep blue-mauves, and several toning or contrasting shades planted together create a lovely *pointilliste* effect. It's surprising that these are not more available in England as they are hardy up to a point. As a safeguard you can take a few cuttings, which succeed readily, and in any case it's good to snip them over regularly to keep them bushy and flowering. The scarlet *grahamii* seems to be the hardiest, and eventually forms a substantial clump.

Buddleias of all denominations and the very tough catmint (*nepeta*) also flower reliably even in dry and/or poor soil, as does *gaura lindheimii*, a plant that forms a low clump of dark pointy foliage from which arises a spray of wiry bendy stems, tipped with delicate pink-tinged white flowers that look almost like a flock of tiny butterflies hovering in the breeze. There is a pink form too but to my mind the white is prettier. Even in poor conditions both the gaura and the nepeta will make large clumps which you can divide up every couple of seasons. They also seed themselves generously.

Another later flowering herbaceous plant that can cope with being hot and dry is *ceratostigma willmottiana*, which makes a carpet about a foot high of neat glossy foliage with intense blue phlox-like flowers from July on. These contrast with the reddish tones the foliage takes on in late summer. It spreads fairly rapidly but its stringy roots are easy enough to pull out if it goes too far, and it is a useful filler between subjects that have already had their turn at flowering.

Naturally all the aromatic semi-shrubs are at home in hot, dry conditions: the lavenders, cistus, sages, phlomis, thymes, helianthemums, etc. It's worth noting that some lavenders, such as *lavandula grosso* and *lavandula stoechas*, go on flowering through most of the season. (To keep lavenders in good shape, clip them lightly when they've finished flowering, then prune them carefully in spring when the new growth starts, back to 3 or 4 leaf joints. Otherwise they soon make long woody stems which will not resprout. If you inherit any old lanky ones, the only thing to do is chuck them and start again.) Perovskia (Russian sage) is another tough aromatic semi-shrub, which makes a good clump of spreading shoots (up to 3ft) clothed in silvery ferny foliage and tipped with spires of blue flowers. Ideal for stabilising a hot dry slope as its deep roots spread horizontally, but think twice before planting it as it's not easy to get them all out again if you decide to move it somewhere else.

Another 'evergrey' gem is *convolvulus cneorum*, with its narrow shiny silver leaves and white trumpet flowers in early summer. Good as a highlight in the front of a border or edge of a terrace as it can easily be kept to a silvery dome of about 2ft high and wide. Finally there's the delightful *caryopteris clandonensis* with its grey-green crinkled leaves and fans of lavender blue flowers, a hardy shrub that makes a dome of arching stems 3-4ft high and across, which continued flowering in my gravelly garden through several months of intense heat. If you want to add more colour among these smaller shrubs and extend the flowering season, you can always tuck in some spring and/or summer bulbs and/or appropriate bedding plants among them.

No doubt you will want some roses on your garden, and you need not hesitate to plant them provided you have a reasonably deep and healthy soil for them to live in. Most roses do very well in warmer climes – after all many of the ancestors of our present roses came originally from the Middle East. In drier or windier spots the *rugosa* roses are unbeatable, and they flourish even along the central reservation of miles of motorway in the south – what less hospitable place could there be? Roseraie de le Haye is a special favourite, with fragrant double cerise-violet flowers most of the season, followed by round orange-red hips. It reaches 5ft each way eventually. The lower single pink Frau Dagmar Hastrup is another pretty and vigorous grower.

My particular favourites are the hybrid musks, shrub roses with sprays of small full flowers that continue flowering in fragrant abundance through rain, shine, heat or chill. Their red-tinted foloage is an added asset. They reach 5-6ft up and across when fully mature, and blend in happily with other kinds of shrubs and flowering plants in the famous mixed border. If you don't already know them, look out for Cornelia, Felicia, Penelope, Prosperity, Buff Beauty and their friends and relations.

One 'rose' I'd ban if I had my way is the Queen Elizabeth, surely the most boring and ungainly rose ever foisted on an undeserving public, and not a whiff of fragrance to redeem it. If it was called the Powder Pink Giraffe they'd know what to expect, and would realise that the only thing to do with it, especially here where it grows extra tall, is to chop it almost to ground level every season. But why bother, when there are so many gorgeous, graceful and super-fragrant roses available nowadays which are so much more worth giving garden space to.

For instance the gem *rosa chinensis mutabilis*, its abundant and delicate red-tinted foliage a perfect setting for its single flowers which open pale peach and turn slowly through coral and pink tones to a deep raspberry as they age. A bush in full flower, which it is most of the time from April to November, looks as if a flock of many coloured butterflies is feasting on it. Its fragile appearance belies its resistance to disease and to all kinds of weather, and in this climate it will grow eventually to a spreading 8-10ft. When it is not actually in flower it is still in leaf, and its pretty foliage provides an added pleasure even in the duller months. Best to give it a firm stake or tripod arrangement to prevent it getting blown about by the wind.

One of the springtime glories in warmer spots is another Chinese rose, *rosa banksiae lutea*, a very vigorous climber which creates enormous festoons of fresh green glossy foliage smothered for several weeks in May and June with uncountable tiny yellow button roses. Unfortunately no fragrance, but their abundance more than makes up for that. Gorgeous in the company of a wisteria, provided they are planted not too close and you can get in to prune them. There is also a white form.

No talk of roses would be complete without invoking the name of David Austin. Many of his most popular varieties are on sale here, and others of course can be mail ordered. They are rightly renowned for their old fashioned beauty and scent, allied to their modern vigour and resistance to disease and to the vagaries of the weather. Meilland, Delbard and André Eve are other names and catalogues to look out for. Those who love old roses will need no reminding that the French were pioneers in introducing and breeding hundreds of rose varieties in the 19th century, many of them derived from the longer flowering varieties discovered in their colonies. Some of these originals and many of their descendants can be found in the specialist catalogues and the better *jardineries*.

Other plants

The choice of plants available nowadays in France is truly wonderful, not least as a result of the new-found enthusiasm in the gardening domain for *le look british*. All through spring and early summer there is a dazzling array in the markets of plants for bedding, pots and troughs, as well as an increasing range of herbaceous things and shrubs. To find other suppliers look in the local papers or Pages Jaunes for *pépinières* (nurseries) or *jardineries* (garden centres). Plant fairs with a full range of plants, including more unusual ones, are also becoming more and more popular.

There are some great gardening magazines available such as *Mon Jardin et Ma Maison* and *Ami des Jardins,* so look in these for dates of said fairs in your area and addresses of specialist plant suppliers, as well as for advice on the plants and the monthly jobs appropriate for the area you live in. (But ignore their planting plans, alas often bizarrely unrealistic.) The magazines give you scope too for fantasising about other kinds of garden: I now know how to prune my palm trees, which kinds of mimosa will give me blossom through the year, which shrubs flourish in Atlantic breezes and how to protect my alpine gems, how to plant the agapanthus avenue and keep the oleanders blooming around my sun-baked terrace in Provence . . .

There is a great surge of interest too in rescuing old varieties of vegetables and wild and medicinal plants, and from at least one of these seed merchants you can obtain seed of up to 300 kinds of tomato, should you wish to do so! Some of these exotic tomatoes are beginning to appear in the local markets too, both as plants and as the finished article – truly delicious. More mundanely, you will also see on the stalls in spring and early summer bundles of seedling lettuces, leeks, cabbages, artichokes, etc, ready for planting, as well as numerous varieties of tomatoes, peppers, and so on, so if you have the right conditions for creating a *potager* you will be off to a flying start. The people selling the plants will be more than happy to advise you in making your selection according to your garden conditions and the time you want to enjoy your harvest (*la récolte*). Early varieties are *précoce* or *hâtive*, late ones are *tardive*.

Major garden centres such as the Jardiland chain have a huge choice of plants, from alpines and indoor orchids to major trees. Their prices may be slightly higher than elsewhere, but their plants are of good quality and healthy, and are guaranteed. What the few extra euros are buying you is actually something precious, ie time, since plants that have been well cared for, and have not been set back by neglect or becoming pot-bound, will flourish and flower for you that much sooner. The humbler local *jardineries* often have a reasonable choice too but you'll have to select the healthier plants more carefully. More or less similar ranges of garden equipment and garden furniture as in the UK are available in garden centres and the larger *bricos* and supermarkets - with the added bonus of weather that makes it worth investing in!

Container plants

One important caveat if your garden is anywhere other than in an ideal well-watered and sheltered valley: resist the temptation to go round the *jardineries* and choose the largest plants you can see. Go for the smaller specimens instead, and those that have a good shape. Don't forget that many container grown plants, especially the larger shrubs and trees, will have spent several seasons in their pots and therefore their central roots may well be in a more or less solid ball which it is impossible to disentangle without seriously setting the plant back and/or having to prune back lots of its top growth to compensate. So for larger subjects it's better to be patient and plant them bare-rooted in the autumn or early spring.

The truth is that growing things will only survive the extremes of summer drought and cold spells in the winter if their roots are well spread out and can grow freely in any direction they need to. And don't forget, a plant cannot untangle its roots by itself! So unless you are handling peonies, hellebores, hostas or anything else that hates being moved, it's best to tease out the root ball and trim off any very matted roots (as well as to peel off the top layer of soil in the pot, often full of weed seeds). If you start off with smaller plants, add plenty of feed and root encouragement when planting and water them well at the beginning, you will have happier plants that will settle in quickly, and in fact will soon be as big as the ones you wanted in the first place. With this useful difference, that they will resist when the weather begins to play tricks, while the bigger ones, which looked fine for a season or two, have started dying back and dying off.

Local trees

There's little beech in these southern areas, it's too hot and not damp enough except in some river valleys, but hornbeam is happy and in fact grows all over the place, often to a considerable height. As do evergreen oaks, which though they grow slowly make wonderful trees of character, the nearest substitute for olive trees in places too cold for the real thing. Other oaks, ash, sycamores in profusion (including the pretty *érable de Montpellier*, with clusters of small three-lobed leaves that turn gold and coppery peach in autumn), acacias and fruiting chestnuts also flourish in the wild.

A word of warning about acacias: leave them in the wild, where they light up the woods and hillsides wonderfully with their creamy fragrant blossom in April/May. They grow fast and look gorgeous in flower, but have an unfortunate habit of dying off in chunks even before they reach maturity. They seed themselves everywhere, the roots throw up suckers, most new growth has vicious spines, and they are almost impossible to eradicate, until they die off, that is . . . you have been warned! One point in their favour, their wood is hard as nails (which is why the Egyptians used it for their sarcophagi) and it makes great fence posts - if you need some, look for *piquets d'acacia*.

If you are fortunate you may inherit a walnut tree or two, trees which in fact are able to survive in comparatively sparse conditions, though of course they produce more nuts if they have a measure of damp and some reasonable soil. For planting olive trees the Dordogne valley seems to be about the northern limit. They will survive in a sheltered or frost-free spot, but don't be surprised if a spell of winter cold sets them back. Umbrella pines are happy in the Dordogne hills, though they only grow wild in a few places. Italian-style cypresses will also flourish.

Favourite shade trees are the horse chestnut, lime, catalpa (large leaves and white flowers resembling the chestnut), paulownia (ditto leaves and purple flowers but unpretty lumpy seedpods), *mûrier platane* (plane tree crossed with the mulberry, non-fruiting), real mulberry (the fruits are delicious but sticky and attract all the wasps of the neighbourhood), and *albizia*, a mimosa relative that makes a delightful spreading canopy of feathery foliage crowned with fans of very fragrant frondy pinkish flowers. There are some magnificent mature ones in this area which must be several decades old, having reached 30ft high and 20ft across. Other varieties of mimosa also flourish here in sheltered spots.

Other good specimen trees include *cedrus deodara* and the Atlantic cedar *cedrus atlantica glauca* (blue-green) or *aurea* (greeny-gold), which forms a graceful broad based pyramid of frondy foliage. It grows fairly quickly and will eventually reach an imposing 30-40ft high and 15-20ft across, so it needs plenty of room. Somewhat smaller is the liquidambar, a narrower pyramid shaped tree that reaches 20ft or more, with large maple-type leaves that turn the most amazing colours in autumn. The kaki or persimmon tree is another a good choice, a standard with large dark green leaves that turn gold before they drop in autumn, leaving the oval orange fruits hanging on the bare branches like early Christmas decorations.

The splendid *ginkgo biloba* also thrives in fairly poor conditions, provided it gets off to a good start. The species has flourished for the last 160 million years, and one huge tree in Hiroshima even survived the bomb blast. It reaches 40-50ft eventually, and its fan shaped leaves turn a wonderful gold in the autumn. There are some magnificent ones along the Champs Elysées.

Another lovely little tree (grown as a standard or a large shrub) that blossoms reliably from July onwards goes by the cumbersome name of *lagerstroemia*, unfair for something which is very pretty with its oval glossy leaves and thick pointy clusters of frilly blossom in white, pinks, cerise and mauves that flourishes miraculously through the summer heat like an enthusiastic lilac. Hence its local name, *lilas des Indes*. You'll see them in street planting too where they survive with the minimum of attention and water. As a final bonus the foliage turns golden or copper in the autumn, and even when the tree is bare you can enjoy its mottled plane-like bark. It has been bred to be pruned, so to keep it flowering don't hesitate to cut it back in early spring. If left to itself it will grow eventually to a spreading 15ft high and 10ft or so across.

Another gem is a large shrub/small tree called *clerodendrum trichonomum*. Its large heart-shaped leaves frame clusters of pink buds which open, from July onwards, into white tubey flowers which are wonderfully fragrant. Great to plant near the terrace as the slightest breeze will waft their exotic perfume about. The flowers are followed by extraordinary berries, each one set like a small blue bead in a five-pointed star of red sepals, which last for several weeks. A similar size (up to 10-12ft eventually) is *vitex agnus castus*, a substantial graceful shrub with willow-type silvery leaves and spires of white, lavender-pink or mauvey-blue flowers from midsummer. The whole plant including the wood is aromatic, and it is hardy enough to resist severe cold spells.

Most splendid of all flowering trees is the *magnolia grandiflora*, introduced into France via the botanic gardens of Montpellier in the 1840s or thereabouts. For several decades this magnolia was a must in every grand garden in the warmer parts of the country, and in many classic leafy residential areas magnificent trees from this time, now forty or fifty feet high and lit up in summer by their superb orbs of creamy flowers, gaze down in lordly elegance upon the bustle and scurry of our lesser world.

Though you may not live to see yours attain the same heights, it is still worth planting one, and they can be found in good nurseries as standards. Provided it has a good start it will withstand both heat and cold, up to a point – or rather down to a point, in the case of the cold. Look out for them in your area to assess whether or where you could plant one. Again, good to put in a situation where you can savour its memorably exotic perfume, but leave it plenty of space. Many other magnolia varieties can withstand high temperatures provided they have a deep root run, and in fact the very hot summer of 2003 encouraged some local ones to flower all over again in September just as plentifully as they did in spring.

Hedges

As any experienced gardener knows, the wind can be as drastic as the heat in drying out plants and soil, so if there isn't any already in position, it's wise to create some sort of wind protection in the form of hedges or suitable trees. It may seem contradictory, but where there are strong prevailing winds, a partly permeable barrier that acts to slow down the wind gives more shelter than a solid wall or dense hedge, behind which the wind may create more turbulence.

But consider carefully what you plant – definitely no *leylandii*!! For one thing it will grow like a rocket and soon need lots of pruning and chopping about, since its instinct is to reach its natural height of 40-50ft as soon as possible. That is, if it doesn't die first of heat and drought, as thousands of them around here did in the hot summer of 2003, leaving miles of local hedges, as well as major trees, toasted brown or very blotchy, and in need of being grubbed out and replaced.

You will be much better off with laurel (the Portuguese cherry laurel, *laurus lusitanicus*, has fragrant flowers, smaller leaves, and is prettier than the ordinary *laurus nobilis*), plain eleagnus, or a mixed evergreen hedge combining for instance photinia, *viburnum tinus*, choisya, cotoneasters (the arching *lacteus* or *franchetti*, rather than the *horizontalis* with its ungainly spiky growth), evergreen ceanothus, eleagnus, *abelia grandiflora*, osmanthus, etc. A hedge of this kind, with 4 or 5 varieties, gives you the welcome bonus of flowers and berries, as well as some fragrance, through the seasons.

If you need a solid boundary hedge you can choose a single kind, or a couple of similar habit, plant them 3-4ft apart and let them grow into a solid line. You could also, on the belt and braces principle, put in a chain link fence as a barrier and to help defend them while the shrubs are growing big enough to do the job by themselves. If it's to be a decorative hedge with several types of shrub, plant them far enough apart for each to keep its own shape. There is now a law against planting evergreen hedges and trees that are not in keeping with the local vegetation, and there are specific rules about heights of hedges: they must be planted at least 2m within your boundary, and if they are closer than 3m they must be kept to a height of 2m.

Grass

On the subject of grass, if you cannot enjoy your summer unless you are surrounded by acres of carefully striped green velvet, don't choose a property south of Tours, unless it is in that lush well-watered valley with perfect soil! Anywhere else will be too dry for the velvet effect, and if you tried to achieve it you would be using criminal amounts of water. For a real lawn, having the right soil is as important as having enough rainfall, so if this matters to you keep this factor in mind. If you want to plant one, do so in spring, or better still in September/October so that it has time to settle in and prepare for the summer heat - after March it may well be too dry for it to root properly. In July and August you will probably not be allowed to water it anyway, so there's not much point in being too ambitious. Ask in your local *jardinerie* or agricultural merchant for the kind of grass (*de l'herbe à semer*) that suits the local conditions, and don't be too disappointed if it isn't the velvet variety.

Feeding

As for feeding, your plants will be undyingly grateful for a regular dose of a magic formula called Or Brun, available in sacks in all the usual garden/*brico* places. It is a mixture of manure, seaweed and other treats that growing things find delicious, it is concentrated, easy to use - being of more or less compost consistency - and not too smelly. A distinct advantage over manure is that it is clean and doesn't bring weed seeds into the garden. A generous amount mixed into a planting hole will encourage root growth, vital to your plant's future health and happiness. In early spring you can spread it on your flowerbeds or around shrubs, climbers, etc, then work it into the top layer of soil, and give them another dose if you see things flagging mid-season. Also great in potting mixture for keeping up the enthusiasm of your terrace plants.

Another traditional tip being reintroduced by the organic brigade is the use of a magic potion called *purain d'orties*, a nettle stew made very simply by dumping fresh nettles into a tub of cold water about 5 times their volume, and leaving them to soak for 24 hours. During the following 24 hours the liquid is very effective as an insecticide, specially on greenfly, and after that it makes a very good plant food, since nettles, for all their unpopularity, are full of things that other plants appreciate and thrive on (especially tomatoes, so put a layer of nettle leaves in the planting hole to give them a good start). Horsetail (*prêle*), a prehistoric fern-type plant that thrives locally in ditches and damp conditions, can also be added to the *purain* mixture.

Tree pruning and clearing the ground

Chopping large trees about is one task that it's as well not to meddle with, and to leave to the professionals. If you haven't already tried it, believe that it is more dangerous than it looks, and if you have, you'll know this already. Any high or sizeable branches need the proper tackle to remove them safely, and if there are whole trees you need to get rid of, then a professional size chainsaw and/or bulldozer, handled by someone who knows how to make the tree fall in the desired direction, will do the job much more safely and speedily than you could do it yourself.

Of course if you want to replant in the same space, or if it's the kind of tree that will resprout, you'll need to have the whole stump (*la souche*) taken out. In this case it should be cut down to about a metre high so that there's enough left to put a chain round and drag out with a tractor or digger. Any scrubby trees or shrubs can be dug out very rapidly with a *pelleteuse* or *tracto-pelle*, a digger or JCB that will simply scoop them up bodily and dump them wherever you wish, to replant, to rot or to burn. The men who operate these machines are usually very skilled and efficient, and booking one of them for even half a day can save you weeks of exhausting and ineffective work. The secret of success is to ask them to come beforehand and have a good look at the terrain, gradients, access, etc, and to explain exactly what needs to be done – scouring out old stuff, making planting holes, moving shrubs, regrading slopes, levelling for a terrace or whatever.

If you have any amount of land to cope with you'll need a hefty strimmer, and to be very careful when using it specially if there are random stones lying about, as there are over most of the country! For a strimmer and a chainsaw it makes sense to buy the best you can afford, specially ones that start reliably, since with cheaper ones about 20 per cent of the time allocated for the job tends to be spent trying to get the dratted thing going. A tip for smaller hand tools: before you plunge into the undergrowth, stick some bright coloured tape round their handles – you'll be less likely to leave them there, or to dump them by mistake on the bonfire! Speaking of tools, you may notice if you look for garden forks, spades or other such things, that many have a long straight handle (*une manche*) instead of the D handle type normal in the UK. The straight variety is usual in the south since the shape is Roman in origin, while in the north you may find the familiar D ones, which are in the Germanic tradition.

To clear awkward things such as scrub and saplings, brambles or rough grass, ask around (eg at the *mairie* or in your local bar) for a someone with a *gyrobroyeur*, a ride-on machine with a vicious horizontal scything blade that can deal with most things of this kind very speedily. After a couple of cuts you'll be well on the way to having something manageable, and the brambles or whatever needs spraying can be treated more effectively. For treating ordinary to tough weeds, look in the *jardinerie* for glyphosate, the generic and *very* much cheaper form of a brand-leading weed killer you probably know already. After using it you can plant again a week or so after the weeds have died down, but if they are tough ones, leave them longer than this and dose them again to make sure they are really dead. It's no news to experienced gardeners that trying to do things in the garden in a hurry usually takes longer in the end! For more drastic treatment you can use sodium chlorate (*chlorate de soude*) but then you'll have to wait several months before replanting.

The most effective, though temporarily unlovely, way to clear all weeds, overgrown flowerbeds and unwanted tangles of growth, is the permaculture method: cut everything back as near to ground level as possible, then cover the whole patch you want to clear with a thick layer of black plastic (available in broad widths from any agricultural merchant), or anything else that will keep out the light. Leave it untouched for 6 months while it all rots away, and when you take the lid off again, hey presto, there is lots of undisturbed and useable soil, with a flourishing bacteria and worm population that will help it to stay healthy.

In fact permaculture research has also shown that different types of bacteria live and work in different layers of soil to which they are specifically adapted, so it is counter-productive to dig over the soil so deeply that you bury the top layer and expose the deeper ones. You may have to dig deep to begin with in order to get out any major shrubs, resistant weeds, etc, but after that it is as well to hoe only the top layer of soil to keep it aerated, and to leave the deeper layers undisturbed to do their own thing. If the soil is naturally heavy and compact, dig in some grit or other bulky material at the beginning to help correct the drainage.

A tip to save time and mess when clearing out old plants, doing a pruning blitz, clipping a hedge, etc: start with a groundsheet or *bâche*, a large tough plastic sheet (available in several generous sizes in any *brico*) which you lay on the ground as near as possible to where you are working and on which the debris can pile up. Then you can drag it to wherever you want to dump the rubbish, with far fewer trips than it would take with a wheelbarrow, or even a garden trailer, and much less mess to rake up. If it's going on a bonfire don't let the stack get too high otherwise you may have a Guy Fawkes event on your hands! This is all just common sense, but that's something that can get overlooked when you are in the first flush of enthusiasm for reclaiming your new domain, and are perhaps working on a larger scale than you are used to.

Back for a moment to the trees: as a glance around many town squares will indicate, especially in early spring, the traditional French notion of tree shaping has more in common with the butcher's trade than that of the sensitive surgeon. Fortunately the old-fashioned short-top-and-sides approach is being mellowed by a style derived from the Japanese, called *élagage douce*, which respects the natural shape and proportions of the tree. If you need a tree surgeon look in the Pages Jaunes for *élagage/un élagueur*, and avoid the *bûcherons* who are loggers.

But don't be in a hurry to get rid of mature trees until you are sure you don't want them, for shade or shelter or privacy, or to hide a less than lovely part of the view. It is easy enough to take them away but somewhat harder to put them back again! And an old apple tree, for instance, that is past its best can provide an ideal ready-made support for a climbing rose or clematis (or even for some annual convolvulus - morning glory - which will spiral up to amazing heights if it is kept watered), so the tree can flower all over again.

A general comment about pruning things: it may be tempting to hack into any overgrown shrubs, climbers, trees, etc, but it's a fact that if a healthy plant is pruned hard it will, nine times out of ten, react by growing more vigorously. This means that although it will be smaller for a while, it will probably end up bigger than it was in the first place, specially if it already has an established root system. Thus if you are trying to sort out overcrowded shrubs you may do better to select the most promising ones and get rid of the duds completely, instead of trying to keep them all, and to keep them all in check. Climbers are easier to deal with since they can be cut back to the main stems and then trained in again to wherever you want them to go.

Keep in mind that new growth will usually start from a leaf joint just below wherever branches and stems have been cut, so generally it's better to take out some main branches right from the tree trunk or from 10-15ins above the base of the shrub, rather than to chop them off half way, because that tends to make them resprout in all directions and become very lumpy. Of course thinner branches and outer growth can be trimmed back, while keeping leading shoots that are growing in the desired direction. The main thing is to keep the basic shape of the shrub or tree as far as possible, because this is what keeps it in proportion and gives it its character. If it is hacked about too severely this governing matrix is destroyed and the plant then grows any which way and becomes even harder to control – so go carefully.

One other factor to keep in mind about any trees you inherit or plan to plant: they must be kept well clear of any phone or electric lines. This is partly common sense, in view of the violent storms that seem to strike us increasingly often nowadays, and partly because if you don't keep the electricity lines on your property clear, the EDF will come and do it for you; that is to say, they will do a hatchet job chopping back or even chopping down any trees they deem to be a threat to their lines. They have a divine right to go onto anyone's land for this purpose without notice, and in February or so they appear in gangs, complete with a crane hoist, to trim trees along the roadside or anywhere else they consider necessary. You have been warned!

Watering

It goes without saying that you'll need an efficient watering strategy for your property, but bear in mind that 'efficient' means using less water not more, especially when you have to pay for every drop you use. Keep in mind too that at the height of summer just when everything is at its thirstiest, there may well be a complete ban on watering, so prepare your plants for this by doing the best for them the rest of the year. But this does not mean overdosing them; the more water they have the more they will want - read on!

The main factor in your watering plans is of course the permeability of the soil you are on. If it's gravelly or sandy then you'll need to add manure and any other vegetable matter you can find. If it's clay then it's even more important to improve it, otherwise it will bake rock hard in the summer. Some coarse gravel or a few sackfuls of the tree bark sold for mulch can help break it up (use the medium or small grade). To feed and balance your soil, ask around locally for well rotted manure, *fumier bien pourri*. If you want topsoil ask for *terre végétale*. Usually this is supplied by companies who do earth moving (*terrassement*) and *travaux publics* – look for them in the Pages Jaunes if your neighbours can't advise you. But don't count on getting rich loamy soil, unless you are lucky it may be sandy or lumpy clay, and need further improvement so that you get a good balance between drainage and water retention.

If you want to do serious gardening it's worth putting in one of the watering systems with perforated plastic pipe that lets out a trickle of water at or just beneath ground level.

- Pluses: the water goes to the roots of the plants where it is needed, and is not wasted just getting the leaves wet. After all, what plants need water for is drawing up nutrients from the soil. You can lay out the pipe network and then connect it to a timer on the tap so that sections of the garden get watered in turn, or control it manually.

- Minuses: the pipes look messy and artificial until the plants cover them. You can't place the pipework exactly until the planting is done, but then it may be harder to get among the plants to lay the pipes. The pipes sometimes spring leaks you don't notice and a lot of water can be wasted. The timer/control units are not infallible.

However this is still a more efficient way to use water than sprinkling the plants with a hose, which is wasteful and can anyway only be done once the plants are out of direct sunlight. (Don't be tempted to shower them even if they are wilting under the grilling sun - it does them more harm than good to get a sudden cold drenching, and they'll perk up again when the sun has passed.) But *don't* leave the system to run constantly. Apart from the bill, plants won't bother to make proper roots if they have an easy supply of water. Time it so that they get a good dose every 2 or 3 days, and they will root well *and* flower for you gratefully!

Apart from any summertime ban on watering, be sure to reduce the supply when growth slows down and to stop it well before the cooler weather comes, to avoid waste and prevent possible frost damage. Also check now and again that the water isn't trickling right onto the trunk of shrubs or trees. Remember they absorb the water through their roots, not through the bark, which is designed to be watertight and may split if it stays wet a long time.

A final PS about hoses which you may not think of if you are not used to the heat: store your hose if possible in the shade because if it's in the sun with the water in it, the water will get scalding hot and have to be run off before you put any of it on the plants. Not very good for the hose either. Also if you leave it full and lying on the grass in blazing sun it may make scorch marks. Leave seeds and bulbs too in a cellar or somewhere cool, not in a shed or greenhouse where they will bake.

Another vital water-reducing measure: putting down a mulch (*un paillage*), of coco shell, hemp (*chanvre*), shredded tree bark (the finer one works best in a border) or whatever you can find locally. Purists have their own preferences, but whichever you use, the main point is to cover the exposed soil thickly in spring while it is still cool and before the weeds get going. Make sure the ground is well watered or rained on before you cover it up, as once the mulch is in place it takes a lot of water to penetrate it. Work from the edges of the area being covered towards the middle, so that you flatten the mulch as you go and don't have to tread on the wet soil.

Laid on thickly enough, the mulch will prevent evaporation, discourage any annual weeds from sprouting, and make it easier to see and to treat any perennial weeds that come through. Most bark mulches are acidic, which is no bad thing if you are on the limestone soil that is common in much of the south and in hill country. They gradually rot away into the soil and will need topping up every couple of years or so depending on your local conditions. The mulch also proves its worth in the winter, protecting the soil from heavy rain and keeping frost away from plant roots. (And it hides those black watering pipes!) Only disadvantage, it discourages plants from seeding themselves, but you can always gather the seeds when they are ready.

Garden refuse

It's not worth using grass cuttings for a mulch, as they are generally full of weed seeds and are too compact to rot properly, they just go slimy and smelly – and the high summer temperatures bring out the smells something chronic! Best to create a proper compost heap and add them to it gradually, along with any other rottable refuse. This is the only sensible thing to do anyway with garden rubbish. The communal rubbish bins are for household stuff and your neighbours will not be happy to see them fill up with your weeds or prunings! Besides, much of this rubbish is burnt in incinerators which don't do a lot for the environment or the communities living near them, so it's best not to add to it unnecessarily. In the Lot *département* there is now a scheme to provide compost-making bins to any household prepared to pay a token sum for one. How's that for being planet-friendly?

Bonfires are allowed most of the year except when it's too dry, ie from June to mid September, more or less. Your *mairie* will tell you when you can or can't. A few reminders about bonfire techniques may be useful if you've forgotten how. If you have a large garden to overhaul or a lot of ground to clear then you'll probably amass an impressive mound of stuff to be burned. When you come to do this, choose if possible a day with a light breeze but no strong wind. Don't leave the heap until it is dry, as the fire may then get out of hand. Best to burn it when it is still partly damp - but don't just set a match to a corner of it and hope it will go, because it won't!

To do it safely and effectively, you can start the fire by the logger's method: choose a spot on the windward side of the heap and build a small fire just on the edge of it with some really dry material, as if you were lighting a fire in a grate. Build this up until it is hot enough to take a couple of substantial logs. Once these are burning well they will make a core which will stay hot and will keep burning as you dump the rest of the waiting pile in stages on top of them. If you alternate the drier stuff with the damper bits it will all soon disappear. Needless to say, make sure the fire is really out before you abandon it.

The Dordogne valley

To digress for a paragraph or two: For those who are not familiar with it, the Dordogne valley is really a gardener's paradise, since it's cool enough, just, to grow many familiar English plants (provided you have some shade), and warm enough for many more southern ones. The wild plants are a matchless garden in themselves; it never fails to delight me in spring watching the succession of blossom which goes on for four months or so, from late January to May: blackthorn, wild plum, cherry, apple, wild viburnum, judas tree, honeysuckle, pistachio, hawthorn, tamarisk, wild roses, acacia and many other nameless things – and that's not counting the wild flowers: snowdrops, cowslips, tiny daffodils, pulmonarias, sages, campanulas, euphorbias, aquilegias, cranesbills, scabious, wild orchids in umpteen varieties, innumerable daisies, thymes and thousands of rock plants, all growing happily in their favourite corners and making a wonderful tapestry.

And even from the fairly scruffy hedgerows around our village one can gather apples, plums, bitter cherries, luscious figs, walnuts, hazelnuts, blackberries - what more could one ask? In fact when you are surrounded by the wonderful gardens of nature it seems impertinent sometimes and even pointless to garden in one's own little patch - but there we are, it's a habit that brings a lot of pleasure, in spite of its occasional frustrations.

Useful vocabulary

clay	*l'argile* (f)	mulch	*le paillage, mulch*
compost (bag)	*le terreau*	peat	*la tourbe*
compost (heap)	*le compost*	sand	*le sable*
earth, soil	*la terre*	topsoil	*la terre végétale*
gravel (rough)	*la castine*		
gravel (rounded)	*le gravier*	arch	*l'arceau* (m)
humus	*la matière végétale*	avenue	*l'allée* (f)
manure	*le fumier*	bank	*le talus*

border (edging)	*la bordure*	standard (rose)	*(rosier) sur tige*
border (flowers)	*la plate-bande*	tree	*l'arbre* (m)
decking	*le caillebotis*		
drive	*l'entrée* (f)	annual	*annuel/le*
flowerbed	*le massif, la parterre*	arching	*retombant/e*
hedge	*la haie*	deciduous	*caduc*
lawn	*la pelouse, le gazon*	dwarf	*nain/e*
pond	*la mare, l'étang* (m)	early (variety)	*hâtif/ve, précoce*
terrace	*la terrasse*	evergreen	*persistant/e*
tunnel, arcade	*la tonnelle*	hardy	*rustique*
trellis	*la treille*	late (variety)	*tardif/ve*
wall (low)	*le muret*	non-hardy	*gélif/ve*
		perennial	*vivace*
bark	*l'écorce* (f)	shrubby	*arbustive*
berry	*la baie*	spreading	*tapissant/e*
branch	*la branche*	variegated	*panaché/ée*
bud	*le bourgeon*	weeping	*pleureur/euse*
cutting	*la bouture*		
flower	*la fleur*	in full sun	*en plein soleil*
flower cluster	*la grappe*	in semi-shade	*à la mi-ombre*
foliage	*le feuillage*	in shade	*à l'ombre* (f)
graft	*la greffe*		
leaf	*la feuille*	axe	*la hâche*
plant	*la plante*	bucket	*le seau*
root ball	*la motte*	chainsaw	*la tronçonneuse*
root	*la racine*	garden fork	*la fourche à bécher*
sap	*la sève*	garden spade	*la bêche/pelle-bêche*
seedling	*le plant*	hoe	*la houe, binette*
shoot	*la pousse*	hose	*le tuyau de jardin*
stem	*la tige*	mower (tractor)	*la tondeuse (autoportée)*
sucker	*le rejet, gourmand*	pickaxe	*la pioche*
thorn	*l'épine* (f)	rake	*le rateau*
trunk	*le tronc*	secateurs	*le sécateur*
twig	*la brindille*	shears	*la cisaille*
weed	*la mauvaise herbe*	shovel	*la pelle (-terrassier)*
		stake	*le tuteur*
annual plant	*l'annuelle* (f)	strimmer	*la débroussailleuse*
bedding plant	*la plante à composition*	tap	*le robinet*
biennial	*la (plante) bisanuelle*	watering can	*l'arrosoir* (m)
bush	*le buisson*	wheelbarrow	*la brouette*
climber	*la plante grimpante*	wire	*le fil*
grass	*l'herbe* (f)	vine eyes	*les yeux de vigne*
ground cover	*le couvre-sol*	fertiliser	*l'engrais* (m)
herbaceous plant	*le vivace*	insecticide	*l'insecticide* (f)
moss	*la mousse*	weedkiller	*l'herbicide* (f), *le désherbant*
shrub	*l'arbuste* (f)		

to cut back (plants)	*rabattre*	to stake	*tuteurer*
to cut down (a tree)	*abattre*	to strim	*débroussailler*
to cut the grass	*tondre le gazon, faire la tonte*	to thin out	*éclaircir*
to dig	*creuser*	to turn over (soil, etc)	*retourner*
to graft	*greffer*	to water	*arroser*
to harvest	*recolter*	to weed	*désherber*
to hoe	*biner*		
to make cuttings	*bouturer*	to fade	*fâner*
to train against a wall	*palisser*	to flower	*fleurir*
to plant out	*repiquer*	to grow	*pousser*
to prune	*tailler*	to self-seed	*se resemer*
to prune trees	*élaguer*	to spread (runners)	*drageonner*
to rake	*ratisser*	to sprout (seed)	*germer*
to sow	*semer*	to wither	*flétrir*

Swimming pools

This is a fraught topic which deserves a chapter of its own. Pool disaster stories abound, so if and when you decide to take the plunge (. . . *groan*), the first thing to do is find a reliable contractor to do the work. There are several national groups of pool designers and distributors such as Desjoyaux and Piscines Ambiance, with certified local sub-contractors: look in the Pages Jaunes for *piscines*.

Generally it's wiser to avoid the one-man-band type who can do a bit of everything and who offers to dig out a pool for you more or less in his spare time (provided you pay a hefty sum up front for the materials), or else who just happens to have a couple of months free in which he could get it done - oh yeah? If he's so good, how come he's so available? But there's the catch, the people who know how to do it properly are busy doing it properly, and a well done pool is a fairly complex job. So plan well ahead of the day you want to take your first dip!

The first step is obvious: finding out what kind of soil and/or rock will have to be got through to make the hole big enough. If you can't tell, ask a nearby farmer for his opinion (*un avis*), and/or any builder in the neighbourhood. Ask also if there are any springs (*sources*) or underground streams (*courants souterrains*) which might interfere with the plans – there often are such things in limestone country. One thing to avoid is siting it on or near any rubble, backfill (*remblai*) or recently turned over soil. The weight of water added to the weight of the pool walls will shift any underlying soil that is not really solid. If this situation is unavoidable then the pool structure and the earth around it should be left to settle for *several months* before it is filled and the surround (*la plage*) is finished.

Next hurdle, apart from being nice to your bank manager, is the planning permission required. Start at the *mairie* (see the chapter on Houses, p. 96). If you live in a conservation area there are strict guidelines about pool siting and visibility, also about the colour of the inside, so before you start digging be sure to get expert advice and find out exactly what you are allowed to do. As of January 2004 it is obligatory to have a childproof safety fence (*une clôture de sécurité*) surrounding a pool on a property that is let and around all new ones, and by 2006 around all others, so you'll need to check carefully on these requirements (which to nobody's surprise are very complex) and make sure they are incorporated correctly in the overall design.

As far as the actual construction is concerned there are of course several options to suit the amount of space and cash available for the project, ranging from the small scale pre-formed pool (though these are now becoming available in bigger sizes) to the mega infinity pool. If you've been in one of these you'll know the uncanny feeling of being able apparently to swim all the way to the horizon. Sad that this particular thrill comes with a hefty price tag, not least from having to top up the water level fairly frequently.

For those who can't quite manage the Hockney effect with something lined in hand-tinted ceramic, there is the more realistic option of a heavy rubber liner which is custom made to fit exactly the contours of your particular pool. Needless to say the finish of the inside of the pool has to be satin smooth so that there is no risk of the liner being pierced. The contractor will check this when they come to measure up for it. A lining of this type is of course less resistant than tiling, but with due care will last for a good many years, and will make a noticeably smaller hole in the pocket.

It seems that more options in design, cleaning methods and widgetry (eg robot cleaners) come onto the market every few months. As usual with any big project, it's a matter of juggling fantasies versus realities, not least of these latter being your budget. On this point remember that you have to allow not just for the excavation and construction of the pool but for ongoing maintenance: running a continual pumping system, keeping the water clean and free of bugs or leaves, topping it up when it evaporates, etc – and having someone do these things for you if you are away for any length of time during the season, or too busy to do them yourself. These tasks are not complicated, but it's essential that they are done correctly and on time if you want to avoid the water going murky and having to clean out everything and refill the pool. And then it will need packing up for winter, ideally under a substantial cover.

There are various systems available for keeping the water clean, so it is possible to avoid overdosing everything with chlorine. In fact it is now illegal in France to put a chlorine system in a new pool, it has to have a saline system. This works by electrolysis, which releases the chlorine in the salt to do its job of cleaning the water. It is then reconverted by UV rays back into salt. Needless to say the water cleaned in this way is much more pleasant to swim in. A tip from friends who have one of these: if you have a cover on the pool, leave it open during the day even if the weather's not very bright so that the cycle of salt to chlorine and back to salt again is not interrupted.

You will no doubt want a shower somewhere nearby, and there are very effective solar heated models on the market. Ditto for a solar system for heating the water if you want to, in which case it is worth investing in a proper roll-over cover. In any case it's as well to have a cover of some kind to avoid losing too much heat overnight, and to prevent leaves, bugs and bits falling into the water. Speaking of which, it makes sense when you are planning your poolside planting to avoid anything near the water that will shed a lot of leaves. The aromatic and 'everygrey' plants mentioned in the section above work well, and provide a foil for the brighter colours which look so good in the brilliant sunshine. One poolside border seen a few years ago and still clear in my mind's eye was a shimmer of blues, whites, silvers and a few grasses which swayed and billowed in the passing breeze with a wonderful seaside effect.

10 Formalities

Making arrangements

If you plan to live in France for more than a day or two you will no doubt have to deal with some members of the ubiquitous administration. These *fonctionnaires* are notorious for keeping you waiting and making you sign everything in triplicate – but usually it's not their fault, they are trying to deal with a ridiculously cumbersome system. Attempts are at long last being made to streamline it, ie reduce the avalanche of paperwork the average person has to deal with down to a mere snowdrift or two.

In the bureaucratic jungle we encounter a central contradiction in the French national character: on the one side the devotion to form, forms, the done thing, the hierarchy, the system as hallowed by our predecessors - largely attributable to the Roman aspect; and on the other, the rebellious individualism, flights of fancy and showing off, largely attributable to those noisy wild Gauls, who are still alive and well in spite of all the efforts of the *legionnaires*, past and present. Thus it can happen that just when you have committed some culpable oversight or have become entangled in the deepest thickets of bureaucritania, some kindly functionary will take pity on you, smile at you sweetly, waft aside with a shrug whatever regulation it was tripping you up, and let you go with a pat and a friendly caution and six months in which to pay up or whatever it was you were supposed to do.

But don't count on it. If you come up against the diehard *fonctionnaire* you will discover that they stick to the tiniest footnote of the law and are completely impervious to any human feeling, let alone to any common sense. So whenever you receive any official looking document, cancel all other engagements, get out the dictionary and READ IT VERY CAREFULLY, especially the smallest of the small print and any bits with numbers in them. If there is something in it you really don't understand and you need authoritative advice in English, you can call the nearest English Consulate (for phone numbers see p. 157). If you can cope with the answers in French, then go to your *mairie* to ask what it is all about. They are usually very helpful as they are responsible for administering large chunks of the system, and if they don't know the answer themselves then they probably know somebody who does.

The *mairie* and the paperwork

In fact it is a golden rule to go to the *mairie* first for information, notification and/or permission if you are planning to make any external changes to your house or property, or to start *chambres d'hôtes* or any other money-making activity. If you live in a conservation area you will need planning permission from the Monuments de France and/or the *département* architect's office for any externally visible changes to your property, and the *mairie* will point you in the right direction to start the obstacle course. (More on all this in the Houses chapter.)

Unless it is a complex matter you don't need to make an appointment at the *mairie*, you can just turn up during the opening hours posted outside it. In some cases you may be asked to provide an authenticated photocopy of a document, eg of a birth certificate if you apply for registration with the health service. Go to the *mairie* with the original and the photocopy, which they will validate with a convincing red stamp. (On the subject of documents: you will often be required to provide even simple documents like a birth certificate translated into French by a certified translator. Some members of the profession charge a great deal for their services, so it is worth knowing that your nearest British Consulate will do standard translations for a modest fee.)

It is also wise to present yourself at the *mairie* of your commune once you have moved in, if you have not already done so during the purchase transactions. Much of the mechanics of daily life in France are regulated via the *mairies* and they are generally an invaluable source of advice and information. They are the first stop also for several paper chases you need to start on once you have really arrived and if you are planning to be a resident, ie live here for more than 6 months per year.

They will also advise you about recent changes in legislation, for instance in the matter of the *titre de séjour*. The laws on immigration, as on so many other aspects of French life, have recently changed, with the result that it is no longer necessary for EU citizens to have a resident's permit unless they are planning to undertake a professional activity. At least that's probably what the law implies. Not for the first time, there are certain ambiguities in the legislation, which will no doubt be clarified in the course of time. However all foreigners who plan to stay in the country for more than 3 months are supposed to go to their nearest *mairie* to present themselves, and to provide proof of their address (*un justificatif d'hébergement*), that they have sufficient means to live on (*des moyens d'existence*) - though no amount is specified - and that they have medical insurance including cover for costs, treatment and repatriation should they become seriously ill. There is no mention of a penalty for not doing this.

Making an appointment

A: Bonjour, je voudrais prendre rendezvous avec Monsieur --/le Docteur --/ Maître -- s'il vous plaît.
  Hello, I'd like to make an appointment with Mr --/Dr --/Maître -- please.

B: Bien sûr, monsieur, ce serait pour quand?
  Of course, monsieur, when for?

A: Le plus tôt possible.
  As soon as possible.

B: Vous préférez le matin ou l'après-midi?
  Would you prefer the morning or the afternoon?

A: Dans la matinée si possible.
  In the morning if possible.

B: Je regarde le planning . . . il serait disponible ou le jeudi 16 à 10 heures ou le mardi suivant, le 21, à 14 heures.
  I'm just looking at the diary. . . he would be available either on Thursday 16th at 10 o'clock, or on the following Tuesday, the 21st, at 2pm.

A: Vous pouvez le répéter, s'il vous plaît? Un peu plus lentement?
  Could you repeat that, please? A little more slowly?

B: Bien sûr. Vous pourriez venir ou le jeudi 16 à 10 heures, ou le mardi 21, à 14 heures.
  Of course. You could come either on Thursday the 16th at 10 o'clock, or on Tuesday the 21st at 2pm.

A: Merci. Je réflechis . . . le jeudi je ne peux pas, donc plutôt le mardi.
Thank you. Let me think . . . I can't on Thursday, so rather the Tuesday.

B: D'accord. Pour le mardi 21 à 14 heures. Vous êtes Monsieur . . . ?
Very well, Tuesday 21st at 2pm. You are Monsieur . . . ?

A: Monsieur Stevens, Alan Stevens.

B: Ça s'écrit comment?
How do you spell that?

A: S-T-E-V-E-N-S.

B: Merci. Vous savez où se trouve le bureau/le cabinet/l'étude?
Thank you. You know where the office/surgery is?/chambers are?

A: Pas exactement, mais si vous pouvez m'expliquer un peu - j'ai le plan de la ville.
Not exactly, but if you could explain a bit - I've got a map of the town.

B: Bien - vous voyez là-dessus la cathédrale?
Well - can you see on the map the cathedral?

A: Un moment, je la cherche - ah oui, voilà!
Just a minute, I'm looking for it - oh yes, there it is!

B: Et en face du parvis, la rue Maillot qui part tout droit vers la place Gambetta?
And on the far side of the square outside it, the rue Maillot which goes straight on to the place Gambetta?

A: Oui, je le vois.
Yes, I see it.

B: Donc vous trouverez le bureau/le cabinet/l'étude sur la gauche de cette place, au numéro 18.
You'll find the office/surgery/chambers on the left of the square, at number 18.

A: Numéro 18, vous avez dit? Bien, je le note.
Number 18, did you say? Fine, I'll make a note of it.

B: D'accord. Donc c'est pour le mardi 21 à 14 heures.
Very well. So it's for Tuesday 21st at 2pm.

A: D'accord, je comprends.
Fine, I understand.

B: C'est bien. Bonne journée, monsieur.
That's good. I wish you a good day, monsieur.

A: Merci, vous de même, au revoir.
Thank you, the same to you, goodbye.

B: Merci, au revoir.
Thank you, goodbye.

Car registration and insurance

If you are definitely going for resident status you can embark on the application for a French driving licence (limit one year), and for replacing English plates on your car with French ones (limit 3 months). The usual information is needed for the former, plus of course your English licence details. Provided you have applied within the time it is more or less a formality, and you do not need to take any further test. Replacing your UK licence is now optional, as licences issued in any EU country are in principle valid throughout it. However if you commit an offence for which points would be deducted from the licence (ie anything other than a parking offence) then you need to apply for French licence (*un permis de conduire*) so that they can be taken away from it. The French driving test is rigorous and includes a serious written part. One more reason for sticking to the rules of the road!

Getting registration plates (*les plaques d'immatriculation*) changed can be a really lengthy and expensive business, but unless you return regularly to the UK you need to persevere in order to keep your vehicle insured. A UK policy will automatically give you third party cover in France, which is obligatory, but will not cover damage to your own vehicle or its contents. A green card issued in England, which provides your usual cover, is usually only given for a few weeks, and most French agents will not insure a car with foreign plates unless they have proof that you have started the application for the change.

I say started, because to complete it you need first of all the application form, from an organisation called the DRIRE (ask at the post office for the address of the nearest office, or else look on the site www.pagesjaunes.fr on Pages Blanches, putting DRIRE in the *'nom'* box and the *département* number in the *'département'* box). Then you need to obtain a letter from the manufacturer (*une attestation de conformité*), even if it is a French-made car, giving the exact date it was made (deduced from the chassis number which you must tell them), and declaring that it meets EU standards on safety, emissions, etc. There is often a hefty fee for this letter and it usually takes a few weeks to arrive, so do this next!

Then you need to contact the nearest *préfecture* or *sous-préfecture* to ask for the application form for a registration document, called a *carte grise* from its charming grey colour (*une demande de carte grise*). Next stop your local tax office to obtain a certificate proving that the VAT on your UK car has been paid abroad, or to pay it on arrival. For this you'll need to produce proof of the original purchase if possible, and the UK registration document.

One change to a UK vehicle always required by the DRIRE is the realignment of headlight beams, so you need to get this done at a garage, and be sure to obtain proof of same. On some cars this can be done with the flick of a switch but on others it means replacing the whole headlight unit, something which tends alas to cost more than sixpence. Ditto for rear fog light and reversing light, which have to change sides. (While we're on the subject: if you are considering bringing over a camping car and getting it adapted to French requirements, don't, as it will be almost impossible to make it comply with them short of rebuilding the whole thing.)

Next stop, the MOT/*contrôle technique* centre for a complete health check of the vehicle - Pages Jaunes under *contrôle technique* for the nearest Autosur or DEKRA test centre or equivalent. This test (current cost 50€) is now very thorough, and anything that isn't up to French standards has to be corrected. Provided the major things pass, a provisional *certificat* will be issued on condition that you get any minor things done within the next 2 months. Proof of this has to be provided to the test centre before they'll issue a final certificate. Then add your UK registration document to the pile. Lastly – whew! - there's the little matter of proof your identity and address, ie for the first, a photocopy authenticated by the *mairie* of your passport, plus for the second a bank statement, EDF bill, etc. Then you need to gather up all the original documents and make two complete sets of photocopies, one to send in with the originals and one to keep. When you have collected all this - it's just a little rehearsal for dealing with the bureaucrats! - you have to go to a *tabac*, buy a tax stamp to the value of the required fee, stick it on the form, check that you have got everything asked for, check again, put it in a tough envelope, put that in the post, treat your self to a stiff drink - and keep your fingers crossed!

Once all these pieces of paper have been digested by the system and you have received your *carte grise* with your new number, you can have the plates made, a service provided at a garage, shop or boutique that makes keys, etc, and who will probably mount them for you as well. In contrast to the UK law, a French car may change identity several times in its life. If in the future you move to another *département* then you must apply again, within a month of moving, for new plates and a new number including that of the *département*. If your move is within the same *département* you still have to get the address on the *carte* updated, which means a visit to the nearest police station or *gendarmerie*. The vehicle tax was abolished a while ago so that is one thing you can add to the (shortish) list of problems you *don't* have!

All of which means that, unless you are desperately attached to your UK vehicle, it's easier to buy another one over here. There are plenty of good quality second-hand ones on the market, which is carefully regulated, and it is now possible to buy new ones at a discount through dealers who are not tied to selling a single make. If you're in a right-hand drive car it's annoying to be on the outside of the road all the time, where you often can't see properly beyond the vehicle in front of you. If you've been through all this rigmarole but eventually want to sell, it is not easy to get anything like the real value of a right-hand drive car in a left-hand drive country, and it's another palaver to re-register it in the UK if you take it back there to sell.

Insurance

Insuring your car may be cheaper here, unless you live in a busy town and/or have a very up-market vehicle, and there are plenty of attractive offers around. Several grades of policy (*une police*, confusingly) are available, ranging from minimal third party (*au tiers*) plus fire and theft, to *multi-risque collision*, which covers damage (*les dégâts*) done by an identifiable person or agent, to fully comprehensive (*compréhensive*), which covers all possible kinds of damage. All policies include cover for public liability (*la responsabilité civile*), which is obligatory for all car owners. If you keep a car at a holiday property for occasional use then the basic policy will be adequate, but of course if you are doing a lot of kilometres then the more cover you have the better, considering the general standard of driving on major routes and the not negligible risks from the freakish weather we have had in recent years.

When you apply for a policy you will need written proof from your UK insurers of your no-claims bonus (*le bonus*) so that it can be taken into account in assessing your premium (*la prime*), which is decided on the factors you'd expect: the area you live in, your age and driving record, if your car is garaged or on your own land, etc. The premium is payable either when the policy is issued or monthly by direct debit. It will be cheaper if you agree to a voluntary excess (*une franchise*), and will continue to be reduced (though only to 50%) if you don't make any claims.

If you do, you will lose a proportion of your bonus calculated according to the circumstances of the accident and your degree of responsibility for it (though if you've had the maximum bonus for 3 years then one accident will be excused and won't dent your bonus). For this reason it is important, if you do have a bump, to get the accident statement form filled in accurately (see p. 36) and to nab any possible witnesses. In a crisis it may not be easy to keep your head and do everything necessary - for instance make a sketch of the position of the cars involved if they have to be moved to clear the road - so it's a good idea to take a look at this form in some quiet moment to make sure you understand it and are prepared in case the worst happens. In fact it follows the standard EU format and matches the English version. After an accident you'll need to check also the form filled in by the other driver(s), make sure it is accurate and then sign it. They will do the same with yours.

Two more things to keep in mind: you will be insured only for the car specified in your policy, so if you plan for any reason to drive another one (other than a hire car) for a short time, you must contact your insurers and give them its details so that you remain covered (they may charge you for this, and in fact not all companies will do it). And as with health insurance, you can only cancel (*résilier*) your policy after a year on the anniversary date, having given three months' notice by registered letter (*un courrier recommandé*) - unless you replace the car, in which case you can replace the insurers too.

When you receive your insurance certificate you should stick inside the windscreen the square green coupon that is part of it, and put the rest of it with your other documents in the car. As we've mentioned, the items you must keep there include your licence, the *carte grise* and a European Accident Statement (*Constat Européen d'Accident*), which your insurers will send you, as well as a red warning triangle for accidents and a set of spare bulbs for all the external lights on the vehicle. You can be fined for not having all these things in the car. Remember that you should in any case always carry your *carte de séjour* or passport on you.

Another matter to keep in mind is the *contrôle technique*, the equivalent of the MOT. This is strict, especially on the matter of emissions, and any car sold second hand (*une voiture d'occasion*) must have a certificate issued within the previous 6 months. The *contrôle* is carried out by specialist test centres, currently costs 50€, is obligatory for every car that is 4 years old, and has to be repeated every 2 years. If your vehicle fails the test for any reason, you must have the necessary work done and take the proof of this, and the car, back to the test centre within 2 months for a *contre-visite*. It will be checked again, free of charge. Past this time limit, you will have to put the vehicle through the whole test again and pay another fee. The fine for not having an up to date *contrôle* is ginormous.

TV licence

All owners of a TV set are obliged to have a licence, and to pay a fee for it (*la redevance audiovisuelle*) which goes towards financing some of the state owned channels. It is expensive – currently 117€ for colour, less for black and white - but the good news is that one licence covers any number of sets belonging to the same owner. It is issued by the Centre Régional de la Redevance Audiovisuelle, and you can find the relevant address from your nearest post office or the Pages Jaunes site. The fine for not having a licence is substantial. If you buy a new TV here then your name and address will be sent by the shop to the licensing authority.

Applying to join the Health Service

This conversation appears in this chapter as a typical example of its kind and as an introduction to adminspeak. See the next chapter for more on the health service itself.

Je voudrais faire une demande d'inscription auprès de l'assurance maladie;
I'd like to apply to be registered for health insurance;

est-ce que vous pouvez me renseigner sur les démarches à suivre?
can you give me some information about the procedure to follow?

Bien sûr, madame. Permettez-moi d'abord de vous poser quelques questions:
Of course, madame. First allow me to ask you some questions:

Votre nom? . . . votre état civil?. . . et votre nomme de jeune fille?. . . votre adresse?
Your name? . . . your marital status? . . . and your maiden name?. . . your address?

Vous êtes résidente définitivement en France? Vous êtes installée ici depuis longtemps?
Are you permanently resident in France? Have you been living here long?

Vous êtes propriétaire ou locataire?
Do you own your house or are you a tenant?

Pour préparer votre dossier il nous faut une attestation de la part du service de santé brittanique que vous avez droit aux soins médicaux, la formule E160.
To prepare your application we require proof from the British health service that you are entitled to health care, the form E160.

Avec cela vous devez nous envoyer une copie de votre pièce d'identité,
With that you need to send us a copy of your proof of identity,

une copie conforme de vos actes de naissance, et de mariage s'il y en a,
certified copies of your birth certificate, and marriage certificate if there is one,

avec un justificatif de domicile en France, ainsi que vos coordonnées bancaires ou postales
with proof of your place of residence in France, as well as details of your bank or post office account

si vous voulez recevoir les remboursements directement sur votre compte.
if you would like the refunds to be paid directly into your account.

On va vous envoyer un formulaire à remplir et vous monter un dossier, et dès qu'on a tous les éléments en main pour le compléter, vous serez inscrite.
We'll send you the form to fill in and set up your dossier, and as soon as we have all the documents in hand to complete it, you will be registered.

Ensuite on vous enverra votre carte vitale avec votre attestation,
Then we will send you your carte vitale with your attestation,

ainsi que votre numéro d'inscription provisoire auprès de notre service.
along with your provisional registration number for our service.

Le numéro définitif vous sera communiqué dans les meilleurs délais.
The permanent number will be sent to you as soon as possible.

Bien sûr, si vous avez des questions vous pouvez toujours nous rappeler pour des plus amples renseignements.
Of course if you have any questions you can always ring us again for further information.

Writing letters

Formal letters

A few things which the French do differently when writing a letter:

- The writer's *name and address* go in the top left hand corner of the page.
- The addressee's name and address go on the top *right* of the page.
- The French don't say 'dear' someone unless they mean it. Formal letters start simply *Monsieur, Messieurs* or *Madame*.
- The date has a *le* before it but no capitals for days of the week or months: *Le mardi 12 juin.*

Useful phrases in bureaucritania

Some of the following are 'them ' and some are 'us' – take your pick.

Suite à notre conversation téléphonique du mardi 12 juin, je vous confirme que . . .
Following our phone conversation of Tuesday 12 June, I confirm that . . .

Suite à votre courrier de mardi 12 juin je tiens à vous préciser que . . .
Following your letter of Tuesday 12 June I wish to make it clear that . . .

Merci de bien vouloir . . .
Please would you . . .

- remplir ce formulaire . . .
  fill in this form . . .

- nous envoyer des informations complémentaires sur . . .
  send us further information about . . .

- m'envoyer la documentation sur votre service/le modèle n° xxx à l'adresse ci-dessus.
  send me your brochure/information about your service/model n°xxx at the above address.

Merci de nous préciser les circonstances exacts du sinistre . . .
Please give us exact details of the circumstances of the accident/fire/calamity. . .

Merci de nous faire parvenir . . .
Please send us . . .

- les pièces suivantes qui sont nécessaires à l'établissement de votre dossier.
  the following documents which are required to make up your dossier.

- les pièces citées ci-dessus afin de mettre à jour/compléter votre dossier.
  the documents listed above so that your dossier can be updated/completed.

- des pièces justificatives concernant le coût des réparations de votre véhicule afin que nous puissions vous faire rembourser correctement.
  written proof of the cost of repairs to your vehicle so that we can arrange your refund.

Afin que l'instruction de votre dossier puisse se poursuivre, il est nécessaire de . . .
In order for the completion of your dossier to progess it is necessary to . . .

Veuillez nous signaler tout changement eventuel de votre situation qui serait susceptible à entraîner une modification de votre éligibilité à bénéficier des dîtes pensions . . . etc etc etc . . .
Please inform us of any change in your circumstances which might affect your entitlement to these allowances, etc

Merci de bien vouloir répondre dans les 7 jours à compter de la date d'envoi de ce courrier.
Please be sure to reply within 7 days from the date of this letter.

N'oubliez pas de dater et signer ce document dans les cases désignées à cet effet.
Do not forget to date and sign this document in the boxes indicated for this purpose.

Merci de nous transmettre vos questions ou remarques éventuelles sur . . .
Please send us any questions or comments you may have concerning . . .

Veuillez nous indiquer quel jour vous conviendrait pour prendre rendezvous . . .
Would you please let us know which day would be convenient for a meeting . . .

Suite à votre annonce dans *La Dépêche* de jeudi dernier, je voudrais vous demander . . .
In response to your advertisement in last Thursday's Dépêche, *I'd like to ask you . . .*

Veuillez nous faire savoir par retour du courrier si . . .
Would you please let us know by return of post if . . .

Merci de nous tenir au courant.
Please keep us informed (of progress).

Auriez-vous l'amabilité de nous faire savoir dès quel moment on pourrait espérer une réponse définitive à notre demande dont le dossier vous a été envoyé fin octobre 2003, concernant l'aménagement en gîte des dépendances situées sur notre propriété, le lieu-dit Les Vaches *etc* . . .
Would you be so good as to inform us when we might hope for a definite answer to our request conveyed in the dossier which was sent to you at the end of April 2002, concerning the conversion into gîtes of the outbuildings on our property, Les Vaches (and so on and so forth . . .)

Winding ups

N'hésitez pas à nous contacter pour des plus amples renseignements.
Do not hesitate to contact us for fuller information.

Je me tiens à votre disposition pour toute information complémentaire.
I would be pleased to give you any further information.

Je reste à votre disposition pour un entretien éventuel.
I would be available to meet you for a possible interview.

Je me ferai un plaisir de vous fournir la documentation sur l'hébergement que nous proposons.
I will be glad to send you full details of the accommodation we offer.

Vu l'urgence de la situation, nous vous serions très reconnaissants de nous répondre dans les meilleurs délais.
In view of the urgency of the situation, we would be very grateful if you would reply as soon as possible.

Dans l'attente de vous lire prochainement, je vous prie, etc
Hoping to hear from you shortly, I remain . . .

Dans l'attente d'une réponse favorable de votre part, je vous prie, etc
In the hope of a positive answer from you, I remain . . .

Endings

Endings for formal letters are at first sight absurdly elaborate, but in fact they contain infinite nuances of meaning, an echo of the 18th century aristocratic milieu in which the exact angle at which a hat was doffed and the exact depth to which a bow was bowed were calculated to a millimetre and could make or break a reputation among the gilded mirrors of Versailles . . .

If you are replying to a letter that ends in one of these fol-de-rols you can simply repeat it in your reply if it is appropriate, or choose another. Here are a few not too ridiculous ones – no point trying to translate them! If you can't be bothered with any of these, *'Salutations sincères'* or just *'Sincèrement'* will do.

> *Je vous prie d'agréer, Monsieur/Madame, l'expression de mes sentiments distingués* or *de mes respectueuses salutations* or *de mes salutations cordiales . . .*

> *Je vous prie de croire, Monsieur/Madame, en l'expression de mes sentiments les meilleurs* or *mes salutations les plus sincères . . .*

> *Je vous prie de croire, Monsieur/Madame, à l'assurance de ma considération distinguée.*

Other official phrases

A qui de droit.	*To whom it may concern.*
Rayer le mention inutile.	*Delete the option that does not apply.*
cochez la case	*tick the box* (put an X in it - the French don't use ticks)
le cas échéant	*as the case may be*
sous réserve de	*on condition that*
sous huitaine/quinzaine	*within a week/fortnight*

Things in writing

une affiche	*notice, poster*
une aide-memoire	*memo, reminder*
une (petite) annonce, un publicité	*(classified) advertisement*
[un avertissement	*warning*]
un bilan (de santé)	*balance-sheet, full (health) report*
un bon	*coupon, chit*
un bon de commande	*order form*
une carte postale	*post card*
une carte de voeux	*greetings card*
un compte-rendu	*report (of meeting), minutes*
un courrier	*letter*
un dépliant	*leaflet*
un document	*document*
un dossier	*file of information, documents for application, etc*
une étude, une expertise	*detailed report, survey*
un faire-part	*note to announce a birth, engagement, etc*
un feuillet	*flyer*
une fiche	*notice, filing card, set of instructions, etc*
un fichier	*document, file of information, etc*
un formulaire	*form*
un (petit) mot	*'a word', 'a line'* (ie a short note)

Informal letters

Some possible endings for a personal letter, in ascending order of friendliness:

Bien à vous	*all the best*
Cordialement	*cordially*
Amicalement	*'friendlily'*
Bien amicalement	*'really friendlily'*
Très amicalement	*'very friendlily'*
Pensées chaleureuses	*warm thoughts*
Pensées amicales	*friendly thoughts*
Toutes mes amitiés	*'all my friendlinesses'*
Je t'embrasse	*I kiss you*
Gros bisous/Grosses bises	*big kisses*

Tous mes/nos remerciements pour . . .   *with all my/our thanks for . . .*
En vous remerciant encore une fois pour . . .   *thanking you again for . . .*

Je garderai longtemps le souvenir de votre hospitalité/gentillesse.
I shall long remember your hospitality/kindness.

Other comments

J'espère avoir bientôt de vos/tes nouvelles	*I hope to hear from you soon*
Dans l'espoir de vous/te lire bientôt	*hoping to hear from you soon*
Portez-vous/porte-toi bien	*stay well*

Faites-moi/Fais-moi savoir si . . .
Let me know if . . .

- vous pensez/tu penses faire un petit tour dans cette belle région . . .
  you think of making a little trip to this lovely area . . .

- vous arrivez/tu arrives à décrocher ce nouveau poste . . .
  you manage to get that new job . . .

- vous recevez/tu reçois des nouvelles de la part de . . .
  you hear any news from . . .

11 Health

The French health system

There are a number of key differences between the health system in France and that in the UK. First of all, it works. Although there is a shortage of hospital services in some parts of the country, in most areas it is possible, indeed normal, to obtain prompt and reliable treatment for any ills that may befall you, whether minor or major.

A few examples that come to mind: an elderly friend recently diagnosed with a sizeable abdominal cyst had a successful operation ten days later in the local hospital, with a week of convalescent care to follow as part of the service, and a couple of weeks of home help. A neighbour advised to have a blood test before an appointment with a specialist was called on early the following morning by the local district nurse, who took the sample as requested. Within 24 hours the results had been sent to the patient, to their doctor and to the specialist. The nurse was surprised by our surprise, her only comment, *"C'est normal!"* And she added that if it had been "really urgent" the results would have been sent right away by fax!

Some American friends on holiday nearby were alarmed when their little boy of 18 months developed an inflamed ear and ran a high fever one evening. The doctor on call advised them to go to the emergency service at the nearby hospital, where they were received half an hour later by a doctor who spoke some English and had an English dictionary on hand. All was explained, the child examined, medicines prescribed and the nearest pharmacy reopened (by then it was about 9pm) to provide them. What more can one ask?

Another significant difference is that as a patient in France you have much more autonomy in managing your own health care. There is no obligation to be registered with any particular doctor, although of course it makes sense to establish contact with a local practitioner who will if necessary be able to make a house call. But if you start with one doctor and then are dissatisfied or don't get on with them, you are perfectly free to go to another one. Your notes will in theory be forwarded to the new practitioner in due course.

Nor is there any hocus pocus about keeping a diagnosis secret from you. If you need to have an X-ray then you can make an appointment at a specialist centre which will take and process the X-rays on the spot, and give them to you to hand on to the doctor, dentist or whoever is treating you. In fact everyone is entitled to see their own medical records, though this is a recent law and it may take longer in some places than in others to obtain them. But it is reassuring to know that you can do so, if ever you have a query about the correctness of a diagnosis or treatment or about medication prescribed, if you have a problem following an operation, a dispute with your insurers, etc.

Likewise if you feel the need to consult a specialist for some reason you can simply look in the Pages Jaunes (where they are listed by category under *médécins*), to find one of the right variety near you, and you can make an appointment with them directly. They will probably apologise if they can't see you within a couple of weeks. Again, it makes sense to tell your doctor what you are doing, but there is no obligation to do so. Indeed there is nothing to stop you consulting more than one specialist if you want to, and each appointment will be refunded on the usual scale by the health insurance system.

One downside of all this freedom of choice, of course, is that it does create a hypochondriac's heaven, and state spending on the health service is colossal. The

French top the charts in Europe for consumption of tranquillisers, anti-depressants and antibiotics, though there is now a policy afoot to reduce the latter, and to encourage patients to accept generic medicines by reducing the refunds on branded ones to the cost level of the generic. With many citizens, especially those *d'un certain âge*, their health is a topic of burning interest, and you may well overhear a group of them, as you loiter on your favourite café terrace, gleefully exchanging blood pressure statistics and regaling each other with alarmingly detailed accounts of their latest symptoms.

If the problems that concern you are minor ones, you will find excellent advice at your nearest pharmacy. A pharmacist's training is rigorous and they pride themselves on being well informed and finding the appropriate medication for their customers. Some also have special ranges of herbal and essential oil remedies. Of course they do sometimes try to sell you more medicines than you need – a friend who once asked a pharmacist to remove a foreign object from her eye was recommended to buy eye drops, something antibiotic "just in case" and something else anti-inflammatory - but on the whole they can be relied on and are very efficient and helpful.

You can spot a pharmacy from the street by the green neon cross above the door, which will be flashing when the place is open (don't forget they shut at lunchtime like everyone else). But in each town there is always one pharmacy open for emergencies. The weekly rota is posted on their doors, or you can ask in any bar which is the current *pharmacie de garde*:

"S'il vous plaît, où se trouve la pharmacie de garde pour cette semaine?"
"Please, where is the late night pharmacy for this week?"

Joining the system

How to participate in this wonderful health system? First of all, it is open to all EU citizens, so if you are in the country for less than 6 months and are equipped with the famous form E111 (*'cent-onze'*), you pay the costs of your treatment and medication, and claim a refund on the usual UK scale when you return, backed up of course with clear proof of payment. If you are a resident, then you can obtain from the DSS the form E106 which proves your entitlement (although legislation on this topic is changing, so check for the latest information).

Contact the nearest office of the Caisse Primaire d'Assurance Maladie, the CPAM (see the conversation on p. 131 for this) who will send you a form to fill in and request your E106 and proof of your identity, ie certified photocopies (get them stamped at the *mairie*) of your birth certificate and passport. They will also ask for your bank details, if you want the refunds to be paid directly into your account. They have an office in the main town in each *département*, which you can find in the phone book, or you can look on the Pages Jaunes site on the Pages Blanches page, putting in CPAM as the name and the *département* name or number in the *'département'* box.

Within a couple of weeks usually you will receive a document called an *attestation vitale*, a provisional Social Security number (eventually replaced by a permanent one) and a green plastic card, the *carte vitale*, with the number on it. This is proof that you are in the system, which works as follows. When you go to the doctor, dentist or other practitioner, you pay for the session or treatment, X-ray or whatever, and at the end of it you will be handed a form *(une feuille de soins)* indicating the type of treatment given and the costs incurred.

Then you fill in your name, address and Social Security number, sign the form and send it off to the nearest CPAM. (The form for dental work should be returned within two weeks.) Within a week or so you will receive the refund of a proportion of the costs, assessed according to an arcane scale of percentages which nobody outside the CPAM understands. However for everything except glasses and dental crowns, etc, it is about 70%. (For these items, the refund rates are what you might call *dérisoire*, ie next to nothing.)

Some practitioners, usually those working in a group practice or larger health centre, have a direct link to the CPAM, and if you produce your *carte vitale* they will deduct immediately the amount covered by the state, so you only have to pay the balance of the total indicated on your *feuille de soins*. The same is true at a pharmacy. When you buy medicines on prescription they will give you a *feuille de soins*, and the larger ones will accept your *carte vitale* as part payment.

So the next thing to do is to top up the state cover with a policy from a *mutuelle*, a company providing private health insurance. There are a large number of these in the market, mostly vying with each other by offering the best refunds on optical and dental care, and extras on their hospital cover. Compare the options carefully as you are only allowed to cancel (*résilier*) the policy after one year on the anniversary date, and then only after giving 3 months' notice by registered letter (*courrier recommandé*).

Once you are registered with your chosen *mutuelle* they will contact your CPAM to confirm this. Subsequently the CPAM will inform them directly of any claim you make, and they in turn will forward their top-up of your refund directly to your bank account. They are also fairly prompt, in fact many of them claim to refund you within 48 hours. They vary in their readiness to refund treatment with complementary medicines. Some *mutuelles* belong to a private card system, in which some practitioners and many larger pharmacies are enrolled. If you go to one of these you can pay the costs of your prescribed medicines with your *carte vitale* and your *carte mutuelle*, and don't have to hand over any cash or wait for a refund.

Complementary medicines

It is a typically French contradiction that the official line is against complementary medicines (*les médécines douces*), but in fact they and their practitioners flourish openly in many places. One tradition that is officially accepted is homoeopathy, and many doctors practice this alongside conventional medicine. Homoeopathic remedies are available in many pharmacies, but it has been decided recently that they will be only partially refunded. Attitudes to alternatives are softening somewhat, in face of all the incontrovertible evidence that these other methods work very well (not to mention the ginormous deficit of the social security system).

Osteopathy has now been officially recognised, and you may find it possible to have acupuncture sessions prescribed. Herbal remedies are widely available, and essential oils are becoming increasingly recognised for their effectiveness – both these being domains in which the French have long been specialists. Again, they can be found, along with advice on using them, in many pharmacies as well as health shops. Your doctor may prescribe sessions with a masseur/physiotherapist (*kinésithérapeute*), and of course you can go to one independently (find them in the Pages Jaunes).

Massage and aromatherapy are widely available, as is acupuncture, and as might be expected in view of the historic links between France and the Orient, there is a long standing interest in the range of martial arts and their associated philosophies. In many towns, even comparatively small ones, you can find classes in T'ai Chi, judo and/or yoga, and some of these are even provided in some old people's homes as part of a policy to counteract the effects of ageing.

To track down any of the above, ask at your nearest health shop (in the Pages Jaunes under *diététique*), which usually has its finger on the pulse, you might say, of the local possibilities. Or else look in the magazine stands for an issue of *Psychologies* which has loads of information and addresses on *médicines douces* and various therapies, alongside other health magazines such as *Top Santé*. And if it appeals, in the countryside all the locals know the phone number of the nearest healer or *guérisseur/euse* (often a woman), who usually works with herbs and/or psychic energy, and of *le raboteur* (often a man), a bone-juggler who can work wonders with a twisted knee, dislocated shoulder or aching back. These skills are mostly passed down from one generation to the next, in a chain that has resisted all the efforts of the Church and of 'medical science' to break it, simply because they are effective.

One may or may not believe in such traditional methods, but after all it's thanks to them that the human race survived in considerable numbers and over a considerable period of time long before the first pharmacy was opened! And of course still does, where it is allowed to do so. Is it not one of mankind's most searingly tragic ironies that the value of 'native wisdom' (including medical knowledge) is at last being recognised just when the few remaining groups of authentic 'natives' are being finally wiped out, either physically (mostly through the environmental damage caused by commercial greed and recklessness) or by the insidious invasion of those 'Western' so-called values that we in the West are growing, literally, sick of.

Organics

Spurred on by the recent crises which have revealed just how health-destroying commercial methods of food production can be, for man and beast alike, there is a growing enthusiasm in France for organic products: *les produits biologiques*, or simply *bio*. Many local markets now have a stall or two devoted to *produits bio*, and you will find them too in many supermarkets, particularly eggs and milk - as well of course as in health shops, such as the La Vie Claire chain. The most authentic are marked with an AB label and *'issu de l'agriculture biologique'*, and to earn this, growers and producers have to adhere to a very strict set of rules.

Hence organic producers are in the forefront of opposition to the cultivation of GM crops (OGMs), since this poses a real threat to their own hard-won accreditation. There is a strong tide of public feeling in France as elsewhere against OGMs, and although in spite of this the EEC is still (at the time of writing) wavering on banning the import and production of GM foods, at least there is now a law requiring them to be declared on product labels. If you care about the meat you eat and want know exactly where your Sunday joint comes from, buy it from a local butcher - most of them are in the habit of labelling the carcases hanging in their shop with full details of their origin. Or go for the Label Rouge packs in the supermarket, which denote meat which, if not entirely organic, is at least from animals that are reared sanely. For poultry, next best is *élevé en plein air*, ie free range.

In conclusion, it seems to be much easier to stay healthy in a country where, unless you are locked into a stressful job, there is so much more space and so much more scope for being outdoors, and for enjoying the wonderful fresh food available in all the markets – accompanied of course by medicinal doses of the local beverages . . . And perhaps part of the feeling of *bien-être* is the added peace of mind from knowing that if any health problems do arise, you have excellent chances of finding appropriate treatment and making a quick recovery.

FOR AN EMERGENCY: see useful phrases p. 148, phone numbers on last page.

Useful vocabulary - general

Parts of the body

artery	l'artère (f)	bowels	les intestins (m)
blood	le sang	breasts	les seins (m)
bone	l'os	buttocks	les fesses (f)
joints	les articulations (f)	calf	le mollet
ligament	le ligament	chest	la poitrine
limb	le membre	elbow	le coude
muscle	le muscle	finger	le doigt
organ	l'organe (f)	foot	le pied
vein	la veine	genitals	les organes génitaux
		hand	la main
face	le visage	heart	le coeur
cheek	la joue	heel	le talon
chin	le menton	hip	la hanche
ear	l'oreille (f)	kidneys	les reins (m)
eye	l'œil (m)	knee	le genou
eyes	les yeux (f)	liver	le foie
gums	les gencives (f)	lungs	les poumons (m)
head	la tête	nail	l'ongle (m)
jaw	la mâchoire	neck	le cou
lips	les lèvres (f)	rib	la côte
mouth	la bouche	shoulder	l'épaule (f)
nose	le nez	skin	la peau
nostril	la narine	spine	la colonne vertébrale
tongue	la langue	stomach	l'estomac (m)
tooth	la dent	thigh	la cuisse
		throat	la gorge
ankle	la cheville	thumb	le pouce
arm	le bras	toe	le doigt de pied, l'orteil (m)
back	le dos	varicose veins	les varices (f)
belly	le ventre	wrist	le poignet

Diseases

AIDS	SIDA	diarrhoea	la diarrhée
angina	l'angine de poitrine (f)	flu	la grippe
arthritis	l'arthrite (f)	German measles	la rubéole
asthma	l'asthme (m)	hay fever	le rhume des foins
bronchitis	la bronchite	headache	le mal de tête
cancer	le cancer	heart attack	la crise cardiaque
chickenpox	la varicelle	hepatitis	la hépatite
cold	le rhume	measles	la rougéole
constipation	la constipation	mumps	les oreillons (m)
cystitis	la cystite	nervous breakdown	la dépression nerveuse
depression	la dépression	pneumonia	la pneumonie

rheumatism	*les rhumatismes*	stroke	*l'attaque cérébrale* (f)
smallpox	*la variole*	TB	*la tuberculose*
sore throat	*le mal à la gorge*	throat infection	*l'angine* (f)
stomach upset	*la crise de foie*	ulcer	*l'ulcère* (m)

Symptoms

abscess	*l'abcès* (m)	sprain	*l'entorse* (f)
bleeding	*le saignement*	stiffness	*la courbature*
blister	*la cloque, l'ampoule* (f)	sunstroke	*l'insolation* (f)
blood group	*le groupe sanguin*	temperature	*la température*
blood pressure	*la tension artérielle*	tingling	*le picotement*
breathing	*la respiration*	trembling	*le tremblement*
bruise	*le bleu, l'ecchymose*	wound	*la blessure, la plaie*
burn	*la brûlure*		
cut	*la coupure*	to become infected	*s'infecter*
fever	*la fièvre*	to bleed	*saigner*
fracture	*la fracture*	to cough	*tousser*
infection	*l'infection* (f)	to feel bad	*se sentir mal*
itching	*la démangeaison*	to hurt	*faire mal*
lump	*la boule*	to pull a muscle	*se froisser un muscle*
migraine	*la migraine*	to redden	*rougir*
pain, soreness	*la douleur*	to shiver	*frissonner, trembler*
period	*les règles* (f)	to sneeze	*éternuer*
pulse	*le pouls*	to stiffen	*raidir*
rash	*l'éruption* (f)	to sweat	*transpirer*
scar	*la cicatrice*	to swell	*enfler*
scratch, graze	*l'engratignure* (f)	to twist an ankle	*se fouler la cheville*
spot	*le bouton*	to vomit	*vomir*

Treatment

ambulance	*l'ambulance*	operation	*l'intervention chirurgicale* (f)
at the rate of	*à raison de* (dosage)	pill (contraceptive)	*la pillule*
bandage	*le pansement*	poultice	*la compresse*
capsule	*la capsule*	prescription	*l'ordonnance* (f)
check-up	*la contrôle*	sticking plaster	*le sparadrap*
blood pressure check	*la contrôle de tension*	stitches	*les points*
clinic	*la clinique*	surgeon	*le chirurgien*
doctor	*le médecin*	tablet	*le comprimé, la tablette, pastille*
doctor on call	*le médecin de garde*	treatment	*le traitement, les soins*
doctor, your (GP)	*votre médecin traitant*	X-ray	*la radiographie (la radio)*
dose	*la dose*		
emergency department	*les urgences*	to check	*contrôler*
hospital	*l'hôpital* (m)	to cure, heal	*guérir*
medicine	*le médicament*	to examine	*examiner*
ointment	*la pommade*	to get better	*se remettre*

| to heal over | *cicatriser* | to take care of | *soigner* |
| to prescribe | *prescrire* | to treat | *traiter* |

At the pharmacy

I need something . . .	*J'ai besoin de quelque chose . . .*
to soothe pain	*pour soulager/apaiser la douleur*
to reduce constipation	*pour aider le transit intestinal*
for my digestion/to help me sleep	*pour favoriser la digestion/le sommeil*
to relieve stress/itching	*pour calmer le stress/les démangeaisons*
to reduce inflammation	*pour réduire l'inflammation*

against . . .	*contre . . .*
diarrhoea	*la diarrhée*
headaches	*les maux de tête*
headlice	*les poux*
insect bites	*les piqûres d'insectes*
period pains	*les douleurs de règles*
a rash	*une éruption*
stomach burn	*les brûlures d'estomac*
sunburn	*le coup de soleil*

Describing your symptoms

NB: Normal temperature is 36.8°C in the morning and 37.5°C in the evening.

I don't feel very well.
Je ne me sens pas bien.

I feel worse in the evening.
Je me sens pire le soir.

I feel better in the morning.
Je me sens mieux le matin.

I've got a temperature.
J'ai de la fièvre.

I often feel hot./ I get hot flushes.
J'ai souvent chaud./J'ai des bouffées de chaleur.

I feel cold even when it's hot.
J'ai froid même lorsqu'il fait chaud.

It's better/worse than before/than this morning/than yesterday.
C'est mieux/pire qu'avant/que ce matin/qu'hier.

It's getting bigger/smaller.
Il grandit/il diminue.

I have a bad cold.
Je suis très enrhumé.

I've hurt my knee.
Je me suis blessé au genou.

I've cut my finger.
Je me suis coupé le doigt.

My throat/ear/knee/back is painful.
J'ai mal à la gorge/à l'oreille/au genou/au dos.

I find it hard to breathe/to digest/to get to sleep.
J'ai du mal à respirer/à digérer/à m'endormir.

I've noticed some palpitations.
J'ai remarqué des palpitations/des anomalies cardiaques.

I have a problem with my circulation/a heart problem/my breathing.
J'ai des problèmes de circulation/des insuffisances cardiaques/respiratoires.

I had a kidney operation 5 years ago.
J'ai subi une intervention chirurgicale sur les reins il y a 5 ans.

At the doctor's - Chez le médecin

A: Bonjour, Docteur Bernard.
Good morning, Dr Bernard.

B: Bonjour, M. Martin. Dîtes-moi, qu'est-ce que je peux faire pour vous?
Good morning, Mr Martin. Tell me, what can I do for you?

A: C'est mon genou qui est très douloureux, le genou droit.
It's my knee that's very painful, my right knee.

B: Ça a commencé quand?
When did it start?

A: C'était hier, j'ai trébuché en descendant les marches de la terrasse, et je suis tombé sur la jambe droite, avec le genou coincé dessous. D'abord ce n'était pas très grave mais pendant la nuit il s'est mis à enfler et maintenant c'est vraiment pénible. Je ne peux presque plus le bouger.
It was yesterday, I tripped on the terrace steps, and fell on my right leg, with my knee stuck underneath me. At first it wasn't too bad but during the night it started to swell and now it's really painful, I can hardly move it any more.

B: Déshabillez-vous, s'il vous plaît.
Please take off your trousers (clothes).

A: Bien sûr . . .
Of course . . .

B: Ah oui, je vois . . . est-ce que ça vous fait mal?
Ah yes, I see . . . does that hurt?

A: Pas trop . . .
Not too much . . .

B: Et ça?
And that?

A: Aiee, c'est affreux!
Ouch, that's awful!

B: Mes excuses . . . mais je crois quand-même que ce n'est pas trop grave, pas besoin de faire des radios. Vous pouvez vous rhabiller.
I'm sorry . . . but actually I don't think it's really serious, there's no need to do an X-ray. You can put your trousers on again.

A: D'accord.
All right.

B: L'essentiel c'est de ne pas faire trop d'effort, mais il faut le bouger un peu de temps en temps pour rétablir sa souplesse. Je vous fais une ordonnance pour une pommade qui va aider à reduire l'inflammation. Vous n'avez pas d'allergies à certains médicaments – aux antibiotiques, par exemple?
The important thing is not to strain it, but you need to move it a little from time to time to get it supple again. I'll give you a prescription for an ointment to help reduce the swelling. You don't have any allergies to medicines, to antibiotics for instance?

A: Non, je ne crois pas.
No, I don't think so.

B: Bon . . . la voici, et la feuille de soins aussi. Donc ça devrait aller nettement mieux en 48 heures, mais si jamais ce n'est pas le cas, n'hésiter pas à revenir me voir.
Good . . . here it is, and the form for your insurance too. Well, it should be noticeably better in 48 hours, but if by any chance it isn't, don't hesitate to come back and see me again.

A: Merci beaucoup, Docteur, je suis rassuré. Je vous dois 20€, n'est-ce pas?
Thank you very much, Doctor, I'm reassured. I owe you 20€, don't I?

B: Oui, c'est ça . . . merci.
Yes, that's it . . . thank you.

A: Merci à vous, Docteur Bernard, je me sens mieux déjà.
Thank you, Dr Bernard, I'm feeling better already.

B: C'est bien! Alors, au revoir, M. Martin.
That's good! Well, goodbye, Mr Martin.

A: Au revoir, Docteur, et encore merci.
Goodbye, Doctor, and thank you again.

Other possible questions and comments

Vous avez remarqué des circonstances particulières qui déclenchent les symptomes?
Have you noticed any particular circumstances that set off the symptoms?

Pas vraiment, ça se produit sans raison évidente.
Not really, they come on without any obvious reason.

Oui, je le remarque surtout le matin quand je me lève, ou dans la journée si je me mets debout brusquement.
Yes, I notice it specially in the morning when I get up, or in the day if I stand up suddenly.

Est-ce que vous avez déjà suivi un traitement pour ce problème?
Have you already had treatment for this problem?

Quels médicaments avez-vous pris pour cette condition?
What medicines have you taken for this condition?

Est-ce que vous prenez d'autres médicaments en ce moment?
Are you taking any other medicines at present?

Est-ce que vous avez d'autres problèmes de santé? De circulation sanguine, d'allergies, de maux de tête?
Do you have any other health problems, with your circulation, allergies, headaches?

D'abord on va faire des analyses de sang et des radios. Dès qu'on a les résultats on va décider pour la suite.
First of all we'll do some blood tests and X-rays. As soon as we have the results we'll decide what to do next.

Je vous conseil de prendre rendezvous avec un spécialiste.
I advise you to arrange an appointment with a specialist.

Je peux vous recommander quelqu'un de bien.
I can recommend someone very good.

Il faut suivre le traitement à la lettre.
It's important to follow the treatment to the letter.

Faites-moi savoir si vos symptomes s'aggravent.
Let me know if your symptoms get any worse.

Making an appointment at the dentist

A: Bonjour, le cabinet du Dr Michelet, en quoi je peux vous aider?
Good morning, Dr Michelet's surgery, how can I help you?

B: Bonjour madame, je voudrais prendre rendezvous avec le Dr Michelet s'il vous plaît.
Good morning madame, I'd like to make an appointment with Dr Michelet please.

A: Vous êtes madame . . . ?
Your name please?

B: Gilbert, je suis déjà venue deux fois.
Gilbert, I've already been a couple of times.

A: Bien sûr, Mme Gilbert. Alors, qu'est-ce qui vous arrive? Est-ce que c'est urgent?
Of course, Mme Gilbert. So what's happened? Is it urgent?

B: Oui, c'est urgent, c'est une couronne de devant, et le support s'est cassé. Ça risque de partir à tout moment.
Yes, it's urgent, it's a front crown and the pin has broken. It could fall out at any moment.

A: Et cela vous fait mal?
And does it hurt?

B: Pas vraiment, mais la couronne est partie deux fois déjà et j'ai bien peur de la perdre.
Not really, but the crown has fallen out twice already and I'm afraid of losing it.

A: D'accord, je comprends. Je regarde le planning . . . Vous pouvez venir en fin de matinée jeudi?
Fine, I understand. I'm just looking at the diary . . . Can you come in at the end of the morning on Thursday?

B: Oui, bien sûr - je suppose que ce serait assez rapide pour la remettre?
Yes, of course – I don't suppose it will take long to fix it in again?

A: Probablement pas, donc on peut vous recevoir à midi moins le quart.
Probably not, so you can come in at 11.45.

B: Merci, madame, c'est rassurant.
Thank you, madame, that's reassuring!

A: On est là pour ça, vous savez!
That's what we're here for, you know!

B: Ah oui, et tant mieux! Donc à jeudi madame, et au revoir.
Yes, and so much the better! Well, till Thursday, madame, and goodbye.

A: Au revoir, Madame Gilbert.
Goodbye, Madame Gilbert.

Useful vocabulary - dentist

anaesthetic	*une anesthésie*	gums	*les gencives*
bridge	*un bridge*	injection	*une pîqure*
crown	*une couronne*	plate, etc	*une prothèse dentaire*
enamel	*l'émail (m)*	tooth	*une dent*
filling	*un plombage*	X-ray	*une radio(graphie)*

12🌸 Appendix

Asking for help

Could you . . .

repeat that (slowly), I didn't understand	*le répéter (lentement), je n'ai pas compris*
help me/us a moment	*m'/nous aider un moment*
help me, I need some/a . . .	*m'aider, j'ai besoin de/d'un(e) . . .*
give me/us some information about . . .	*me/nous renseigner sur . . .*
explain something to me/us	*m'/nous expliquer quelquechose*
help me find my bearings	*m'aider à m'orienter*
tell me/us how to get to XXX?	*me/nous dire comment aller à XXX?*
show me/us how it works?	*me/nous montrer comment ça marche?*

Pourriez-vous . . .

I'm looking for . . .

the market	*le marché*
a car park nearby	*un parking dans le coin*
the road to Beaune	*la route de Beaune*
a bakery that's still open	*une boulangerie encore ouverte*
the late night chemist	*la pharmacie de garde*
a reasonably priced hotel	*un hôtel pas trop cher*

Je cherche . . .

Where is . . .

the market/the post office	*le marché/la poste*
the tourist office	*l'Office de Tourisme*
the nearest service station	*la station service la plus proche*
the bus stop for the station	*l'arrêt de bus pour aller à la gare*
the central bus station	*la gare routière*
the fresh milk/the eggs	*le lait frais/les oeufs* (in the supermarket)

Où se trouve . . .

How do I . . .

get from here to the airport?	*aller d'ici à l'aeroport?*
find your office?	*trouver votre bureau?*
find your house?	*arriver chez vous?*
find a taxi around here?	*trouver un taxi dans le coin?*

Comment je fais pour . . .

I don't understand . . .

what you're saying	*ce que vous dîtes*
what's happening	*ce qui se passe*
what I'm supposed to do	*ce qu'il faut faire*
this notice/this sign	*cette affiche/ce panneau*
the directions	*les directions*
the instructions	*les consignes*
the message	*le message*

Je ne comprends pas . . .

I can't manage to . . .

understand the map

find the right road

get this appliance to work

loosen the nuts

connect the aerial properly

shut off the tap completely

Je n'arrive pas à . . .

comprendre la carte

trouver la bonne route

faire marcher cet appareil

déserrer les écrous

brancher l'antenne correctement

fermer la vanne complètement

There's an emergency . . .

There's been an accident.

Someone's been hurt.

It's my wife/husband/a friend.

It's a guest who's staying with us.

Il y a une urgence . . .

Il y a eu un accident.

Quelqu'un est blessé.

C'est ma femme/mon mari/un(e) ami(e).

C'est un(e) de nos invité(e)s.

He's fallen down the stairs/on some steps/off a ladder.

Il est tombé sur l'escalier/sur des marches/d'une échelle.

He's hit his head and he's unconscious.

Il s'est cogné la tête et il a perdu connaissance.

I think he's broken his ankle.

Je crois qu'il s'est cassé la cheville.

He's in a lot of pain.

C'est très douloureux.

He can't move/breathe properly.

Il ne peut pas bouger/respirer normalement.

He's bleeding badly.

Il saigne beaucoup.

He's got very severe pains in the chest.

Il a des douleurs terribles dans la poitrine.

He's got an asthma attack.

Il a une crise d'asthme.

He's burned his hand very badly.

Il s'est brûlé la main très sévèrement.

He's cut his leg with the chainsaw.

Il s'est coupé la jambe avec la tronçonneuse.

What happened exactly?

Qu'est-ce qui s'est passé exactement?

Is he losing a lot of blood?

Est-ce qu'il perd beaucoup de sang?

Does he feel hot or cold (to the touch)?

Est-ce qu'il sent chaud ou froid (au toucher)?

You definitely mustn't move him.

Il ne faut surtout pas le déplacer.

Cover him up well and keep him warm.

Il faut le bien couvrir et le garder au chaud.

Give him some water but nothing else.

Donnez-lui de l'eau à boire mais rien d'autre.

Where are you now?

Vous êtes où actuellement?

Where do you live exactly?

Vous habitez où exactement?

How can we recognise your house?

Comment répérer votre maison?

Don't worry, we'll be there right away.

Ne vous inquiétez pas, on arrive tout de suite.

You can take him straight to the hospital yourself, I'll tell them you're coming.

Vous pouvez l'amener à l'hôpital vous-même directement, je vais les prévenir.

Is he under medication?

Est-ce qu'il prend des médicaments?

Has he had this problem before?

Est-ce qu'il a eu ce problème déjà?

Who is your usual doctor?

C'est qui, votre médecin traitant?

Enjoying a conversation

Here are some responses you can make to encourage your local friends in one of their favourite sports: talking about the latest events and telling stories. Note the *vous* or *tu*: the *vous* can be adapted to the *tu* context but not the reverse.

C'est . . .	That's . . .		
bien!	*good!*	amusant!	*amusing!*
super!	*great!*	marrant!	*funny!*
formidable!	*terrific!*	curieux!	*peculiar!*
une bonne nouvelle!	*good news!*	bizarre!	*weird!*
merveilleux!	*marvellous!*	absurde!	*absurd!*
magnifique!	*magnificent!*	dingue!	*crazy!*
fabuleux!	*fabulous!*	affolant!	*enough to drive you mad!*
passionnant!	*fascinating!*	ahurissant!	*astounding!*
étonnant!	*amazing!*		
remarquable!	*remarkable!*	affreux!!	*awful!*
extraordinaire!	*extraordinary!*	honteux!	*shameful!*
inimaginable!	*unimaginable!*	lamentable!	*deplorable!*
époustouflant!	*breathtaking!*	epouvantable!	*horrifying!*
inouï!	*unheard of!*	le comble!	*the limit!*

Quelle histoire!	*What a story!*	Quel dommage!	*What a pity!*
Quelle surprise!	*What a surprise!*	Quel horreur!	*Oh, how awful!*
Quel bonheur!	*What a joy!*	Quelle folie!	*What madness!*
Quelle miracle!	*What a miracle!*	Quel désastre!	*What a disaster!*

Que c'est beau!	*That's really beautiful!*	Que c'est drôle!	*That's really funny!*
Que c'est bon!	*That's really good!*	Que c'est dingue!	*That's really crazy!*

Qu'est-ce qui se passe?	*What's going on?*
Qu'est-ce qui vous arrive/t'arrive?	*What's happened to you?*
Qu'est-ce que tu racontes!	*What rubbish are you telling us!*
Qu'est-ce que tu penses!	*What did you think /expect!*
Qu'est-ce qu' elle imagine/invente?	*What does she think she's doing?*

C'est vrai!	*That's true!*
Comme vous dîtes!	*As you say!/ You're quite right!*
A qui vous le dîtes!	*Look who you're talking to! Tell me about it!*
Ça, alors!	*Fancy that!*
Quand-même!	*Well, really! I should think so too!*
A ce point-là?	*As much/As bad as that?*

Tu parles!	*You don't say!*
Tu rigoles!	*You're joking!*
Sans blague!	*You're kidding!*
Vous plaisantez!	*You're joking!*

Ce n'est pas vrai!	*It's not true!*
Ce n'est pas possible!	*It's not possible! It can't be true!*

Ce n'est pas très sérieux!   *That's not very right and proper!*
C'est n'importe quoi!   *It's not at all as it should be!* (done without regard to the rules)

Alors, raconte(z)-nous!	*Now, tell us the whole story!*
C'est arrivé comment?	*How did it happen/come about?*
Qu'est-ce qui s'est passé exactement?	*What happened exactly?*
Combien de temps ça a continué?	*How long did it go on for?*
Qu'est-ce qui s'est passé ensuite?	*What happened after that?*
Et ensuite?/par la suite?	*And then?/after that?*
Et maintenant?	*And now?*

Je le vois d'ici!	*I can just picture it!*
Ce n'est pas rien, ça!	*That's quite something!*
C'est la vie!	*That's life!*
C'est dire!	*That's saying something!*
Ça va sans dire.	*That goes without saying.*
C'est le cas de le dire.	*It couldn't be more true.*

Comme quoi . . .	*It all goes to show . . .*
Il fallait s'y attendre.	*It was only to be expected.*
Je m'en doutais.	*I thought as much. That's what I expected.*
J'en doutais.	*I didn't think so. (It's not what I expected.)*
On verra bien.	*We'll see what happens/how it turns out.*
Tu m'étonnes!	*You stun me! (= I'm not at all surprised)*
Cela m'étonnerait.	*That would surprise me.*
Je n'en reviens pas!	*I can't get over it! I'm amazed!*
C'est la moindre des choses.	*That's the least one/they can do.*
Là, elle exagère!	*She's really overdoing it/going beyond the limit!*

Pourvu que ça dure!	*Long may it last!*
Le plus tôt serait le mieux.	*The sooner the better.*
C'est la cerise sur le gâteau!	*It's the cherry on the cake!*
Ça fera le bonheur de tout le monde.	*That'll keep everybody happy.*
Tout est bien qui finit bien.	*All's well that ends well.*

Other things people say

Vous voyez/Tu vois ce que je veux dire?	*Do you see what I mean?*
Ce n'est pas la peine.	*It's not worth it, don't bother.*

Je n'en sais rien.	*I've no idea.*
Je n'y suis pour rien.	*I can't do anything about it/the situation.*
Je ne le ferais pour rien au monde.	*I wouldn't do it for anything in the world.*
Cela n'a rien à voir./à voir avec . . .	*That's got nothing to do with it./with . . .*

Je le croirai quand je le verrai.	*I'll believe it when I see it.*
Je l'ai vu de mes propres yeux.	*I saw it with my own eyes.*
Je n'en croyais pas mes yeux.	*I couldn't believe my eyes.*
Cela m'a fait froid dans le dos.	*It sent shivers down my spine.*
Cela m'a réchauffé le coeur.	*It warmed my heart.*

Allons-y!	*Let's go! Let's get on with it!*
C'est parti!	*Here we go! Let's get on with it! There it goes! They're off!*

Miscellaneous useful info

A few tips on eating out

Snacks: Curiously, in many smaller towns there are comparatively few places where you can stop for a coffee, tea or a glass of something and have a nibble alongside it, if it is not officially meal time. To some this may not matter, but for those who get that 'time for a little something' feeling in the middle of the morning or afternoon, it is good to know that the bars and cafés which serve drinks don't mind if you bring in a sandwich, *pâtisserie*, biscuits, etc, to eat with whatever you are drinking.

If they serve food themselves you may be able to order a sandwich or a slice of something in between meals, but many places serve drinks only with no food at all in sight, not even a peanut - though they may have croissants available at breakfast time. Bringing in your own food can provide an alternative too if you are out and running late for lunch, since the midday service in most cafés and restaurants stops by 2pm, except in a *brasserie* or similar establishment with service *à toute heure* (all the time).

Coffees: For a standard small black coffee ask simply for *un café*, for the same in a larger cup diluted with hot water, *un café allongé*. A small coffee with a dash of milk is *une noisette*. For white coffee - *un café (à la) crème* - the formula varies, but usually *un grand crème* is a double dose of coffee topped up with frothy steamed milk, and a small one (*un petit crème*) is a single dose ditto. To be sure you get *un petit crème* and aren't palmed off with a *noisette*, ask for your coffee *avec du lait bien chaud*. A *café au lait* is usually made with boiled milk, as served at breakfast time, traditionally in a bowl.

Booking: Remember that many French people eat out at lunchtime, rather than in the evening. The busiest period for a restaurateur is Sunday lunch, when many families reserve their tables well in advance. At other times it's not always necessary to book but restaurants appreciate knowing that you are coming, and you'll often get a better table if you do reserve. In this case they will expect you to show up and will hold your table if you are late, so it's only polite to phone them if you are delayed, or if you have to cancel, the sooner the better.

Tips: In a café a tip will always be appreciated but not insisted on, but in a restaurant it usually says *service non compris* on the menu and it is normal to leave something extra. If you are having a large meal the service, usually 10%, may be added to the total, so check the bill. Otherwise tips are entirely at your discretion.

Cooking ingredients

Plain flour = *la farine*, self-raising = *la farine de gâteau*, wholemeal = *la farine complète*. French flour has more gluten in it than the English variety so you need less of it for making sauces, etc.

Baking powder = *la levure chimique*, in sachets or packets. Yeast = *la levure de boulanger*, sold dried in packets, or fresh in cubes at a bakery. Bicarb = *bicarbonate alimentaire*.

Double or whipping cream = *crème entière*, pouring cream = *crème liquide* (both sold in a square carton or *brique*). Or you can buy real cream ready whipped (*crème chantilly*) in a spray can, but don't stand it next to the shaving cream! Cottage cheese doesn't exist, but there are several other species of soft cheese, *fromage frais, fromage blanc, crème fraîche* (slightly soured cream), etc, all clearly labelled with their fat content.

Butter: salted = *demi-sel*, unsalted = *doux*. For a treat try *baratte*, farm butter in a slab.

Cheese for cooking: most recipes prescribe Emmenthal or Gruyère, but when they melt these become very stringy. Easier to handle is Cantal from the Massif Central, available everywhere. It has more the consistency of Cheddar and has similar degrees of age and taste: *jeune* (young) is fairly bland if it's in a plastic packet, more tasty cut fresh from a whole cheese; *vieux* (old) is mature and sometimes has a real sting in its tail; *entre deux* ('between the two') is tangy and usually just right for cooking. Ask to taste them before you make your choice: "*Je peux le goûter?*"

If you see *cuillère à soupe* in a recipe, think of the big spoons the French use for soup, and you'll realise the UK equivalent is a tablespoon.

Mushrooms

What are these doing here, you may well ask? Are we lucky readers about to get some tips on hunting the 100€-a-sliver truffle? Sorry to disappoint, here we are talking wild woodland mushrooms, about which passions also run high. Read on . . .

At certain times of the year whole families disappear mysteriously for hours on end, normally loyal *fonctionnaires* call in sick, there is a rash of urgent family funerals to go to, and a curious increase is seen in the number of vehicles parked along the wayside in the deeper darker reaches of the woods . . . while their erstwhile occupants can be spotted, if you look really hard, searching and scouring the undergrowth for the much prized but elusive mushroom. You may think all this is an exaggeration but believe me it is not.

If you want to try partaking in this age-old ritual, there are a few points to keep in mind. First, disguise yourself as a local by borrowing a little white van and a large black beret . . . well perhaps not, but be very careful that while you too are searching for the prize, you aren't treading on someone else's patch. How to recognise it? You can't, until you've lived among the locals for a few dozen years, and maybe not even then, because the best place to find a particular kind of mushroom at a particular moment of the year is a jealously guarded family secret handed down from one generation to the next, and the owners of same will never, but never, tell anyone else where it is. So all you can do is be discreet and hope you don't bump into someone else who might think they have more of a right to a mushroom than you do.

Second, if you do find any, don't eat them until you have had them vetted by someone who knows which are which. In principle the local pharmacy will check them for you, but they are not infallible, as I happen to know from a sad tale I will not burden you with. The pharmacists have charts of numerous varieties to refer to, but these show only a tidy version of each one, and unless the person you ask has trudged through the woods and seen the real thing in its various stages of growing and decomposing, they may not give you the right answer. Preferable to go to an aged neighbour for a verdict, and the older the better, since they wouldn't have reached the age they have if they didn't know a good 'un from a bad 'un . . .

Other wayside harvests include apples, plums, walnuts, chestnuts, etc. It is legal to pick up windfalls on the road or within one metre of the edge of it, but not to pick fruit or nuts off the trees growing by the road – they all belong to someone. Blackberries can be picked from the road side of the hedge.

Public toilets

A café is probably the easiest place to find a toilet when you are out. As you have probably discovered, the sophistication of the facilities varies directly with the class of the establishment, and many of the simpler cafés still retain the traditional 'Turkish' toilets which, while perfectly functional, are in fact little more than a ceramic-lined hole in the floor with a flushing system. To be really courteous you can buy a coffee or drink if you want to use a café's toilets, but they will rarely turn you away if you ask politely:

"Est-ce que je peux utiliser la toilette, s'il vous plaît?"
"May I use the toilet please?"

Many towns and cities have in the last few years, thank goodness, replaced their smelly public *pissoirs* with clean, automatic toilets concealed in those shiny silver kiosks you'll see here and there, looking like something waiting for Dr Who. They may seem intimidating but they work very well, and sometimes even have music. They are usually stocked with toilet paper and they clean themselves automatically. Put the number of coins indicated into the slot, the door will slide back and in you go. When you have finished just open the door and leave, the machine does the rest on its own. Museums, tourist offices and many public buildings also have presentable public toilets.

Door locks

Modern French outer doors have a security system with a retractable metal bar inside the outer edge (derived from the metal bar with handle used to secure older doors and windows). To lock one of these doors, close it firmly then turn the handle upwards to the vertical position, which slots the bar into place, and then lock it, turning the key twice.

Electric kettles

These are still something of a novelty as the French traditionally heat the water for making coffee in a saucepan. However there are plenty of them in the shops so if you are setting up a second home worry not. But if you are coming to a *gîte* run by French people don't count on finding one – best to bring your own if you'll be miserable without that familiar bubbling purr!

Washing machines

For some reasons best known to themselves, many continental washing machines (though not all) have very long cycles of over an hour, even for a delicate wash. This is something to check if you are considering buying one over here, as these models use far more electricity than necessary and tend to thrash the clothes. If you already have a model you are happy with it may be worth bringing one over, but note that the local variety fill on a cold supply only, so plumbing in a UK model will take a little extra pipework. Also, thermostats for hot water in immersion heaters, etc, are by law set very high, so this is something else to check on your washing machine if you don't want your clothes to get stewed.

Washing powders also differ (having been designed originally to work with cold water) and even the usual leading brands seem to have a harsher formula which can be hard on fabrics and on colours. There are now special milder ones on the shelves such as Mir Couleurs. If you want to bother and are driving over, you could bring some of your usual from the UK.

Furniture

If you are interested in buying furniture locally you may want to take a look at what is available second hand. One place to find such things is in a *brocante*, where the stock is usually a mixture of antiques (*antiquités*) and more recent things. Another possibility is an establishment called a *depôt-vente* or *troc*, where you can often find good pieces which are brought in to be sold by their owners and have not passed through other dealers' hands. The local papers will tell you about *brocante* fairs, *marchés aux puces* (flea markets) etc, but if you go, be prepared to wade through a lot of unbelievably junky junk to find the good bits. There are also lots of bargains to be found in the classified ads in the local free papers, if your vocab and your phone repertoire will stretch to it, and also in the *vide-greniers* ('attic emptyings'), local events equivalent to a car boot sale.

Running *gîtes*

Herewith a few hints on making things run smoothly for yourselves and your visitors, from friends who know something about that of which they speak.

- Booking form: make sure it is foolproof and covers everything, including clear conditions for cancellation, insurance, liability, etc. Explain all the practical details so that clients know what to expect and what to bring: laundry facilities, if there's a phone available, sports facilities nearby, etc.

- Prepare a clear map and foolproof directions to send out with the booking confirmation, including advice on an easy place to stop for shopping on the way.

- If guests tell you that they are going to arrive late, you could offer to do a basic shop for them.

- Make clear the times guests should leave and can arrive, and allow yourselves enough time between the two for doing the change-over, cleaning, etc, without panic.

- Decide what to do about cleaning: whether to include it in your prices, or to give guests the choice of doing it themselves or paying to have it done.

- Make it clear on the booking form if they can or need to bring linen, pool towels, etc. If you're providing sheets and towels it's worth having quality ones (but preferably non-iron!), which make a good first impression and will stand up to regular laundering. You'll need enough to provide a complete change of linen, kitchen towels, etc, every week even if guests are staying for longer.

- *Keep everything very clean and in good running order*, especially the pool. The cleaner things are to begin with, the more careful people will be and the more likely to leave the place clean when they go.

- Extras appreciated by guests include a bottle of something chilled in the fridge when they arrive, welcome drinks with other guests and an occasional barbecue (with food provided or contributed jointly) to give them the chance to mingle.

- Make up a file of local visits, restaurants, etc, for each *gîte*, and be prepared to make bookings for guests if their French is wobbly. (Also have some spares of a good local map.)

- Be prepared to spend time with your visitors if they want to chat.

- Have spares on hand of household extras including a full gas bottle, light bulbs, glasses and mugs, spare kettle, etc, so that guests aren't hanging about while you make a quick dash to the shops to solve their little problems.

- Keep all the accounts clear and up to date, and as separate as possible from your own household expenses. Supermarkets will provide a TVA (VAT) receipt if you need one.

- Have bills ready the evening before people leave so that they can get away early.

- You might want to prepare a simple questionnaire for them to fill in at the end of their stay to highlight what they did or didn't like about your establishment.

- Have some flyers of it available so they can spread the word among their friends!

Temperatures

°F	°C
32°	0°
50°	10°
60°	15.5°
70°	21°
80°	27°
90°	32°
100°	38°
150°	66°
212°	100°

Oven settings

setting	°F	°C
1	160-170	70-77
2	200-220	93-105
3	225-275	107-135
4	285-325	140-163
5	350-400	177-205
6	410-450	210-232
7	475-500	245-260
8	525	275
9	550	288

Quantities, measurements and containers

une borne	milestone, kilometre (slang)	la barrique	barrel
centaines (f)	hundreds	le bidon	container for liquid
dizaines (vingtaines, etc)	10s, 20s, etc	le bocal	glass jar
une douzaine	dozen	la boîte	food tin, box
une goutte, larme	a drop (of liquid, drink)	la bombe	aerosol can
une hectare	hectare (about 2.25 acres)	la botte	bunch (carrots, flowers), bale
un lieu	league (distance), place	le bouchon	cork
une livre	pound (lb), £	la bouteille	bottle
[un livre	book]	la brique	'brick', carton for milk, juice, etc
un mètre carré	square metre	le cabas	shopping basket
un mètre cube	cubic metre	le cageot	wooden vegetable crate
un mile	mile	le cartable	school satchel
un pied	foot	le carton	cardboard box, cardboard
une pouce	thumb, inch	le casier	pigeonhole, locker, storage box
une rame(ette)	ream/pack of (printer) paper	le chargement	load (in truck, etc)
une stère	cubic metre (of firewood)	le colis	parcel
		le contenant	container
le bout	end, bit, scrap	le conteneur	freight container
la demi-bouteille	half bottle, etc	le contenu	contents
l'échantillon	sample piece, swatch	le couvercle	lid
les miettes	crumbs	[la couverture	blanket]
la moitié	half	l'emballage (m)	packaging
le morceau	piece	l'enveloppe (à bulle) (f)	(bubble) envelope
la part	share, piece	le flacon	small bottle
la partie	part of	le fret	freight
la pièce détachée	spare part	le fût	barrel
[la pièce	room]	le jeu	game, bunch (of keys), set of cards, boules, etc
la portion	portion	la panier	basket
le quart	quarter	le paquet	package
les restes	remains, left-overs	la poche	pocket, plastic shopping bag
le tiers	third (third party)	la porte-monnaie	purse, wallet
la tranche	slice	le récipient	container, recipient
le calibre	calibre, grade	le sac	sack, plastic (bin) bag
les dimensions	dimensions, measurements	le sac à dos	backpack
l'épaisseur (f)	thickness	le sac à main	handbag
le gabarit	size, calibre	le sachet	small plastic or paper packet, plastic shopping bag
[la grandeur	grandeur]	la serviette	briefcase (towel, serviette even!)
la hauteur	height	le tonneau	barrel
la largeur	width	la trousse de clés	bunch of keys
la longueur	length	la trousse de toilette	toilet bag
la masse	mass	le tube	tube
le poids	weight	la valise	suitcase
la pointure	shoe size		
la profondeur	depth		
la quantité	quantity	le mètre	tape measure
la taille	size, waist	la règle	ruler
le volume	volume, room space	peser	to weigh

Useful contacts and sources of information

British Consulates in France

Biarritz: British Consulate (Hon.)   05.59.24.21.40
7 av Edouard VII, Barclays Banks SA, 64202 Biarritz cedex

Bordeaux: British Consulate-General   05.57.22.21.10
353 bd du Président Wilson, BP 91, 33073 Bordeaux cedex

Boulogne-sur-Mer: British Consulate (Hon.)   03.21.87.16.80
c/o Cotrama, Tour Administrative, Hoverport, 62200 Boulogne-sur-Mer

Calais: British Consulate   03.21.96.33.76
c/o P&O European Ferries, 41 pl d'Armes, 62100 Calais

Cherbourg: British Consulate (Hon.)   02.33.44.20.13
c/o P&O European Ferries, Gare Maritime, 50101 Cherbourg

Dinard: British Consulate (Hon.)   02.99.46.26.64
La Hulotte, 8 bd des Maréchaux, 35800 Dinard

Dunkerque: British Consulate (Hon.)   03.28.66.11.98
c/o L. Dewulf, Cailleret & Fils, 11 rue des Arbres, BP 1502, 59383 Dunkerque

Le Havre: British Consulate (Hon.)   02.35.42.27.47
c/o Lloyds Register of Shipping, 124 bd de Strasbourg, 76600 Le Havre

Lille: British Consulate-General   03.20.12.82.72
11 square Dutilleul, 59800 Lille

Lyon: British Consulate-General   04.72.77.81.70
24 rue Childebert, 69288 Lyon cedex 1

Marseille: British Consulate-General   04.91.15.72.10
24 av du Prado, 13006 Marseille. Also deals with Monaco.

Nantes: British Consulate (Hon.)   02.40.63.16.02
L'Aumarière, 44220 Couëron

Nice: British Consulate (Hon.)   04.93.82.32.04
8 rue Alphonse Kerr, 06000 Nice. Also deals with Monaco.

Toulouse: British Consulate (Hon.)   05.61.15.02.02
c/o Lucas Aerospace, Victoria Center, 20 chemin de Laporte, 31300 Toulouse

Newspapers

Le Monde - traditional, serious news coverage   www.lemonde.fr
Le Figaro - mainline, more social and chat   www.lefigaro.fr
Libération - current affairs seen from the left   www.libe.com
Les Echos - business information   www.lesechos.fr
Le Canard Enchaînée - equivalent of Private Eye
L'Equipe - all the sports results   www.lequipe.fr

Magazines

News

Paris Match   www.parismatch.fr
L'Express   www.lexpress.fr
Le Nouvel Observateur   www.lenouvelobs.fr

| Le Point | www.lepoint.fr | |
| Marianne | www.marianne.fr | Irreverent and well informed. |

Science and environment

Sciences & Avenir
Science & Vie
Ca m'Intéresse

Gardening

Mon Jardin et Ma Maison
L'Ami des Jardins

Travel

SNCF:	www.voyages-sncf.fr
Raileurope:	www.raileurope.co.uk
Air France:	www.airfrance.com
easyJet:	www.easyjet.com
Ryanair:	www.ryanair.com
Europcar:	www.europcar.fr
Eurolines:	www.eurolines.com

Utilities

EDF: www.edf.fr
France Telecom: www.francetelecom.fr

Yellow Pages: www.pagesjaunes.fr Also Pages Blanches and international directories, map facility, English option.

TV channels (*chaînes*)

TF1	www.tf1.fr	News, chat, lots of game shows, thrillers, etc.
France 2	www.france2.fr	Slightly more serious than the above.
France 3	www.france3.fr	Local and regional news plus more serious fare.
France 5	www.france5.fr	Culture/arts/sciences channel, quality documentaries (good for listening practice).
Arte	www.arte-tv.com	(same wavelength, in the evenings) Quality fare, run jointly by France and Germany.
M6	www.m6.fr	News, science, lots of sci-fi, American series, etc.

Other sites

For those whose French is up to it, there are some interesting sites which give a few glimpses into the workings of this country and some of its assets.

Culture

www.culture.fr - cultural resources and events, virtual museum tours, archaeology sites which accept amateurs, etc.
www.monum.fr - virtual tours of lots of wonderful buildings.

Government

www.elysee.fr - information about the president and presidential programme.
www.internet.gouv.fr - information about the government and current issues.
www.premier-ministre.gouv.fr - about the prime minister and current issues.
www.service-publique.fr - info on government departments and local government.
www.ladocumentationfrancaise.fr - library of official publications of all kinds, recent political speeches, etc.

Property information

General publications with some property info

French News   www.frenchnews.com
   Monthly paper packed with news and info for the English, up to date information on changes in the law, etc, plus lots of useful classified ads.

Living France Magazine   www.livingfrance.com
   Everything in and about France. Regular features on language, legal info, etc.

France Magazine (UK)   www.francemagazine.com
   Cultural news and background, lots of practical information on daily life in France.

France Magazine (USA)   www.francemagazine.org
   'Official' magazine for the American market, lots of current and cultural info and interesting site links.

Maison Française   Gorgeous glossy with mouthwatering houses.

Bonjour Magazine/France Review   www.frenchtouristoffice.net
   Official publication of the French Tourist Office (French and English editions).

Property for sale

French Property News   www.french-property-news.com   Essential, excellent links.
www.buy-the-best-online.co.uk/french-property.html
www.europropertynews.com
www.frenchpropertydigest.com
www.francevoila.com/property
www.france-for-sale.com

Le Journal des Particuliers and *De Particulier à Particulier*
Thousands of properties all over France sold by private individuals (no agents' fees).
www.toutlimmobilier.fr
www.bienvenu-immobilier.fr
www.century21-france.com

Holiday property

For booking your holiday or for advertising your property to let:
www.vacances-france.com   *Good deals for advertising.*
www.cheznous.com   *Expensive to advertise in but excellent reputation.*
www.gites-in-france.co.uk
www.discover-france-holidays.co.uk
www.ferryprice.co.uk/ferry-to-france *Useful link for all the ferry companies.*
www.le-guide.com   *For the southern half of France, lots of info and purple prose.*

General information

For general information on the workings of the country and on the rest of what you need to know, both before you come and when you get here, an excellent source is David Hampshire's *Buying a Home in France* and *Living and Working in France*, published by Survival Books (www.survivalbooks.net). Herein you will find the nitty gritty on lots of topics, though if you are buying it is still advisable to make sure you have the most recent information, as rules and regulations do change. The author also provides an excellent reading list of general and practical titles which it would be impertinent and pointless to duplicate.

Emergency numbers

SAMU - ambulance or medical emergency	15
POLICE	17
POMPIERS – fire and general rescue service	18
European emergency number	112

Local phone numbers

Doctor:

Hospital:

Mairie:

Poste:

Station:

name	number